LIZA WITH A 'Z'

The Traumas & Triumphs of Liza Minnelli

LIZA WITH A 'Z'

*The Traumas & Triumphs of
Liza Minnelli*

Michael Freedland

ROBSON BOOKS

To Beth, Ellie, Ben, Jamie and Jacob
All that they say about the joy of grandchildren is true

This revised and updated edition published in Great Britain in 2003 by Robson Books, The Chrysalis Building, Bramley Road, London, W10 6SP. First published in 1988.

An imprint of Chrysalis Books Group plc

British Library Cataloguing in Publication Data
A catalogue record for this title is available from the British Library.

ISBN 1 86105 681 8

Typeset by FiSH Books, London
Printed by Butler & Tanner Ltd, Frome and London

Acknowledgements

I chose Liza Minnelli as a subject for this book simply because she is a character who is almost a throwback to a past age – an entertainer who sings, dances, acts and pulsates with the kind of vitality that has always been fascinating, but which is becoming increasingly rare. Rare subjects always make the most interesting books.

That certainly was the impression of the dozens of people I interviewed for this project. I should like to thank them all, even though very many of them, for reasons I always respect, preferred that I didn't mention their names. Among those to whom I particularly want to offer my thanks were:

The late Fred Astaire; Charles Aznavour; Wendell Burton; Sammy Cahn; Saul Chaplin; the late Bob Fosse; the late Judy Garland in a 1962 BBC radio interview; Joel Grey; Jacqueline Hyde; Lorna Luft (for a lengthy magazine article); Sidney Luft – to whom I would like to give particular thanks for an obviously difficult and intimate assessment; Debbie Reynolds; Walter Scharf; Tony Wells; George Abbott; Jerry Lewis.

There was tremendous help from Barbara Paskin, for which I am extraordinarily grateful. Particular thanks are due to the librarians of the Academy of Motion Picture Arts and Sciences in Beverly Hills as well as those of the British Film Institute and the British Library.

To my dearest wife Sara my thanks for everything.

MICHAEL FREEDLAND
London, 2003

Prologue

She's the woman who defied expectations – all of them, except the one that said she was destined to be a superstar.

But it's the surprises that set her apart from practically everything said about other top stars. They amounted to a simple formula – as the daughter of one of the icons of twentieth-century show business, there was no way she could match the starry heights of her mother. Judy Garland, after all, was in her time not just big, but huge enough to be one of those – to use a horrible term that conjures up images of lavatory cleaners as much as the glittery lives of Hollywood – household names. So reaching those heights? Forget it.

Then there were the details of her private life – doomed, of course. She was a depressive, so would she end up the way her mother did while she was in her 50s? The possibility of her being dangerously depressed is one to be considered but has never really been proved.

She was a drinker? Much too much for anyone's good. She took drugs? No doubts about that. So she couldn't recover. But somehow, if all the tales are true, she did. She had an illness totally apart from her dependence on narcotics and one, so serious, that was known to fell people at the point of diagnosis. She recovered. She could barely talk. A leg was virtually dead, yet a year or so afterwards she was dancing. And singing.

So just a comeback kid? No, she was a hard worker. 'I'm a terribly strong woman,' she said after her ill-fated 2002 marriage to producer David Gest and her promise to lay off all the drugs and booze. 'And I've come through all kinds of things.' It wasn't going to be a replay of all that had happened to her mother. 'The disease got her. And I know it's a disease . . . there was no help. It was awful.'

Always there was the question of her reprising everything terrible that happened to her mother – the drugs, the drink, the men. Was she really running parallel to Judy? 'Yes,' she said, 'almost. But there was no help for my mother. No Betty Ford Center.'

She made no pretence now to hide her problems or what they brought. They made her suffer, she said, from 'isolation, thinking you're not good enough...'

The trouble with comeback kids is that they do come back – but do so all too often for reasons of sentiment. But no sentiment in the world could guarantee the kind of rave reviews that came the way of Liza Minnelli – Liza with a 'Z'.

As her mother once said: 'Liza is all show business'.

It was the kind of show business that declared it was just another kind of love affair, and she has had plenty of experiences of both kinds. Fred Ebb, the lyricist of her greatest triumph, *Cabaret*, nicely put the way she looked on her theatrical commitments. 'Her total eagerness to win an audience and her total eagerness to please them.'

And as a journalist once noted: 'Like her mother, Minnelli exudes an aura of the little girl lost who just wants to be loved and proves it with a gurgling giggle of a laugh that could so easily trickle into a tear.'

But always there were questions. Not quite as unusually as some of the other disasters that she turned around into something quite different, there were the disastrous marriages that began – as they always do – like a bright sun in the height of summer and ended like an electric storm on a grey miserable winter's day. Could she recover from that sort of blight? She said she had. But then circumstances changed all that – yet again. Liza would be the first to point out that the one lesson we learn from history is that we don't learn from history.

Undoubtedly, being a child of the superstar could never have been easy for her. For all the talk of theatrical dynasties, the star-inlaid pavements of Hollywood Boulevard are littered with the corpses of hopeful off-spring of stars with acting careers that never lasted long enough to see the bright lights.

Chapter One

BREAKING INTO show business isn't the most difficult thing in the world to do. Staying there is.

Every year a thousand anxious youngsters line up outside agents' offices hoping for the big break that will take them to the top, make them *the* discovery of the decade, turn them from understudy into star overnight. Many of them know in their hearts that it probably won't happen. They won't admit their doubts – even to themselves; to concede the possibility of failure would be to recognise that the goods they have to offer are second-rate. If they don't have confidence in themselves, no one else is going to give them a second chance.

Having said all that, take, as a matter of argument, the one who does manage to make it. Just occasionally Broadway, Hollywood or the pop factories of New York, London, or Memphis, Tennessee, create what our misguided age calls a superstar: a Marilyn Monroe, an Elizabeth Taylor, a Barbra Streisand, an Elvis, even a Madonna.

There's also always the overnight sensation – a sensation overnight whom everyone forgets come the daylight. It happens more often than some theatrical historians would care to admit.

Then there is another category: the performer who has had a few doors opened to him or her. We know them well, the shapely youngster who found her way on to the screen via the old route of the casting couch, a route no more secure than the springs in the upholstery. Let her fall out of favour and her career disappears like a page of script caught up in the stream from a Hollywood sound-stage wind machine. Or the youngster who is the friend of a friend of the producer who is offered a bit part for old times' sake and then, having exhausted the producer's good will, starts a new career selling life insurance or crimping hair.

The hardest category of all is the 'child of the superstar' – the one who is carried on to a set in mother's arms as a baby and then makes regular Christmas appearances on television until he or she is ready for the Big Début. There's no doubt that the début will come. Parental influence will ensure that and if not parental influence then that of mama's or papa's agent. The opportunity will definitely arise, for the very reason to which no one would openly admit – the desire to see that star, albeit vicariously, fall flat on his or her face.

Despite all that Isaac Newton wrote and scientists or philosophers have been saying for years, apples do frequently fall quite far from their trees. The chances of a child of a really outstanding performer matching his or her parent's talent are so small they are not worth contemplating.

These performers are exploited as 'So and So Junior' because, for curiosity's sake, people will pay good money to see what they can do and then go out of the theatre shaking their heads and muttering disapproval or worse. Meanwhile, others in the profession that is alleged to be all heart are happily laughing their heads off. Such an entry to and speedy exit from show business is worse than no entry at all.

Liza Minnelli experienced it all. At least nearly all. While still a teenager, she was the one to laugh – and, although she has had her share of tears in the years that followed, she has survived to keep on laughing. Almost everyone saw her work with her mother and felt certain she was going to be merely a Judy Garland carbon copy – no mean feat in itself, but the copycat industry of entertainment likes to think it craves, above all, originality.

In her heyday, she would stand on the near-sacred boards of the stage of New York's Carnegie Hall, throwing out an arm just like her mother did. But it was not Judy Garland reborn, it was Liza Minnelli on her own, playing to audiences much like those that Judy had, rapturous crowds of theatregoers with a fair sprinkling of gay men who perhaps see her as the kind of women many of them would like to have been themselves.

Plainly, one cannot ignore the place that Judy had in Liza's life. But old matters told in other biographies will not be recounted here, except perhaps to dot a few of the proverbial i's' or cross the t's.

The world has moved on since one of the first of her many comebacks 16 or 17 years ago. But much of what could be said then still applies – with one exception, one very vital exception. When she appeared at Carnegie Hall for that comeback concert in 1987, the critics knew that she was her own woman and were happy to say so.

But they all, or at least nearly all, still referred to her as Judy Garland's daughter or compared her with her mother. Nobody does that any more, for the fact has to be faced that there are a great many young adults who no longer know that there was a connection with Judy Garland – or even who Judy Garland was.

Chapter Two

JUDY GARLAND, in the most enthralling routine she ever performed, used to sing of being born in a trunk. It was partly true. She came from a show business family, even though Gumm – her real name – tended to stick to rather than roll off the tongue, and her birthplace, unlike that in the song, was not a hick town in Idaho.

Her daughter Liza was born in the much more pampered, exceedingly comfortable territory known generically as Hollywood. She may have had nurses and expensive toys and the green, green acres of Beverly Hills to look out on from the moment those big, dark eyes opened and registered the scene around her for the first time, but her pudgy little fist may have been clutching a make-up pencil instead of a silver spoon.

It was a showbiz world, with showbiz people constantly in attendance. Could it be anything else when the first voice that the baby remembers hearing is not that of an out-of-tune mother warbling 'Rockabye Baby', but Judy Garland herself giving a personal performance of 'Over the Rainbow'?

This was not the easiest time in Judy's life, but neither was it the hardest or the saddest.

The star who was generally regarded as having the biggest impact on any stage anywhere in the world since the passing of the days when Al Jolson wowed audiences at the Winter Garden on Broadway was in a lull in one of her periodic battles with Hollywood.

No longer was she being given uppers to keep her awake and downers to send her to sleep by the minions of Louis B. Mayer, but the legacy of those days when being a child star was fairly close to being walled up in a luxurious kind of torture chamber, was immense.

Mayer, after all, had not merely cried over Judy the way he had when Joan Crawford tried to break her contract or when Gregory

Peck refused to sentence himself to seven years hard labour in his salt mines. He had ruled her life, behaving as though he were a combination of stern father, bullying headmaster and Adolf Hitler.

Her marriage to the attractive movie composer David Rose (later to become famous for 'Holiday for Strings' and 'The Stripper') took place and was consummated despite a great deal of opposition from both Mayer and Judy's mother, Ethel. Mrs Gumm had put Judy and her elder sisters in the now famous (or infamous) Gumm Sisters act and she was now the stage momma incarnate. But it was Louis B. Mayer who made the biggest decisions – like ordering the nineteen-year-old star of the Andy Hardy movies and, most important of all, *The Wizard of Oz*, to have an abortion. It kept Judy firmly in the MGM stable but did nothing for her marriage to young Mr Rose. They were divorced almost immediately. Judy returned to work after her 'flu' or whatever other phony explanation the studio chose to use at the time to explain her absence in a nursing home.

It didn't make her a happy young woman or well-adjusted enough to go to work in front of a film camera. Yet she was all show business and if you were all show business, when a director shouted 'action', you provided all the action he had in mind. You went mad or felt sick in your own time.

Was it any wonder that she wasn't exactly 'normal' then, nor would she ever be? Can there be any doubt that her unorthodox treatment of her own children had good reason behind it?

Yet when Judy performed – and was allowed to perform – she was superb. She was fairly pretty, although not as cute as Deanna Durbin who was at one time considered her rival, or Elizabeth Taylor, a child star half a generation later. She developed physically a little too early for Mr Mayer who might have liked breasts on women – particularly those who had experienced his casting couch – but not on a little girl who was supposed to dance down the Yellow Brick Road. So he had her bust taped until she felt as though she were acting in a strait-jacket. Hollywood itself was another kind of strait-jacket.

So Judy, as everyone now knows, was temperamental and like a number of temperamental people she was at times more extrovert than was good for her. She needed a quieter existence than she would allow herself. She was an artist who sought out other artists – which was how she came to be married to Vincente Minnelli, often spoken of as the most talented, the most artistic director in Hollywood.

Minnelli has gone down in movie history as one of the men who earned MGM its initials – those that stood for Makers of Great Movies, or Manufacturers of Great Musicals, rather than merely representing Metro Goldwyn Mayer. Since there was no longer a Metro firm and Sam Goldwyn had never had anything to do with the company that bore his name, those words were far more appropriate. MGM made the greatest movie musicals in the world and Vincente Minnelli was making some of the best of them.

That, however, does not do him complete credit. He was also a sensitive, understanding, intelligent director of 'straight' films. Actors and actresses who would never dream of singing a chorus or dancing a single step in front of a camera would say that they preferred to be directed by him than by almost anyone else.

He came from a theatrical family, his family being producers of 'tent shows', a sort of combination of summer stock and circus. Show business was in the Minnelli blood – Vincente was 'acting' in one of their plays at the age of three and a half (which by Judy's standards was already approaching middle age; she had first appeared on stage when she was two). But he quickly demonstrated his abilities as an artist in other directions, too.

In his twenties he was working on Broadway shows, as a designer of costumes and sets. One of his most important jobs was working at the infant Radio City Music Hall, a position that introduced him to an important section of New York theatrical society, including the Gershwins, Dorothy Parker and the pianist-wit Oscar Levant who became a life-long friend.

From Radio City he moved to the Shubert Organisation, headed by Jake and Lee Shubert, two entrepreneurial spirits who had discovered Jolson and who, as a result, behaved as though every inch of Broadway, including the drains, belonged to them. Compared to the Shuberts, Louis B. Mayer was Santa Claus. But they gave Minnelli his first big break, directing shows like their own versions of the *Ziegfeld Follies*.

Immensely talented, Minnelli went to Hollywood, was given virtually a royal welcome – and hated what resulted from it. A contract with Paramount was a dismal failure, producing nothing, so he went back to Broadway. He directed the last Jerome Kern-Oscar Hammerstein musical *Very Warm for May*, a show best remembered for the review comment, 'Not so hot for November'. But it didn't appear to dampen, let alone cool, his reputation.

MGM invited him back to Hollywood and he returned –
apparently with less of a fanfare but certainly with more success.

One of the first people he met was young Judy Garland while
working on *Strike up the Band*, part of a series of 'Gee-let's-get-up-
a-show' movies with Mickey Rooney, which proved what nice, clean,
young people with a few sheets of manuscript paper in front of them
could do if given half a chance.

He devised a musical sequence in the picture in which Rooney
imagined a bowl of fruit as the instruments of an orchestra and
proceeded to conduct them. It made such an impression that he
was invited to direct the immensely successful all-black musical,
Cabin in the Sky. He followed this with a somewhat less auspicious
piece, *I Dood It*.

It was 1944 when Minnelli's career took off with an invitation
from MGM's top musical producer, Arthur Freed, to direct a movie
called *Meet Me in St Louis*.

This was a cosy family story set in the early years of that
century, about a year in their lives that culminates in the St Louis
World's Fair. Minnelli gave it a unique touch – not just the
blending of musical numbers that seemed to dance along with the
girls in frilly dresses and bouncing hair styles, but also by the
imaginative way in which the seasons of the year were shown to
change with the moods of the participants – the main one of whom
happened to be Judy Garland.

Not that they hit it off straight away. By all accounts, Judy was
beginning to strike out at MGM, partly because she didn't terribly
like the story – it seemed like a rehash of all the Andy Hardy tales and
she was fed up with being part of a loving and slightly boring family –
and partly on principle. She was finally realising her own value to the
studio and thought it was about time she let them know it.

Minnelli himself wasn't so sure of the value of the tale either, for
that matter. But Freed talked Judy into starring and Vincente into
directing – the prospect of saying no wasn't exactly enticing with the
threats of Louis B. Mayer always hovering in the background.

It did not appear to lead to a good chemical reaction. Minnelli
knew what he wanted, but Judy didn't. Or if she did, she was uneasy
with his methods. She was not a little frightened of him. Old MGM
veterans remember arguments that led to tears, and tears that led to
storms into Freed's office; not at all the kind of thing the young
Dorothy of *Oz* would have dared to do.

It took one call from Minnelli to 'print' a scene featuring Judy to patch up the problems. She finally thought she knew what he wanted and he discovered she could deliver his idea of the goods. They weren't exactly good friends yet, but they got on well enough, and Minnelli gave Judy one glorious moment of film history – the 'Trolley Song'.

He also found that Judy was still using the Louis B. Mayer-prescribed pills that had dogged her earliest days at Metro. It worried him, although not enough to do anything about it.

Minnelli went on next to direct the musical epic *Ziegfeld Follies* starring, among others, Fred Astaire, Gene Kelly – and Judy.

Then came the picture that would prove to be a formative influence on both their careers. *The Clock* was the first non-musical for both of them.

The story about a girl falling for a GI and then marrying him, all in the course of his twenty-four hour leave, was a gem. It showed that without a musical number to worry about, filming could be a much less exhausting process than she had come to expect. The pills were – for a time at least – put away.

It proved three other things, too: that Judy could be a superb actress without the opportunity to burst into song or to dance down a film-set street; that Minnelli had a lightness of touch that was just as evident with this story as it had been with his musicals; and that, like a scene from the picture, and despite Vincente being gay, the two were in love. On June 13, 1945, they were married.

Their extended honeymoon was spent, *The Clock*-style, in New York. By the time they returned to California Judy was pregnant.

Minnelli went back to work on another Fred Astaire musical, *Yolanda and the Thief*. Judy wanted a break, but the studio saw no reason why she shouldn't carry on with her contractual obligations to play Marilyn Miller in what was supposed to be a Jerome Kern biopic, *Till the Clouds Roll By* (any similarity between the picture and the crusty Kern's real life story was entirely coincidental).

She sang 'Look for the Silver Lining' while a bowl of washing-up hid her expanding waistline, but her bulging stomach was more than evident as she raced around a group of chorus boys, repeating to each one the title of the song, 'Who?' The funny side of that did not escape her.

When the film was completed, she settled down to the life of an almost conventional mother-to-be.

Chapter Three

LIZA MAY MINNELLI was born on March 12, 1946. The name Liza was a tribute to Vincente's late friend George Gershwin. Gershwin's song 'Liza' had been a great hit in the 1920s – largely because Al Jolson had sung it nightly from the stalls of the Broadway theatre where his bride Ruby Keeler was performing – and to Minnelli it was not just a consummate piece of professional song-writing but a very pretty tune. If he said it out loud or not, he could want no better qualities for his new daughter – who, as in the song, would make all the clouds roll away. Judy herself loved the name almost as much as she loved her baby.

The child's father – proudly demonstrating his bisexuality by this new status – was suitably impressed by his new daughter. The name May was his mother's and he considered the fact to be a tribute to her. All fathers think their babies are the most beautiful ever created. All fathers know that they are not alone in those sentiments. But Vincente was convinced that his beliefs would stand up to cross-examination in any court of law. As he wrote in his own autobiography, *I Remember it Well*, 'She was, of course, the most beautiful baby in the nursery. As for those other wrinkled babies around her, all they needed was a cigar in their mouths to look like Eddie Mannix [Louis B. Mayer's studio manager and a formidable Hollywood figure in his own right] . . . There, alone, on a table, was a perfect child with absolutely no wrinkles, letting out a healthy cry . . . projecting!'

Frank Sinatra was the first person to visit Judy when Liza was born. It seemed like an omen. He had been a huge personality and was on a downward slope. But he was going to come back. Nobody at the time could have had any idea of the extent to which he was going to return – or how half a century later little Liza would, too. But that was too far ahead to look.

At that point, everything looked wonderful. Certainly, there seemed nothing wrong with this child who was clearly born to entertain. A paediatrician later diagnosed a slight curvature of the spine – an inheritance from Judy and from Judy's mother, Ethel, but nothing anyone was going to worry about.

As far as people in the business of recording the significant events in the comings and goings of the world of entertainment are concerned, history was made that day in 1946. Practically unique in the pantheon of significant names in cinema history, Liza Minnelli's doings were reported in the world's Press from the moment she was born – not in a tiny paid-for 'Births' announcement which a keen newshound may spy out, but in stories and pictures emblazoned in newspapers on both sides of the Atlantic.

Other stars' children become instant celebrities for a few brief days and then fade into respectable obscurity. This pretty professional entered stage left (the side of page one of the newspapers of the day) and was to stay there for ever after.

The *Los Angeles Times* gushed perceptively: 'Twenty years ago in vaudeville Judy Garland was known as "the little girl with the great big voice . . . " Yesterday, Judy gave birth to another little girl with an incessantly big voice.' And just another historical pointer, the paper added: 'The actress mother and Vincente Minnelli, 33-year-old screen director to whom she was married last June, said they would name the baby Liza.'

Three months later, Liza was christened by the Rev J. Herbert Smith. Kay Thompson, a popular singer and actress who was a close friend of Vincente, was godmother and her husband, Bill Spear, godfather. The occasion at a Beverly Hills church was marked with all the panoply of a Hollywood wedding – crowds, fashionable hats and dresses and the MGM publicity department who were more used to finding excuses for the marital arrangements of the studio's personnel being rather *less* than blissful. The papers were anxious to co-operate. Liza, reported the local *Times*, 'made her first public appearance'. They could not have known how significant the apparently sickly statement really was.

It was surely a pointer to the future. Liza would be thrust into a hoopla world where people sang out loud for a living and in which taking work home meant doing a time step in the living room.

This life was to prove easier for Liza than for her parents. Judy, like many a new mother, was depressed when she took the baby home with her to Evanview Drive and wasn't sure what her new rôle should be. Did she want to be a mother or a star? Or did she want to be both? *Could* she be both?

Her contract with MGM provided most of the answers. She may not have fancied dancing or laughing, but Mr Mayer, Mr Mannix and all the other executives at the Culver City studio had been used to dealing with Garland problems for about eleven years.

They had a new film for her and Vincente was going to direct it. *The Pirate* was going to be the archetypal movie musical, with Judy cast opposite Gene Kelly. It wasn't bad but it wasn't brilliant either and although the audience were supposed to imagine the smell of the greasepaint watching this story of a team of travelling players, the varnish of the sets was much more evident.

Judy was bright enough to see this for herself and it didn't help her depression. Neither did it really assist her marriage. She and Minnelli were not, for the moment at least, getting on as well as once they had – to the point of Judy's insisting that Kelly rather than her husband direct her musical numbers. Liza, however, did seem to act as ballast in the marriage and before long the very presence of the youngest member of the family managed to patch things up between the parents. Minnelli wrote that neither of them could wait to get home from the studio to be with the baby.

On one occasion, they didn't have to rush home. Liza was brought to the studio – something not ignored by the MGM publicity machine, who immediately let it be known that this was young Miss Minnelli's first camera appearance, taken sitting on her mother's lap.

'This is just for fun,' said Judy. 'There'll be no more rôles for Liza until she is able to pick them for herself.' That was also a footnote for the historians. As it turned out, however, it was not to be quite the truth.

In the meantime, Judy was more concerned with her own career than with Liza's – and unfortunately with her own state of mind. Judy spent a short time in a mental hospital ('Mama's gone away,' Vincente is supposed to have explained to Liza, who was not yet at an age when she knew her own name, let alone could understand such a message).

The enchanting *Easter Parade*, in which Judy starred with Fred Astaire, was due to be directed by Vincente, but Judy's psychiatrist thought it would be unwise for them to work together – any pressures they had at home might become magnified on the studio floor – and he was replaced by Charles Walters. After this, the studio earmarked her to play opposite Astaire once more in *The Barkleys of Broadway*. She was so ill, mentally and physically – unable to sleep; unable to keep awake; incapable of working out where she was sometimes or what she was doing – that the studio replaced her with Ginger Rogers in a once-and-for-all return of the famous dancing team (Fred hated that word; he always said it sounded like a coach and horses).

But Judy seemed to recover. She did a couple of songs in another supposed screen biography – this time of Rodgers and Hart – called *Words and Music*. It was a good enough performance for her to be almost immediately cast in a new picture, *In the Good Old Summertime*, an old-fashioned musical with girls in long dresses and wide hats. It was a story about a music store salesgirl who finds that the pen-pal she has been courting by correspondence is none other than the fellow employee she always thought she hated. A remake of the Margaret Sullavan-James Stewart picture, *The Shop Around the Corner* with music, it probably wasn't all that good in artistic terms, but it has much greater historical significance. This time it really did feature a young actress named Liza Minnelli.

Three-year-old Liza appeared in the picture, as Judy walked through the park with Van Johnson. In fact, three-year-old Liza didn't just appear, she sang the title song, twirling a parasol almost as big as herself.

She had learned the song, listening to her mother practise it at home. Naturally, the Press were ecstatic. Louella Parsons, privy to all that went on in the world of the Minnellis, got into nostalgic mood: 'Little Liza Minnelli's first day as an actress was an event at MGM, where old-timers still remember her mother's movie début as a chubby child singer thirteen years ago.'

Vincente gave his daughter a bunch of roses as she relaxed exhausted in her mother's chair at the end of her scene. Her fee: a packet of chocolate wafers.

Liza herself didn't look so happy. She later confessed that she realised she wasn't wearing any panties underneath her pretty frilly dress. Her discomfort was one reason why her appearance was somewhat truncated – and why the historic vocal début of Liza Minnelli was brought to a premature end. Her singing of the song was dropped from the movie.

Judy varied from thin to plump in the course of the film, since it was shot out of sequence, and her weight altered drastically from week to week, in accordance with her wild swings of mood. But despite this she was superb and the critics thought so, too. On its strength, MGM signed her to make the movie version of the Irving Berlin superhit, *Annie Get Your Gun*. She was more than signed; she recorded the entire soundtrack, posed for all the publicity pictures and started shooting.

Liza helped Judy's image immensely. Most of Hollywood still considered her unsuitable for another big role, being aware of her unstable condition, but every time Liza entered the scene, the hearts of the hard-bitten Hollywood studio bosses melted.

How could you resist little Liza walking into Judy's living room twirling a large umbrella?

The writer Adela Rogers St Johns recalled Liza telling Judy that she wanted that umbrella even though her mother said that she didn't. 'How do you know I don't?' she asked. And then the child started talking to herself: 'Don't want an umbrella, Liza, you don't want a bath, Liza, you don't want that dirty old penny, Liza, you don't want that book, that's Mummy's.' She was repeating words that Judy had said the day before. There was a strong little character forming there.

That was how Liza came back into the professional picture. Judy announced her little girl was going to play one of the children who stalk their way through *Annie Get Your Gun*. It read like further good publicity from the Culver City machine, but Judy herself told Louella Parsons that she thought it a good idea. As she said: 'She's a born actress and a scene stealer. I sometimes wonder how I ever lived without that lady.'

Still, her closest friends, to say nothing of her husband, were worried about Judy's mental condition. Not a few doubted that she had considered taking her life. Yet when Liza was around, she could look – and sometimes felt, as did many a manic depressive – the happiest person alive.

'I know it sounds like I'm acting to say it's the most wonderful thing that ever happened to me to have had her, but I mean every word of it,' she said.

Indeed, Liza did lend an element of sanity into a crazy lifestyle. But the idea of her appearing in *Annie* didn't last long. Before the possibility could be taken up by the studio, Judy was out of the picture, replaced by Betty Hutton.

There was another problem which not so many people knew about. The Minnellis' love affair was over – and Liza was just about the only factor keeping them together.

Judy's troubles only increased a thousandfold following her axing from *Annie Get Your Gun* and this time the presence of Liza wasn't going to help. Now she did attempt suicide, slashing her throat with a broken glass tumbler.

Most children's memories go back to the age of four. Sometimes, a certain event is so powerful, so traumatic that the infant brain takes in factors which otherwise might not have registered; a photographic image fixes on a stretch of film that has a stronger chemical coating than normal.

Liza was three years and two months when one such thing happened to her. Judy was sent off to another mental hospital, at the other end of the country, the Peter Bent Brigham Hospital in Boston. Liza went to the station with her father to see her off. Like a scene from a vintage Hollywood 'woman's picture', the horror of it has stayed with her ever since. No one who has experienced anything like it themselves could possibly forget it.

The original plan was that Judy would go off to Boston alone while Vincente and Liza stayed behind. Liza's nurse was part of the scene, too – which would prove useful. A grown-up Liza Minnelli told *Good Housekeeping*'s Muriel Davidson about that day in May 1949:

'When it came time for her to leave, she cried and carried on so much that Daddy hopped on the train and went with her. I sobbed and screamed to be taken, too, but all I could do was stand there and watch the train pull away.'

With her nurse driving and Liza screaming, a new example was found – for far too many bystanders, as it would turn out – of the poor little rich girl.

There was little Liza Minnelli, with her lovely clothes, her beautiful dolls and teddy bears, her decorated nursery and... nothing. When her father returned, he bought Liza a tin drum. She later said that she beat on the toy so heavily that it soon collapsed. One hardly needs to have had a detailed psychiatric training to understand the significance of that – or what happened subsequently. When eventually Judy returned to her family, Liza threw the vestiges of the drum away – in disgust.

And yet little girls and boys are incredibly resilient at three and four, and Liza is not willing to concede that she led a tragic childhood.

Just as clearly as she recalls the heartbreaking farewell to Judy at the station, she is prepared to admit her great pleasure at being sent for by her mother a couple of months later. Judy gave a Press conference in New England to show that she had completely recovered and was now deliriously happy. Liza was trooped out for the occasion to show that their happiness was now complete.

More genuinely happy memories are of the times she went with Vincente to the studio when he was working. Her greatest joy – akin to other youngsters sitting on model trains – was being given rides on the camera booms before her father called out 'Action'.

She later recalled: 'It seemed a long way off the ground. But I was never interested unless he was shooting a musical number or something gay. If he was filming a love scene, I'd slip down and run to another set until I could find someone who was singing or dancing. I used to love to watch Fred Astaire.'

In which case, one wonders whether Mr Astaire was ever aware of a little girl watching him. 'I can't say I ever remember her at the studio, although I was very fond of her father,' Astaire told me shortly before his death in 1987.

If he had been aware she was anywhere near the soundstage, he might have had something to say about it. 'I never liked visitors on the set,' he told me. The man who made Ginger Rogers cry – and her feet bleed – with his insistence on nothing less than perfection was not the most tolerant person with regard to such matters.

Nevertheless, Astaire, even in those early moments of little Liza's life, was the sort of person she related to. 'Cyd Charisse was another of my favourites,' she said in that *Good Housekeeping* article. 'I always thought if I could grow up and dance like her, I'd be in heaven.'

If Judy hadn't quite been born in a trunk any more than Liza herself had been, this was a mere technicality. When Liza was particularly good, Judy would take her up to the loft where she kept a trunk full of her old costumes, and would let her dress up in them. That was the best part of being Judy Garland's daughter. 'I wasn't all that fascinated watching Mama [in the studio],' said Liza. 'After all, I could always see and hear her at home.'

Indeed, she could – and she did. Sometimes to 'Mama's' desperation. Home again (now in Holmby Hills), Judy started thinking about work once more – which meant practising more song-and-dance routines in the living room.

The privileged ones were those who called in for a cup of coffee and a slice of cake and ended up being given a personal Judy Garland performance. Liza, by all accounts, never took these occasions for granted. Like the little girl played by Margaret O'Brien in *Meet Me in St Louis*, she would often sneak downstairs and watch Judy performing, her nightgown around her legs and feet – legs and feet that really wanted to dance, too.

One of those who was granted the opportunity of a personal appearance was Debbie Reynolds. The future star of *Singin' in the Rain* witnessed Liza being constantly tapped on the bottom and pushed off to bed on many a 'show'.

She told me: 'Liza's nurse would try to get her to bed. But she would always get up again and want to be part of the fun. She would sit on the stairs and feel part of it. She just wouldn't go to bed – never. Afterwards, when Lorna and Joey [Liza's half-sister and -brother] came along, they would always go off when told, but Liza never would.'

Sometimes, the teenaged Debbie would put Liza to bed, and then go down to Judy's den where 'she was sitting, telling stories.'

There were more intimate moments that were equally treasured by baby Liza. Like many another infant, her big treat was to go into her parents' double bed and sit in the middle as they began to wake up.

It was such a wonderful experience that she has never forgotten it. 'We'd all go to sleep,' she was to say. 'I didn't dare move, for fear I'd get tossed out. I didn't want that because it was so warm and dark and safe there.'

That was in one of the moments of marital bliss. These were to become fewer as the still tiny Liza gradually became aware of what was going on around her.

At about this time, Judy and Vincente started scrapping; at first that was all it was, but the scraps became fights and one of them was so severe that Judy moved out of the house.

For a time, Liza and Vincente had to live without Mama, which the little girl seemed to accept. However, her father knew that was not what either of them wanted.

One night, however, things looked as though they were getting better. Unexpectedly, he came into Liza's bedroom, held out her bathrobe and told her they were going out – to collect Mama.

It seemed that everything would now be all right. Judy moved back into the house. For twelve months it appeared that all was right within the Minnelli household – unless you were privy to what was really going on. Liza experienced part of this.

One of the problems the men at MGM had occasionally known was the exasperated voice of Judy Garland when the chips of unhappiness were down. Usually, *she* was the victim and most of the time acquiesced in depressed silent sobs at the way she was treated. On one occasion, however, she gave out a piercing, tragic Judy Garland scream. Liza experienced those often enough and she reacted to them with the kind of horror other children reserve for claps of thunder or barks from large, frightening dogs.

At nineteen years old, Liza still shuddered when she recalled the first time she heard that screaming Garland voice that vibrated through her body, seeming to crack her bones and pierce her vital organs.

Liza and her parents had been watching television that day in 1951. It was 'Uncle Miltie', Milton Berle, the vaudeville comedian who in middle age had become the king of American TV. It was generally accepted that his humour converted a television audience into an uncontrollable mass of laughing, shaking jelly. Apparently that was the effect he was having on two generations of Minnellis.

Liza was wearing her favourite Hopalong Cassidy cowboy suit, eating pumpkin pie. Judy was indulging in one of her favourite offstage activities – 'performing' with the character on the small screen, answering him back, singing along with the numbers being broadcast and generally giving her own running commentary on the proceedings.

As Liza told Muriel Davidson, she had a sudden urge to do a 'back flip'. 'I reared back, shot out my legs and accidentally hit Mama right in the head.'

The result was not an occasion to forget – or to relish. Judy's undeniable shock and pain were compounded by what was clearly her mental unbalance. She cried out in pain and screamed in irrational anger – as though Liza had deliberately decided to behead her mother.

The scream was that irrepressible shriek, the noise that was for ever more to fill Liza with unreserved horror. The screaming seemed to go on for hours. Liza was ordered to her room – and this time she went. Doubtless, she was glad of the opportunity to get out of the way. Ultimately, Judy went into Liza's bedroom, gave her a cuddle and told her she was forgiven. The child did not now question that her mother was the one in the right – which was also to be slightly out of character. Before long, Liza would conclude that, no matter how young, she was a member of the family and common democracy allowed her certain rights.

She was to say that both her mother and her father seemed to recognise this and never talked down to her. As Judy herself once put it, 'Why start on the wrong foot? Enough people are going to say "goo-goo, ga-ga" when you're older.' Later, Liza was able to rationalise what her mother meant. As she said: 'In other words, they'll double talk you when you're older, so I'll talk to you straight when you're young.'

The kind of adult status accorded to Liza was to be the envy of her friends – rich, otherwise pampered kids brought up by nurses, who were mainly kept insulated from the world of their elders (and betters?). The richer and the more famous the family, the more the parents were there to be seen and heard but the children only to be seen – and then just when Momma *and* Poppa willed it. That was not the way the Minnellis thought their Liza was to be brought up at all.

They did everything to make sure that Liza was included in everything. Strange though it seemed to their friends – and totally incomprehensible to Louis B. Mayer – Liza was consulted both on matters that concerned her in particular and the family in general.

Have dinner at the Minnelli household and chances were you would have the pleasure of Liza's company at the table, as well as that of her parents or of whoever they might have had as house guests at the time. It was regarded as totally natural. Before long, Judy would depend on Liza so much that Debbie Reynolds told me it seemed that their roles were reversed, a sentiment Vincente himself echoed – and Liza was now sure of her place in the family.

Part of this place was as a member of a showbiz dynasty. Before her fifth birthday, she was thinking of herself as a member of a *corps-de-ballet*. In July 1950, *Photoplay* magazine was showing her wearing powder-puff skirts, a fluffy cap on her head and satin slappers on her feet as wide-eyed Liza 'practised' on the bar at her dancing class – held at the studios of Nico Charisse, Cyd Charisse's ex-husband (though this did not appear to influence Liza's allegiance to Cyd's own dancing performances).

Later, at a school concert, she played a yellow chick. It was child's play to an old trouper who had already appeared in an MGM film.

One suspects that even then, she would have preferred to wear a dress by Irene, the studio's award-winning costume designer.

Judy was as proud as any other mother experiencing the joy of a little girl at her first ballet class. In fact, she was never reticent at showing just how proud she was of her little girl. When, in September 1950, Judy returned from a trip to New York, Liza was at the platform at Pasadena as the train, the *Super Chief*, chuffed in.

'I love you, I love you,' cried Judy for all to hear as she scooped Liza up in her arms and hugged her until, it seemed, there could be no more breath left in her four-year-old body.

Judy had taken a holiday in Manhattan to recover completely from her mental breakdown. In truth, it now seems that this was the worst thing she could have done. Liza was more of a stabilising influence than she knew.

Reporters who had watched the happy reunion, asked Judy about her professional intentions.

'I have no plans further than to have breakfast,' she answered. Eleven days later, Judy announced that she was severing her links with MGM, the studio that had seen all her ups and downs – *Andy Hardy*, *The Wizard of Oz*, *Meet Me in St Louis* and *Easter Parade* as well as what had happened to *The Barkleys of Broadway* and *Annie Get Your Gun*.

A statement by Louis B. Mayer spoke of his great 'regret' at having to accept Judy's 'request'. (He probably cried for the reporters, although he was equally likely to have been considerably relieved that he had no further binding agreement with Garland.) Judy said that she was delighted and was anxious to get back to New York where she had now taken an apartment.

She was going there with her secretary and with Liza. No mention was made of Vincente. It was a significant omission. He had already moved out of the house.

Five months later, she and her husband announced plans for divorce. Liza would not suffer, they said. Judy had custody of the child, but Vincente had as much access as he wished, at least as much as did Judy. It was a settlement unique in Californian law and came to represent what at the time was considered to be the equal influences of both parents on the child. What wasn't known at the time and few would ever recognise, was that Vincente would prove to be the stronger of those influences.

It was the beginning of the strange childhood of Liza Minnelli.

Chapter Four

LIZA WAS to say: 'My childhood may have been awful, but it was truly exciting.'

That it most certainly was and it takes no stretch of anyone's imagination to accept her judgement on the years before and after going to school. She also added: 'Looking back, I wouldn't have had it any other way.' That is perhaps a more subjective judgement and a little more difficult to accept.

Sometimes, she saw things slightly differently. 'I had a horrendous childhood,' she once said – spitting out the syllables so that it sounded like 'horr-en-dous', which it probably was.

The nice thing would have been for her to have learned right from the beginning that she was no different from any other little girl and that her parents were absolutely no different from anyone else's mother and father.

The trouble was that other boys and girls didn't live in houses that were on the route of the sight-seeing buses. That immediately set her out as something special. She knew that people drove up in battered old Fords just to stop and stare. She understood that when buses drove round the corner, they weren't taking short cuts. Even at four years old, she knew that you couldn't just get on a bus and go to town by stepping through the front gate. Buses were for people who were out to rubberneck.

Sometimes if you were four and people stopped outside to look, you got a little conceited. You didn't think they thought your Mommy was anything special, but that everyone had come to look at you.

She was dancing on the lawn once when a car stopped and the driver rolled down the window. Liza curtseyed. She was expecting applause from the lady in the car – perhaps a few cents thrown on to the grass. Instead, the driver looked out – and vomited.

Liza ran in tears to her father, who was in the house that day. It was rejection with a vengeance and she needed a few soothing words and a kiss and cuddle. She got all those and the message that the poor woman in the car would have been sick anyway. It had nothing to do with either Liza herself or her dancing. It made it a little easier, but the event and the feelings it brought on would linger in her memory.

Among the problems was that one familiar to many children of movie and theatrical celebrities. As she admitted in young adulthood: 'I have been reared strangely, differently from most kids. But I was brought up happily and well. The difference between me and any other kid on the block was that when my parents battled, or my mother went to a rest home, it became a matter of public record.'

That hadn't mattered so much before Liza realised there was such a thing as a public record. However, she did suffer the humiliation of knowing, even at that age, that when Judy screamed and shouted at a railway station, there were other people around to hear it.

In the years to come, she would be shunted about rather like a railway train herself – if a very pretty one – even though she was already certain of her station in life. She knew she was going into show business. At every one of the twenty schools she would attend in the ten years following her fifth birthday in 1951, and among the neighbours of the dozen or more houses in which she and her mother lived in the time to come, there were stories of the strange life to which Judy was subjecting her offspring.

It was not the sort of life most people would say they would want to have unchanged. But neither is there any doubt that Liza absolutely thrived upon it. Even as a small child, she rationalised that she was probably happier than her mother ever was.

And she thrived, too, on her relationship with Vincente, who was the parent for fun and excitement, the one who spoiled her so much that his friends took him aside and begged him to be more restrained. With Judy, things were very different. Not just that her mother was stricter with Liza than her father was. That was usual for products of a broken home. No, Liza's relationship with her mother was totally unconventional.

As Debbie Reynolds put it to me: 'I was always struck by the very soulful child that Liza was. I think her eyes expressed it that way.' Maybe she knew then, as Debbie said, 'she was mother to her mother'.

It seems strange that the grown-up Judy Garland would ask her
five-year-old daughter for advice on the various crises of her life, but
apparently that was what she did. Sometimes, it was more easy to
understand. When Judy was in one of her depressed moods, Liza
was on hand to talk her out of it.

Anything that happens when you are five years old, you tend to
think perfectly normal and take for granted. The problems come
later. They would for Liza – much later.

Sometimes, it was the classic question from Liza about Judy's
own childhood that would rock her out of one of the so-painful
moods. Liza would sit enthralled learning about her mother being
carted from one place to another before the Gumms alighted in
California. The stories about Judy's parents brought tears to Liza's
eyes.

Judy held back no punches in talking about her own mother, a
woman she tended to resent as much for depriving her of her
childhood as for subjecting her to what she saw as the pains and the
degradations of Hollywood.

Her father she spoke of differently. When he died in 1935, reported
Judy, she felt quite simply there was no one on her side. Death
haunted her – she told Liza that, too – and she disliked dolls because
they couldn't move and therefore reminded her of the dead. Macabre,
but that was one of the sides of Judy Garland that Liza got to know at
this early, formative age. But she had already worked out what she
assumed was a solution. She would put her arms around her mother's
neck and those soulful eyes were as difficult for Judy to resist as they
were for Debbie Reynolds and her other friends.

By now, Liza was meeting other stars' children, like the year-older
Mia Farrow (daughter of Maureen O'Sullivan) and Candice Bergen
(whose father was the ventriloquist Edgar Bergen – of Charlie
McCarthy fame). They all saw how Judy's depressions would
disappear when Liza took over – sometimes just by talking to her in
that overwhelming little girl voice that was as difficult to resist as
would have been a contract that said all was forgiven, Judy could
work only when she wanted to and then for half a million dollars a
picture.

Sometimes, Liza would sing and dance for her mother. That was
enough for anybody's heart to melt. And when Liza mothered the
poodle her parents had given her for her fourth birthday, all hearts
would dissolve.

There were some people who thought that Liza's effect on her father was perhaps a little too overpowering – which was how his friends put in their fifteen-cents-worth. Vincente was to remember his friend Lee Gershwin – wife of Ira – telling him: 'Vincente, I love her dearly. But Liza is very spoiled. It's your fault, you know. Judy's the disciplinarian with her and tries to instil some character in her. But you give her everything.' As Minnelli recalled in his book, she added: 'You're nothing but a puddle of love. For her own sake, Liza should be disciplined. If she's not, you mark my words. She's going to grow up to be a commuter to an institution.'

It was difficult to treat a five- or six-year-old as an equal in whom you confide and at the same time remember that you shouldn't spoil her – even if it were Judy who was both the disciplinarian and the one who needed to lean on Liza's tiny, immature shoulders.

She was conscious of the way she looked, this little girl – almost as though she were already grown up and competing with other women mixing in her social whirl. Once Vincente took her to see an ice show, but Liza wasn't excited about the performance in store. She didn't like the dress she was wearing. That was all the doting father had to hear. He immediately turned the car round and drove back home – so that Liza could change.

'Daddy,' she said, 'you *do* understand, *don't* you?' That statement was enough to stay in Vincente's memory for the rest of his life. He couldn't understand how a child of that age could respond in that way. He thought it was clever. His friends thought it meant she was exceedingly spoilt.

Whether her grandmother felt the same way or not is not easy to ascertain. Ethel Gumm took it upon herself to take Liza for dancing lessons – until, that is, Judy decided to strike out finally from her mother's barbed-wire apron strings and ordered Liza's nurse, a Mrs McFarlane, never to take her to Ethel again. It could have been pique after a row between the two women; it could have been jealousy. Perhaps it was simply that Judy didn't want her own stage mother to turn into a stage grandmother with too much influence over her own daughter.

Liza observed the row from her favourite position – lying on the floor under the grand piano. When she went to other people's houses, like Lee and Ira Gershwins', she came out from under the piano because she knew she would be the centre of attention.

The Gershwins weren't fussy enough to deny Liza the

opportunity to have her birthday parties at their house – neither Judy's home nor the Minnelli residence was considered big enough to deal with the 100 or more guests who didn't just enjoy cream cakes and games of pass the parcel, but needed the services of an entertainer, previously unseen shorts from the nearby Walt Disney 'factory' shown on professional equipment in the house's cinema, a model train running in the grounds outside, a clown – who for reasons no one was totally able to explain was meant to play 'drunk' – and pony rides for the little girls. There was also the best ice-cream in California served in giant portions.

They were, in their way, as significant Hollywood events as the parties enjoyed by the stars themselves. The public certainly thought so. So many people wanted to line up to see the children of stars – sometimes brought by the parents themselves, although usually by their nannies borrowing the family Cadillac or Rolls-Royce for the occasion – that the police were invariably brought in to block off the streets. Hardly surprising, when regular guests at Liza's parties were Humphrey Bogart and Lauren Bacall, who would bring their own children to the celebrations in person.

These were all children of big stars, but they were children who were spoken to as children. As we have seen, that was not how Liza was used to being treated. Since the age of three, she had been used to her mother confiding her problems about the studios, about Hollywood politics and about agents – while Liza sat quietly listening to what could have been a fairy story. Indeed, she was hearing tales of 'residuals' and percentages and unprintable stories about household names while other children were contenting themselves with Little Red Riding Hood.

She wasn't really much help with the technicalities of her parents' divorce which, inevitably, would be one of the big public events of 1951. Neither would she have liked to have been told of the 'romantic link' between Judy and film producer Sidney Luft. Certainly, Liza would not have been informed of her father behaving, as Judy charged in her action, 'in a cruel and inhuman manner' which caused her 'great mental suffering'.

Part of Judy's suffering was that she had to continually move house. It was the beginning of another episode in Liza's life. For the next few months, 'home' was a hotel room, an apartment or a house that never seemed more than temporary lodgings. Liza later reasoned that Judy wasn't always able to afford the rent and was avoiding the landlords although how Judy Garland could escape anywhere is something of a mystery.

Nevertheless, one of the earliest kinds of 'sport' to which Liza was subjected was the 'game' of sneaking out of a hotel room, four or five layers of clothing on at a time sometimes, in the middle of the night, so that they could avoid paying the bill, without having to carry any luggage. What they couldn't wear had to be left behind with the suitcases.

Liza was to say that she never minded that happening. 'Because Mama always made it fun. You know, she was truly one of the funniest people I've ever known!' As she was to recall for *Cosmopolitan* magazine, Judy would say 'Oh hell! I needed a new wardrobe anyway.'

And she learned how to achieve the confidence of a star. As they sorted themselves out of this little difficulty, her mother would whisper to Liza, 'No problem. Always keep in mind, *I'm Judy Garland!*'

In a similar way, Liza had to get used to the idea that she wouldn't stay in one school for longer than what most children would consider a short holiday. If Judy thought that she was in the money (actually she rarely was) there would be a short stay at a private school for Liza. If she were broke, it would be a neighbourhood state school.

Liza wasn't supposed to notice the disruptions. It certainly was good training for going 'on the road' with her shows in years to come, the experiences of living out of one of the trunks in which Judy was supposed to have been born, but it did contribute to that awful Minnelli childhood, the memory of which only now is beginning to mellow. It has to be looked back on as fun, as character-forming, but then a child living in a slum who becomes a millionaire or an inmate of an orphanage who goes on to be a captain of industry is inclined to look back on childhood with nostalgia. That is the position of the adult Liza Minnelli as she contemplated the in-between stage of not having a father in the house.

But, as she said in her *Good Housekeeping* piece, 'We lived like millionaires and with laughter.'

There was also the other side of things – times when Liza returned from school and would make straight for the kitchen. She wasn't after a snack, but information. There was always the same question to the housekeeper: 'what sort of mood is Mama in today?'

It was indeed hard for a child who knew practically everything there was to know about the way a parent was being treated. Sometimes she could appreciate the times when Judy wasn't working – because they were occasions when her mother enjoyed the rest and loved being with her daughter. At other times, Judy's depressions at not being wanted were the cause of as much pain to Liza as they were to her herself.

The effects of unemployment on the family have become the subject of several learned treatises over the last few years. Few have begun to think of them specifically in terms of the families of the sometime wealthy and famous. No one should think that having an unemployed parent who normally works in a factory or a grocer's shop is any easier, but the phenomenon of the once rich and now insecure is, in its way, every bit as worrying – and dangerous.

Liza could give enough evidence at any such inquiry to make the professional investigators rush to their own psychiatrists. Indeed, it was the beginning of Judy's roller-coaster years; rich one moment, poor the next. At first, money seemed no problem. She took Liza with her on a series of holidays. Then, when she went to Britain to perform at the London Palladium, Liza went along for the ride; a trip she remembers affectionately to this day. It was one of the 'ups' in the Garland life. Her mother was being fêted as a goddess.

It was hardly surprising. Judy Garland on this visit was confirming that the Palladium was virtually the property of American show business. Four years earlier, Danny Kaye had been so sensational at the same theatre that it would never totally recover. Kaye came again and again, but he also whetted the appetites of the theatre's patrons for American performers. Judy was sensational there, second only perhaps to Danny himself. Vincente was as thrilled as anyone in their circle at this triumph and he was even more delighted that Liza was there to see it at first hand.

He as much believed that the child was born to sing and dance as she did herself. This was a good kind of show business for her to see for herself. Not only was Liza's mother being fêted as a great performer in such contrast to her most recent experiences at MGM's empire at Culver City – but it was a superb performance from which, even at this tender age, only good things could be learnt.

Now, however, he might have felt happier if Liza knew the way he felt about her.

The child who was her mother's principal confidante felt that perhaps, for all he said and did, her father didn't show the same degree of appreciation of her capabilities. Whereas Judy would sit and chat to Liza, Vincente just showered her with love – but not with conversation. She wasn't happy with that. One day, however, it was different. Her father came home, plopped himself down in his favourite armchair and started reading the newspaper, while Liza sat dotingly on his lap. Suddenly, something he read in the paper infuriated him. He started muttering to himself. Liza was as excited by this as she would have been had she understood the news story herself. She jumped from Vincente's knees, and ran across the room to Judy – it was one of those occasions when they were all together. 'Mama,' she cried, 'Daddy just spoke to me.' Never had bad news had such a wonderful reaction.

Liza's own talents were instantly recognised in the classroom. In her first 'permanent' school, she was given the role of the Virgin Mary in a Christmas pageant. It wasn't an auspicious 'straight' stage début. As Liza later admitted: 'I walked on stage and dropped the kid!'

Fortunately for all concerned – history would have doubtless taken a different turn had it not been so – the 'kid' was a doll.

Her own life was far more real, as details of her parents' relationships with each other percolated down to her. It was not pleasant for a child who craved not just love – that she was getting – but a sense of normality.

For all Liza's thoughts about paternal neglect, Vincente had as much faith in her latent adulthood as did Judy. He didn't think she needed pampering like other children. Indeed, that showed in the presents he bought her. Judy would give her a gift of a book of nursery tales. If the mood struck him, Vincente could present his little girl with a copy of Colette. He read the French writer's work to Liza, while her friends were having bedtime stories about three little bears. Years later, her father was to say that he didn't stop loving Judy, but that he suddenly realised that he loved Liza and, he admitted, himself more.

A certain degree of stability entered her life when the man she was told was called 'Uncle Sid' entered the picture. Liza was to say that she liked Sidney Luft. She remembers well the day that her mother told her she was going to marry him.

She was watching Judy applying her make-up. As the paint and lipstick went on, the question came: 'How about Uncle Sid and I getting married?' But it was not simple giving an answer. Why on earth would Judy want to marry again? It wasn't that Liza had anything against him, but it did seem a trifle unnecessary.

Well, Judy told her six-year-old daughter, that way she could have brothers and sisters. As Liza told the *Good Housekeeping* writer: 'That made good sense, so I gave my permission.'

What Liza was not told – and judging by the way mother addressed daughter, it's almost surprising that she was not – was just how much it made sense. Judy was two months pregnant when she put Sid fully into the picture in June 1952. The rest came fairly suddenly.

But there were more shocks ahead. Judy made sure that Liza was safely away with Vincente when she had important things to do – and so it was on the evening when father and daughter were sitting in front of a television screen, watching the news. The main story in the bulletin that day was the marriage of film star Judy Garland and producer Sidney Luft.

Liza cried when she heard about it and had to be comforted by her father, who was equally put out. But, Liza later said, 'I rationalised that it wasn't my business when Mama got married, really, or to whom.' Necessity and reality was making little Liza Minnelli work out some very adult problems for herself.

One of the things she worked out was that she and Sid maintained their relationship. They liked each other. Luft was to tell me that 'love' was a much truer description of their relationship.

Almost immediately, they consolidated their feelings about each other with an agreed terminology. Vincente Minnelli remained, and would stay so for ever after, her 'Daddy'. But there was to be something special between Luft and Liza, too. No more was he to be 'Uncle Sid'. Now he was her 'Poppa Sid'. Before long, 'Poppa Sid' became simply 'Pop'.

It was a clever move. It did not mean that he was taking on Minnelli's total parental role – although, as Luft was to tell me, that was how he began to see it for much of the time – but a different title established a demarcation line. 'Pop' was better than 'Uncle'. But it was not – and was not intended to be – quite the same as 'Daddy', who would shower gifts on Liza and would treasure the moments they had together. She would still go to see him at work at the studio, although usually if there were a love scene, she would be sent off in the direction of the ice-cream stand, if there was no 'suitable' musical being made alongside.

And through Vincente, she benefited from the bounties of the studio's costume department. Every October, Liza Minnelli had the most expensive, most elaborate Halloween 'trick-or-treat' outfit, designed by Irene or Adrian. Through paternal influence at the studio, Liza became the proud owner of replicas of dresses originally worn by Cyd Charisse or Leslie Caron.

Liza soon realised how sensible was Judy's reasoning for 'asking permission' of her little daughter to the marriage. But before the nine months of that pregnancy were over, Liza had already found a younger 'brother'. Sid's son Johnny – by his marriage to the beautiful film star Lynn Bari – was eighteen months younger than Liza. She immediately claimed him as a brother, although their relationship would be somewhat taut in those early days. On the whole, however, they appeared to care for each other very greatly.

The family relationship was cemented on November 21 of that year when Judy gave birth to her second child by Caesarian section. Liza now had a sister called Lorna. Officially, of course, her half-sister, but neither of them would consider themselves to be anything but fully related. It was the beginning of a very close, very lasting relationship that many 'whole' brothers and sisters would envy.

It was very much a Luft household. But at the same time, Liza was asserting herself more as her mother's mother than ever she had before. As far as Liza was concerned, this was but totally natural.

'Nobody had a happy childhood,' Liza was to say more than thirty years later. But if such a thing *were* possible to achieve, hers was 'terrific'. Yet, she admitted, she felt 'really assured when I found that out'. As she told *Cosmopolitan* magazine: 'Everything became exaggerated because it was Judy doing it. I was not the only child who was yelled at. I was not an experiment, not a freak. Mama was always there. I got a tremendous amount of love from my parents – and a tremendous amount of garbage.

'I was – how can I say? – crazy. But basically sane.'

That may sound a little crazy in itself, but not to Liza who ought to be able to look to that craziness as the real reason for the immense success that was to follow.

Judy might have known that. 'Watch this,' she would tell Liza, 'I'm going to have to do something crazy.'

If she could survive some of the things that had already happened to her – even now that she was not quite so often being moved from one school to the next and when she no longer had to learn how to creep out of a hotel room literally as a thief in the night – she had to be incredibly sane. Sometimes, the problems were no different from the ones many another child put in charge of a younger brother or sister had to face – except that Liza at that age was never put in charge of her younger sister. On purpose, that is. There was, though, the occasion when she did have to take responsibility.

Lorna's nurse told Liza she was quitting her job – and did just that. The seven-year-old Liza was in charge of a screaming baby sister.

It turned out that the nurse had done quite a bit of screaming herself – and so had Judy. After the tempestuous row – or, rather, in the middle of it – Judy had to go out. The nurse didn't decide to simmer down and take it all as part of the job. She gathered her belongings and left.

The baby screamed more and Liza had no idea how to cope with the delicate situation. Eventually, the older girl had the sense to waken their cook and ask her to deal with the baby until Judy came home. The scene when 'Mama' returned would not have been one for her fans to savour – to say nothing of her detractors and the people at MGM.

Lorna told me herself that she would grow to regard that craziness as nothing less than perfectly normal.

The younger 'Garland' sister would remember duets between mother and sister as part of everyday life.

There were the earliest doses of school homework to go with the songs now. Judy loved to show that she didn't learn all the lessons of life from that trunk in which she was born. She was a bright woman and revelled, even at this stage, in her children understanding how clever she really was. When Liza needed help with the homework, Judy wouldn't let anything interfere with it – unless it was a new theatre tour, a couple of records to make, the chance – the ever-present chance – of a movie comeback, even if not with MGM.

For a time, it seemed that Judy's disenchantment with MGM – and their lack of enthusiasm for her – was good for the still young star (she was twenty-nine when she broke the contract), and a star she remained.

The London Palladium show had been a total sell out, and the news percolated home. As a result of that, Judy was booked again and again into Broadway's own temple of vaudeville (thanks to her, enjoying not so much a renaissance as a resurrection): the Palace. She told Liza all about it, asked her advice on the dresses she should wear on stage and the songs she should sing. Liza told her and, astonishingly perhaps, Judy took notice and followed the advice.

After one tour of duty at the Palace Judy returned to California wearing long black trousers to be met by a delightfully excited Liza. 'Mom, you look fat,' Liza was heard to say.

'I don't worry about my figure any more,' replied Judy – and hugged Liza to prove that there were more important things in her life.

Ask Liza what was most important about her relationship with her mother at this time and chances are she will say it simply: they were friends and it was the friendship she valued more than anything.

By the time she was seven, Liza was experiencing some of her mother's frustrations. 'I worried about Mama,' was how she put it, 'but not in certain ways. I never saw her in a situation that she couldn't handle, even if she was having a tantrum or crying hysterically.'

And there would be the 'yelling' that came – always came – when Judy's prodigious temper was lost or just went missing for a short time. But despite it, she still says that her 'Mama's greatest gift was the ability to laugh.'

On the whole, these were good times for Liza, a Minnelli who sometimes felt she was a Luft, but who was never led to believe she was an outsider.

Their home now was at 144 South Mapleton Drive, in the heart of what was without doubt the film star belt. A few houses away lived Humphrey Bogart and Lauren Bacall; near them, Bing Crosby; down the street, Lana Turner; over the road were the Sammy Cahns.

Cahn, ace song writer of standards ranging from 'High Hopes' and 'Come Fly With Me' to 'I'll Walk Alone' and 'It's Magic', told me he knew that his little neighbour named Liza was destined for big things right from the moment he watched her first performances.

'I have vivid memories of Liza in my little boy's bedroom,' he recalled. 'He's standing up on a cupboard, shining a flashlight on her as she sang.'

And, he remembers thinking about her future: 'By Minnelli out of Garland – that's heavy credentials, heavy, heavy credentials. I started asking myself where she was going to go. I really didn't have any doubts about that destiny.'

She had, he told me, 'a sparrow-like quality'.

In fact, being an insider was sometimes the hardest thing of all at schools like Mrs Emerson's, where other children's parents couldn't help themselves pointing and staring at 'Judy Garland's kid'.

It certainly was not that Liza Minnelli resented being Judy Garland's kid, for even at this time she was nothing but proud of her famous mother, but no child likes being different, and being stared at and pointed out only seems to highlight the problem.

She was happier when it was Mama being stared at. When Judy did her first TV specials, Liza was there to applaud the loudest and to smile the widest when the studio audience got to its feet to cheer.

When she heard that Judy was going back to a film sound stage to work again, her joy was total. This time 'Pop' was producing the film in a new studio for Judy and a new one which Liza could visit every day when she had finished school. *A Star Is Born*, directed by George Cukor, was being shot at Warner Bros' Burbank studios.

It was the beginning of more traumas for Judy, but at first she was simply delighted to be back at work and Liza was ecstatic, hearing her mother sing for the first time about being born in that trunk, 'The Man That Got Away', and her magnificent rendition of 'Swanee' which, if Jolson had not got in first, would have become the greatest of Garland standards.

Meanwhile, as far as Liza was concerned, her Daddy was still on the scene – if facing the agonies of divorced fathers everywhere having to reconcile themselves to being on temporary 'loan' to their children. There is something intrinsically unnatural about a forced day at the zoo or the circus with a child of your own, whom you love and would prefer to simply have sitting at your feet in the living room.

Liza's favourite was the children's park at La Cienega Boulevard. Years later, Liza would tell of hearing the English nannies of her friends sitting on benches, watching their charges and talking to each other about contract deals and film scripts. Her own interest, however, was much more concerned with being with her father.

Vincente took her for long walks. He sat her on the roundabouts and pushed her generously. She sat on the swings and he helped her rides along.

Most of all, it was an opportunity for them to talk. Perhaps, even more than that, it was a chance for them to laugh. It took some time, it turned out, for her to appreciate this. At first, she was convinced that Vincente was laughing at her. But it seemed that she had to learn how to laugh *with* people as much as she had to learn how to perform or sing. Vincente, for his part, liked nothing better than making his beloved child laugh and he succeeded beyond his aspirations.

He admitted in his memoirs *I Remember It Well* that his friends were right: he did spoil Liza 'outrageously', particularly now, with Judy at work and her film in production at Warners, that she was in the neighbourhood, as it were.

Once more, he took her as often as he could to MGM. There she could watch her father's latest movie *The Band Wagon* in production. He was proud of his little girl and loved the attention doted on her by, for instance, Cyd Charisse.

Vincente also said that he smothered Liza with love. If he didn't spoil her, smother her he certainly did. In his book he was to accuse Judy of the occasional 'neglect' of his daughter, which he thought inevitable. Sidney Luft, as he told me, certainly takes exception to that.

The situation in which the father found himself was, however, equally inevitable. Suddenly, he was in a role that was intensely competitive, whether he liked it or not. His weapons were the ones that came easiest and most obvious to him – the love that he quite genuinely felt.

Work and other pressures – particularly his involvement with the woman who was to be his next wife – however, often meant that he had to forgo what he genuinely wanted to do; to spend as much time with Liza as could possibly be squeezed into the day.

He had to reconcile his two worlds and his two loves. Liza was part of his flesh and blood, and he loved her to distraction. But sometimes that love and his responsibility could not be reconciled with his other commitments.

It was a source of pain and anxiety for him, and Liza detected it. She at no time, however, felt as though Vincente were deserting her. Judy was the live-in Mama, and it was she and her problems that caused a great deal more unhappiness for her. Daddy was the man who gave her presents and who provided so much excitement for her on those trips to the film sets.

Vincente knew how Liza felt and the knowledge of it only seemed to heighten his own anxiety. He wanted to give the child a love that was almost overpowering. He knew that generosity and kisses were not enough, but he had to find ways of demonstrating to her the way that he felt, so that she would be left in no doubt as to his sense of devotion and caring.

It was as much a part of the world in which almost every divorced father lives as were the visits to the zoo or La Cienega park. He may not have admitted a sense of guilt, but it is there and every bit as apparent as the senses of love and duty – to say nothing of that of competitiveness.

He went over the top, but somehow and surprisingly the otherwise too mature Liza was managing to avoid the first signs of requiring that commuter's ticket to an institution. Certainly, she was precocious, but that was far more due to the dependence on her shown by her mother than by the doting of her father.

Somehow, when she lived with Vincente – even when Judy was in California, too – she was more of a little girl than when at home in the Luft household. Vincente did not confide in her or ask her advice. Whether she knew that his stance was by far the more correct one or not, she must have sensed that it was better to be treated that way. Also of course, she enjoyed being spoiled.

Sometimes, that spoiling reached excessive dimensions. Once, at a children's birthday party the sight of another little girl sitting on Vincente's lap was more than Liza could take. Suddenly she herself was the little woman scorned. So she had to invoke her position as the most favoured person in his world. Without saying anything, she proceeded towards him like a one-child advancing army, looked him straight in the face and gave him a humdinger of a blow with her fist on his nose.

Of course, she should have been sent home in disgrace. Instead, Vincente laughed and so did everyone else all around. Was there ever such an adorable child! Liza, for one, didn't think there could have been.

It was very clear that she was very much her own person. Plenty of people would be able to decide that for themselves in the years to come.

Chapter Five

IF IT WASN'T easy being the daughter of Judy Garland, it wasn't any simpler having a father who was one of the most famous men in Hollywood, and a stepfather who had just produced a hit musical and was by all accounts one of the most 'bankable' names in Hollywood.

Other children of broken homes have suffered from the problems of having 'two daddies' and there was nothing particularly special in that except that the proverbial goldfish bowl was a highly magnifying instrument through which to see the world and, more importantly, to be seen.

She was to tell the *New York Times*: 'There were no middles, no times when I was just tranquil. I was used only to screaming attacks or excessive love bouts, rivers of money or no money at all, seeing my mother constantly or not seeing her for weeks at a time.' Normality was not on her agenda. It really was a crazy life. The problem was making sure that she didn't go crazy with it.

Her own father tried to make sure that she didn't. He continued to foster his warm, loving, spoiling attention on her between films or other professional engagements and between his own romantic tangles – falling in and out of love; marrying and then planning a divorce.

Liza's visits to the sets of Vincente's films would make movie plots of their own. She went to see him working on the Lucille Ball-Desi Arnaz picture *The Long, Long Trailer*. In one scene, the huge vehicle of the title knocks down a house. The owner – Madge Blake, playing Lucille's aunt – was meant to vent her anger on the caravan.

Liza was so engrossed in this scene that she went up to the old-time actress and asked her, pleadingly: 'Why don't you like that trailer? I think it's a very nice trailer.'

Veteran actress and little girl then sat down to talk. After the usual

35

sort of questions from elder to child about what she liked to eat and where she went to school, Liza looked at Miss Blake with those big eyes of hers and said, 'I have to go and find my Daddy now.'

Miss Blake wrote to Vincente after the incident saying: 'I'd like to tell her that when my second grandchild arrives in September, I hope it will be a little girl as lovely and talented and well-mannered as Liza.'

Vincente was still swelling with pride over that incident when he related the story in his book, *I Remember It Well* about twenty years later. That was an illustration of how normal Liza's life *could* be when given the chance. Normal, that is, if your father is a leading film director and you can forget the fact that he is no longer married to your mother.

But those were matters that could be forgotten, or if not forgotten, then taken for granted. It made life not just tolerable, but wonderful. The other matter about not coming from a broken home was just something that had to be accepted. Besides, young as she was, Liza probably realised that her situation was not very different from that of every other child she knew – particularly those living in the film star belt. Living there was also unreal, but if that's the way things are, you don't question them at that age.

Judy struggled to provide as much kindness and structure to Liza's life as possible, and Sid did too. It wasn't normal for a child to have both a Daddy and a Pop, but to his everlasting credit Sid did for a time make it seem as conventional and as pleasant as a bowl of home-made ice cream.

Certainly it was at least as much a part of Liza's existence as were the traumas and the problems to her own life that they caused – or which her neighbours and the gossip writers believed were caused.

Liza partly blames her mother for most of her acquaintances' fond belief that her childhood was sad and deprived, that she was the poor little rich girl incarnate. But she insists that wasn't so. Judy once told her that she deliberately went out of her way to convince people that she was unhappy. 'Otherwise, they won't cry when I sing "Over the Rainbow".'

That was also something for the psychiatrists. But Liza sees nothing strange in it. 'There's nothing I can do to convince people that I had a happy childhood. They don't want to believe that. But [Judy] ensured my happiness as a kid. I know what happened to me and I know that I'm fine. You know, working and going forward. And

I'm sorry if I'm not unhappy. It's not my fault I'm happy and I have been for most of my life.'

That was not totally true, but Liza would have been a lot more unhappy if she admitted it to herself.

But her mother did provide her with intolerable pressures. Long after Judy's death, Liza was to say that she couldn't even accept the happy moments of life with Mama. Would they last? Should they last? What should she do to make them last? She didn't really know any of the answers. She told a journalist: 'I . . . was trying to find out from my mother whether that was the sort of time when it was all right to laugh all you wanted to. You see, I was remembering the times my mother laughed and was happy, and then later I'd see her crying. And that was something I did not want to do – cry. So I was always in the middle, torn between the laugh and the invisible caution that if I dared to be happy about some things, I would pay for it in tears later, a hundred times over.'

There was deep psychological concern about that. If possible, she would rather have cried first and then laughed – so that it wouldn't always seem like a punishment for being happy, or, as she put it, 'pay for one's happiness before it came. Mother looked at me for a moment and her face was full of sadness.'

'Why should we have to cry at all?' she asked her daughter. But it was a question Liza was no more able to answer than was Judy.

Before long, she schooled herself to be prepared for the time when things wouldn't be so good – so that she wouldn't sit depressed at lost chances of happiness and joy; 'When I wanted sympathy and there would be none, when I would want love and there would be none for me, when I would want to be happy and have nothing to be happy about.'

And yet time has cushioned her. She now maintains that the happy times really did outnumber the sad ones.

Ask her what the happiest ones were and chances are she won't talk about *A Star Is Born* or joining her on stage, but of seeing Judy wearing an apron and baking a cake in their kitchen at Mapleton Drive.

Her life is the only one she has known, so asking her to talk about it is, she says, rather akin to 'asking a princess what it's like being one. She wouldn't know, because she had always been one.'

But princesses didn't have their lives mixed up as though they had been shoved into a food processor. In truth, that was what happened to Liza Minnelli.

If a child experiences the problems of a disjointed life, those difficulties are highly exaggerated for a youngster who is constantly in the public eye, who *has* to behave. The results, of course, are frequently the exact opposite of what is desired – because of the apparent need to seem normal and stable, the problems arise.

On the whole, Liza survived these torments exceedingly well. She had a good relationship with Sid Luft who talked to me of that formative period in her life.

'I am sure that during those years, I was more of a father to her than her real father was. I certainly saw more of her than he did. I loved her as my own and I believe she loved me, too.

'She was reasonably close to her father, but...I wouldn't call Vincente a great father in her growing-up period. He had his own problems to work out at the time. But he certainly loved her. He was a decent sort of a guy, but he was too artsy. For a time he wasn't available to Liza and he was to go through three marriages, but I couldn't say he wasn't a *good* father. He wasn't as attentive as he could have been in the years before she grew up a little.'

Yet, Luft emphasised for me, 'I *was* the father.

'In the formative years, there was no one around except Judy and me. When I married Judy, Liza lived with us. I regarded her as my own child.'

The house at 144 South Mapleton Drive was shaped like a Tudor castle – which might have been considered only right for Hollywood royalty.

Liza was three-and-a-half when Luft first met her. 'And she always had the desire to perform. When I first knew her she was going to a little kindergarten and it was there that she learned to twirl and to love to do so.'

That love to twirl developed into a desire to do much more, which was precisely why Judy suggested and Liza insisted on going to dancing classes.

From the age of five, her sessions at the dancing class were more like regular appearances at church and the dance actions like religious rituals. Sid Luft remembers driving her to those lessons, and their times together on these occasions being some of the most joyous with his step-daughter. Her happiness at going there was positively infectious.

As she grew older, he exercised some of the discipline that fathers are expected to impose. 'Later on, I used to be fairly strict about the time she came in and I liked to know where she was,' he remembered. 'And her mother did, too. But there was no heavy hand needed with her. She was a very good kid, very loving.'

But always, no matter how much they might try to hide it, there was the concern that Liza should feel part of the Luft family, no less and no more so than Lorna. Sid admitted to me that he was always conscious of this and did what he could to put it right. 'I am an early riser – Judy was a night person – so I had breakfast with Liza and the other children every morning.

'I'm a pretty straight guy and I didn't tolerate too much nonsense in the house. I tried to look at everything in its proper perspective as far as Liza was concerned, as I would with everything else. Liza was a wonderful child, really. I can't remember any problems I ever had with her during her growing-up period.'

And there was always the staff there to help things along. There were, in fact, two nurses in the household. One for Liza and another for Lorna.

That may not always have been regarded by the children as a privilege, but it was intended as such by the elder Lufts. They had their pets, a dog called Sam, part collie and part German shepherd, given to Judy at a party by a fellow guest who said he couldn't keep it. Sam came home with her that night and became part of the family. Liza regarded herself as the dog's principal custodian and guardian of his welfare.

The dog was conscious of his responsibilities. 'We'd go out at night,' said Sid, 'and while we were away, he would patrol the house like a night-watchman. When we got home, he would disappear and go to sleep. If the children went down the street, he would walk about ten feet of the back of them to keep an eye on them.'

Sid was also impressed with Liza's nascent talent. You couldn't help but be impressed when you have a young girl around in the house, bursting with the energy that accompanies an ability born into her. As Sammy Cahn said about the pedigree: 'By Minnelli out of Garland...'

And it wasn't just her relationship with her step-father that appeared good and sound. Although that much younger – and years count for a lot at that time of one's life – Lorna was quickly becoming a very dependable friend. 'She was also my own best friend,' Lorna told me years later.

Judy tried to make the two girls seem, to use Lorna's phrase, 'sisterly' by dressing them in identical dresses – but in very different sizes, which made them look like part of a vaudeville act.

The young girl who became her mother's mother – and by now, her confessor, too – was pretty good at being the one to whom Lorna would come with problems, as well, if it were only a broken doll.

Before long, Lorna was copying Liza. The two of them would join in duets – singing, more often than not, the song their mother dedicated to Clark Gable and which followed them both for the rest of their lives, 'You Made Me Love You'.

She would share some of Liza's more exotic costumes – particularly those Vincente had given her but which were now too small – and together they put on shows. The Garland Girls were going places. Their mother appreciated that as well as anyone else.

Sid Luft told me: 'Judy encouraged Lorna right from the beginning to perform every bit as she encouraged Liza. She knew that she was going to have a great talent, too.'

As Lorna told me in our interview: 'I don't understand some of the questions people ask – how could I survive in such a mixed-up household? Well, it wasn't mixed up. It was home. And Judy Garland happened to be my mother – whom I loved.'

Years later, Lorna would decide to go into show business too, an event that could have been foreseen with all those shows. It would have been difficult for her to be a mere bystander when there was so much attention paid to Mama and when Liza had already made it clear that this was where she was headed too.

And then, in 1955, after the triumph of *A Star Is Born* and not a few further bouts of nervous exhaustion, Judy became pregnant again. It provided an opportunity for Liza herself to get into the spotlight. Art Linklater invited her to appear on his daily TV show with three other schoolchildren. Linklater knew about the coming addition to the family. What did Liza want, a brother or a sister?

'A girl,' she replied, 'cos boys are too messy.'

This was one occasion when her wishes were not granted. This time, the baby was a boy, whom she and Sid called Joseph Wiley for purposes of his birth certificate but who from then on would always be known as Joey. Frank Sinatra was godfather.

There was fame of a different, less direct sort that year. Vincente's close friend – and Liza's godmother – Kay Thompson wrote the first of a series of 'Eloise' books, which were based on Liza and, in particular, her relationship with Lorna. No attempt was made to make the children seem in the least deprived. The setting for the story was New York's plush Plaza Hotel, one of the hostelries where they had stayed with Judy – but not, as far as anyone knows, one of the places from which they had had to sneak out in the dead of night.

That, too, was part of the fame game. *Could* a child escape from feeling just a little bit different – not to say superior – knowing that a best-selling book read avidly by her contemporaries had been written about her? It *was* asking too much and occasionally Mrs Gershwin's strictures about the child being spoiled rotten did seem justified – if only one could accept that it wasn't really Liza's fault. Asking her not to be that way was not really fair.

Liza's half-brother seemed almost a generation away from her – nine years can be a very long time at that age. But the bond between them was almost palpable from the moment of his birth.

The three Garland children – and nothing could take that away from them; they were all that – seem to have had an unwritten agreement from that moment on that they were all going to be part of each other's lives for ever afterwards. Despite the pressures and the inevitable small differences that arise, this seems to have been the case.

When Liza was ten, all doubts about her future were finally laid to rest. On the stage of the Palace Theater in New York, she made her professional début.

Well, actually, it wasn't quite a professional début, but the Palace was as professional an institution as you could imagine and Liza knew that full well.

'Pop' had arranged the booking for Judy, more successful and more splendid than even she had ever had at that theatre. It was soon after *A Star Is Born* and audiences from all over America were cramming the theatre to get a 'live' look at that star who, when she *was* born, arrived in a trunk at the Princes Theater.

Rightly, they judged she would perform many of her film routines on the huge Palace stage, a place that had seen some of the greatest triumphs of people like Jack Benny, George Burns, Eddie Cantor and Sophie Tucker, all entertainers to whom Judy was constantly presenting imaginary bouquets.

One night, she had Joey in her arms as she sang to him, 'Happiness is a Thing Called Joe' and warbled her own version of

the Jolson hit, 'Rockabye Your Baby with a Dixie Melody' to Lorna.
But Liza wouldn't be left out of the routine.

Judy was in the midst of the ' Swanee' routine when she stopped
her singing, threw out her hands to dampen down the orchestra – an
old, old showbiz tradition this – and announced that there was
someone very special watching the show from the wings.

'Come on Liza,' she called – and Liza Minnelli, a little gawky
perhaps but with those big eyes drenched by the spotlight and
seemingly returning every one of its beams, ran out.

She looked a little lost on the vast platform that night, but if she
were nervous, she showed no signs of it.

Judy began singing 'Swanee' again and Liza danced to
the melody as though it were the most important thing in her life.

Except that, while every other person put into that situation
would be consumed with nerves, would feel the spotlights burning
into their beings, would be scared beyond reason by the hordes of
people out there – all of them anxious to laugh as well as cheer
kindly – none of these things were matters that bothered Liza. Her
concerns were much more basic and important – were her pants
showing? She may have been only a child, but the mortification of
that possibility was almost overpowering. She could almost not
hear the orchestra or think about the spotlight. Such, no doubt, was
the residue of having gone on the set of *In The Good Old
Summertime* without checking that all her undergarments were in
place. Little girls don't forget such embarrassments. Thinking
about them is almost as unnerving an experience as an adult
woman seeing pictures of herself as a baby lying naked on a
tigerskin rug.

As it was, she need not have worried. Her pants stayed in place
and remained out of sight of the audience who shared Judy's
enthusiasm for the Palace début of her daughter. It might have been
unconventional but, as the songwriter put it, that's entertainment.

(Liza was not totally enamoured of her mother's entertainment
activities. In one scene, Judy had eaten a piece of liquorice. After the
number, she bent down to kiss her little girl, who moved swiftly out
of the firing line. 'Mama,' she said, that stuff you've just eaten smells.')

Equity might have had something to say about it, however – if by
that single action, Liza and her mother weren't giving the image of
the theatre its greatest shine since. . . Judy Garland first appeared on
a stage herself.

Perhaps to keep Equity happy, Sid Luft gave Liza five dollars. 'She put it in a frame that I had made for her,' Sid said afterwards. 'But then she broke into it when, a few years later, she thought she needed it to get to New York.'

Liza's step-father doesn't think that Liza's pride in her successful mother was ever diminished by Judy's illnesses and other problems. 'They tended to come and go quite quickly,' he told me. 'I don't think the children were really aware of those problems. They might have been, but I think that that early on they really were in the growing-up period.

'You would be surprised how pretty normal our house was. A lot of it was more a media hype than anything.'

But what was normal in some parts of the world was excessive in others. Within the film-star belt, love and marriage didn't always go together like a horse and carriage, to quote Sammy Cahn.

The Lufts were certainly already having their problems. Once, according to Judy's biographer Gerold Frank, she was so desperate about their situation that she rang friends to say that she had taken an overdose of 'medication' and that they should arrange for the children to be adopted. Liza and Lorna were to go to live with either Dirk Bogarde, whom Judy had met at his farm in Pennsylvania, or the French film actress Capucine, whom she liked. She would take Joey with her, because she thought he was too young to live with anyone else. Whatever happened, she instructed, they were not to go with Sid.

But like some of the best rows, the anger cooled and they were soon back to what served as normal. Until the next time.

There was another side to this, too. The children, and particularly Liza, were, if anything, a levelling influence on the mother. She spent a of time with them when she wasn't working.

'She was with the children constantly – when we did *A Star Is Born*, when we did the television shows, when we travelled. We travelled with the children.'

She took all the children with her when she starred at the Las Vegas hotels – certainly not the first to do so, but she was wowing them in the casinos before it became *de rigueur*.

When Judy played a club in Brooklyn – not considered to be exactly the pinnacle of showbiz success – she took Liza with her. Her daughter found plenty to occupy herself with, in what would prove to be part of her entertainment apprenticeship. It wasn't the experience of acting, or singing or dancing: instead Liza proved a dab hand at removing stains from Judy's dresses and sewing up falling hems.

She also learned how to be Judy's nurse – an addition to all the other precocious qualifications she was acquiring. She could hear Judy crying in agony in the bathroom. She rushed in to find her mother crouched over the toilet, holding her stomach. Liza was the first person she ever told that she suffered from colitis – it was not a nice thing to talk about. But Liza would understand . . . The little girl was deputed to go to the nearest drugstore to buy some medicine that might make Mama feel better.

Meanwhile, with the increase in the size of the family, Liza's duties multiplied, too. At nine, she was sorting out her mother's fan mail. By the age of eleven, she was answering it. Somewhere, hidden among family albums and other treasures, locked away in old suitcases, or buried among the relics of the past in lofts all over the world, are an unimaginable number of autographed photographs and scrawled notes written by Liza Minnelli which their owners have always thought were by Judy Garland.

That is another strange quirk of fate. In almost any other case, a 'forged' signature by a star's child would be totally worthless. Having a Judy Garland note that was actually penned by a juvenile Liza Minnelli is a different matter entirely.

One can't, of course, know for sure whether little Liza was simply doing her mother a favour at a time when she couldn't be bothered to handle such matters herself or whether she was living out her own fantasies of the time when . . . What is certain is that it provided her with another kind of practice not many other ambitious youngsters ever even begin to enjoy.

It also provided Liza with some spending money – although no fortune, a matter that would rankle with her no matter how young she was. Judy paid her $3 a week for these 'secretarial' duties. Eventually, Liza realised her worth – a factor that managements would quarrel with at their peril – and squeezed a further two dollars out of her mother.

At the age of 14, Liza was retained by Judy to break the law on her behalf. Quite illegally, she had learned to drive. That was all that Judy needed to know. When the family chauffeur was too drunk to do the task himself, Judy got Liza to drive Lorna to and from her school. When Joey was old enough to start school himself, it was Liza who had to drive him, too.

There have been other stories about Liza being entrusted by her mother to hire and fire household staff – a child who checked references! If a maid or a housekeeper wasn't up to it, go the stories, little Liza was deputed to give the erring retainer his or her marching orders.

Sid Luft knocks that one firmly on its unlikely head – the stories those fired staff members would have spread around Hollywood and its environs of the indignity of being told to go by a spoiled brat would have filled the gossip columns for weeks. But it is a story frequently told when recalling Liza's early days, and Liza has told it herself.

'It's a load of malarky,' says Sidney Luft, incensed more as the years since then grow longer and the memories likely to grow dimmer. He remembers the situation clearly enough, he says.

'All that time I was the father. I saw to that sort of thing as a father should see to it. Judy was a devoted mother. She was warm, but more of a disciplinarian than I was. To our way of life, it was a normal household. We had a large number of employees, but it was still a wonderful house there.'

It was an exciting place to be, in the house where Judy Garland could still sing magnificently as she entertained guests and where the early career of Liza Minnelli was taking root.

The conversation in the living room was always about rehearsals and managements who were trying to screw Judy out of her next fee or about other stars who were 'borrowing' her material – and sometimes how good rival performers (who would never be told so to their faces) could be. It couldn't fail to be stimulating to a stage-struck kid. 'It was exciting for me,' her stepfather told me, 'But it was normal for them to have, for instance, the child of Humphrey Bogart as a close friend. I would say it was quite beneficial for them all.'

In the years that have gone by, it has frequently been said about both Garland girls that their 'horrific' childhood had some sort of adverse effect on their lives. Sid Luft tends to think that neither did badly out of it, Liza with her career, Lorna both as a reasonably successful entertainer and as a mother.

'I don't think either of them suffered very much. Lorna now likes to say that she had a problem. But I was in constant touch with Lorna all her life. Maybe there might have been a mild difficulty, but Lorna likes to dramatise – much as I adore her. She tells me, "Dad, you know the problem I had?" Well, I don't know what the hell that was.'

It doesn't appear to have been a problem with each other. 'All three of the children were very close,' Luft added.

Liza didn't see anything strange in that and neither did Judy, who was plainly relieved to be free of yet another obligation. Getting up on stage or on a movie set was one thing, having to do all the other duties was an unbelievable hassle for her; hence the legends about Liza being put in charge of the domestic arrangements.

There could also be another explanation for her various retreats from taking her responsibilities: Judy's yearning for a kind of privacy that was never hers. Interviewing staff meant exposing herself to people who may have come to the house simply to see the star at close quarters. As Lorna told me: 'Mama's idea of heaven was to be able to walk down the street unrecognised.'

Sometimes – just sometimes – Liza may have wanted that, too.

It was the time when Judy wasn't quite as popular as either she or her family would have wished. There was a great deal of adverse publicity about her weight problems.

Liza was at the Beverly Hills Hawthorne School when what was either inherited professional jealousy or downright public unpopularity for her mother struck home for the first time.

'Your mother is a fat pig,' a child called to her. There's nothing like feeling a need to defend a parent to make a kid's blood pressure rise and on this occasion, Liza felt as though she had been hit in the pit of the stomach. She felt dizzy with anger as she reeled under the onslaught.

If she were a little older, she might have kept both her discomfiture and its cause to herself. But she was very young, very impressionable and very, very upset. The first thing she did when she got back to Mapleton Drive was to tell Judy about it.

Her mother, then still in her thirties, was stoical and wise. 'The next time that boy says your mother's fat,' Judy said, as Liza remembered for the *Good Housekeeping* interview, 'look him dead in the eye and say, "My mother can get thin any time she wants to, but your father couldn't get talent if he took twenty years of private lessons from Sir Laurence Olivier."'

Dem's were tough words, as they were known to say in the Southern states. Liza was a lot happier basking in the glory that came to both Judy and her stepfather after *A Star Is Born*. Warner Bros were close to ecstatic about their acquisition.

As a gesture of their appreciation, they gave Judy most of the furniture used in the picture. It sat well in the Mapleton Drive house.

The family lived in the house for seven years – longer than any other home they had. Somehow, however, the strains of moving home were not as hard on Liza as one might think – certainly not as tough as changing schools. But even that she seemed to have learned to accept. As she once said: 'After the first three days it got to be easy.'

The big problem with changing schools was a kind of paranoia the moves induced. Liza now took to listening to the conversations of her fellow students, expecting to hear something unflattering about her if not about her mother. In fairness, that paranoia was more often than not entirely justified. 'Have you seen that new weirdo?' was one of the kinder things she picked up. The gossips may not have been always talking about her, but she believed that they were and she was probably right.

Why her mother and stepfather didn't think of that sort of thing every time they decided on a change of school is one of the questions that can never be fairly answered. Sid Luft told me that he really did not believe it was ever that big a problem for Liza. But it was a huge strain and the fact that Liza recovered would in no small way be a tribute to her stamina.

But she did manage to go through these traumas without disturbing the affection for her of the rest of the family.

Lorna told me that her principal joy at the time was the news that Liza was coming back home for weekends from her new boarding school – Chadwick. Sending her there was partly an attempt to get Liza the best education money could buy (and at this stage of their lives, Judy's and Sid's money bought a great deal) and partly an attempt to make her less spoilt than certain friends had been suggesting she was There was considerable discipline in boarding schools, a fact that did not escape Liza's attention.

She came home every weekend. When Liza did return, she and Lorna would have a lot to keep them occupied. Vincente had bought her a trampoline as compensation for her weeks away. (She was beginning to spend more time with Vincente himself now.)

It was not easy to be in the Luft household, any more than it had been when she was living in a home full of nobody but Minnellis. She was now building up an inner strength – along with the tough outer skin that had been fashioned through the years of her mother's wildly fluctuating moods: alternate bouts of depression so low she was near death and highs that were so high that all reality was lost in the clouds. White fluffy clouds which were all silver linings, front and back. Those moments were the glories of her childhood. The other times were, she now tells herself, perhaps no different to the things that affected most other kids, too.

Liza has allowed her moods to dictate which memories she really accepts of those times. She says she has 'a good filter for keeping out the bad stuff and remembering the good.' Even so, there were the bad times – like the time when she rushed out to buy a stomach pump because she thought Judy was about to take an overdose.

It is partly because of that filter that when, many years later, she told that story herself she could laugh about it. It certainly wasn't all funny. But as we have seen, frequently it was warm and loving.

Like other mothers and daughters Judy and Liza discussed the signs of impending womanhood. Liza was eleven when her mother warned her of the inevitability of menstruation. 'When it comes, we'll crack open a bottle of champagne to celebrate,' Judy told her.

When it eventually did happen soon after that, it was during the time that Sid was anxious about Judy's drinking habits. The drinks cupboard and the wine stocks were all locked away. So Judy hunted through the house – and found a bottle of cooking sherry. It was in that domestic liquid that mother and daughter toasted the younger woman's new-found maturity.

Judy was principally concerned with making Liza feel as much a part of the Luft household as the other children. For that reason, she still dressed Liza and Lorna identically. Liza was to say that this drove her mad. Lorna was five years old at the time. She was eleven.

Things were complicated more now: a newcomer had come into the life of Liza Minnelli – another half-sister; but this time the daughter of her father, a girl who had no Garland pedigree at all.

Tina Minnelli was the daughter of Vincente's second wife, the French-born Georgette. Their father was to say that the girls never really got to know each other until they were both allowed on the same film set together – *Gigi*, which Vincente directed in 1957. He said that Liza treated Tina like a fragile doll. It might not have been that way. The older girl could have regarded the smaller one with spite or jealousy. But she was proud and glad to have a new half-sister.

Besides anything, Liza was only too delighted to watch the *Gigi* fantasy in production.

She would have been happiest of all if she could have been in the cast along with Leslie Caron – her ambition had been to be a second Caron for as long as she could remember. Her own dancing ambitions were curiously uncontested. Not only did they not aggravate anyone – as little girls' theatrical pretensions usually do – but they also gave a great deal of pleasure.

What was obvious now was the drive in Liza Minnelli, a frenetic energy, an inability to sit down, relax, and think about things. Quite clearly, this *was* a direct inheritance from her mother.

There was never any point in walking anywhere if she could run; in talking if she could shout; in sitting still if she could jump around. It was already quite clear that there needed to be a safety valve . The trampoline was one, but it didn't hold quite the same satisfaction or downright joy that came from getting up with 'Mama' on stage or in singing songs with her at home or practising there the dance routines she had learned at school. When those routines were adapted into duets with Lorna and then sometimes into trios with Judy, the Garland Girls provided a kind of little girl's paradise that Liza would never fail to appreciate.

As Sid Luft told me: 'She always had that drive, the quick moving, quick talking enthusiasm other people got to see years later. Liza was very bright and that was hereditary too. Liza's energy was more obvious than was Lorna's. Lorna was a little slower, a little calmer.'

Luft told me of an occasion which seemed to say it all. Liza was about twelve and had cornered her stepfather in his den.

'Pop,' she said, 'You gotta hear this song I want to sing for you.'

As Luft now remembers: 'There was no voice there at all.' But the enthusiasm was there, and so was the innate talent. But it was as hidden as was the woman's body which would take a little longer to develop, too.

For the moment, no one worried too much about her talents or the lack of them. Certainly, her own father did not. She was just his child whom he loved to distraction – which was precisely why he allowed her on to the set of his films, something which his colleagues might have regarded as somewhat unprofessional. Nevertheless, those opportunities for Liza to be enthralled by the movies were chances for Vincente to be excited just by having his daughter around.

When in 1959 he went to Texas to film, it seemed the most natural thing in the world to take Liza with him. Together, they went to the Texan town of Paris, where Vincente was making *Home from the Hill*, starring Robert Mitchum, George Hamilton (before the days of his suntan and sex image) and Eleanor Parker.

Liza loved every minute of it, particularly being with the stars working on this story of a Southern landowner who is something of a ram but who can't keep his own sons in line. The thirteen-year-old Liza was allowed to see the action without really realising what the story was about. What she did understand was that she was having a whale of a time – especially being spoiled by the crew. As she was to say: 'But I never took advantage of it. I was too scared that the happiness would go away.'

The poignancy of that remark said a lot for her. Perhaps she wasn't quite as spoiled as she thought. Possibly she was not taking all the material things that were hers for the asking for granted. Definitely, she knew that what she really wanted was the impossible – two parents who were completely her own, living and loving together. When she went back home, the illusions of the cinema business were left behind in the studios where her father was busy cutting his new movie.

On one of her occasional trips to New York, she thought more seriously than she had before about following in the family tradition. Judy took her, at fourteen, to see the Broadway smash, *Bye Bye Birdie*.

'I'd never seen so many kids running around the stage,' she was to say. 'They looked as if they were having such a good time and I thought, "Oh-ho, that's what it's all about!"'

She also thought about her relationship with Los Angeles and decided she didn't like it. Years later, she said in an interview with the *New York Times* (a paper that was anxious to foster the illusion that nothing good happened west of Manhattan Island) that it was a 'town so filled with lethargy that the people act as though they have sunstroke even when it's raining...I've always loved the razamatazz.'

There was little of that at home, wherever home was. Every time the Lufts moved house, they found themselves living in areas which were not covered by the schools Liza was currently attending. So they were changed along with the houses.

She was at the Buckley School now, which both Judy and Sid thought was suitable for the talents of a young intelligent lady who was undoubtedly more interested in the stage than in algebra or geography. It was a bigger school than ones she had been to before, and was co-ed. Perhaps these were pointers to her desire to go out into a bigger world where there were people of both sexes, all unable to hold back their enthusiasm to see and hear her.

Chapter Six

LIZA HAD her theatrical ambitions, but to outsiders, everything about them seemed to be linked with her mother. And they were ambitions that would be given their full rein when she was but thirteen.

Education was never a big thing with Liza or her parents. However, you could say it was particularly big – since she attended twenty different schools, both in America and Europe, as Judy and her various husbands moved from place to place.

This year of 1959 looked like being a very good one for her. Not only was she going on the filming expedition with her father – an occasion she would never forget – but awaiting her in the wings, as it were, was her own first big professional break; a break that would have been the envy of a hundred thousand other thirteen-year-olds: co-starring with Gene Kelly in a nationally-networked TV special. And if it was all very reminiscent of Judy Garland, well, so be it; that was precisely why, of course, she was there in the first place.

At that age of thirteen – a year younger than her mother had been when she sang about her rainbow, Liza joined Gene singing what had been one of his most memorable numbers – the duet he and Judy had recorded into a million-seller, 'Me and My Gal'. Garland and Kelly had performed the number originally in 1943, three years before Liza was born. Now the child relived the mother's part. The fans who had hoped for a carbon copy of Judy were only a little disappointed. Liza sounded a little like her mother – had Judy's voice been considerably worse than it ever was.

The idea for the show had been born at a party at Ira Gershwin's house. The lyricist brother of George had stayed a family friend and Liza was as welcome as her father at Ira's fashionable house. For the dinner party that night – Frank Sinatra was one of the guests there – Minnelli, newly separated from his wife, was invited to bring a lady. He took Liza. On this occasion, as almost every other time, a party meant a gathering around the piano. Gene started to play 'For Me and My Gal' and Liza joined in. Unlike her stepfather, Kelly liked the way Liza sang and before he himself had got very far into the song, allowed her to finish the number on her own. That was a kind of generosity not usually allowed other professionals, but it was also more than just an indulgence for a perky child.

'I took her aside,' he later recalled, 'and asked if she would like to do the song on my TV show.'

He later admitted that he hadn't really known what to make of Liza. She was merely the daughter of friends, an engaging little girl with big eyes who was like most other girls of that age, a bit on the gawky side. But sweet, too. The evening at the party convinced him that there was a great deal more to her.

Liza admitted she was 'thrilled to pieces' by the invitation – once, that is, Judy had approved it.

'She wasn't as big a voice as her mother,' said Gene Kelly as he limbered into a rehearsal with Liza. 'But her voice makes you think of Judy when you hear it. She's got that same kind of pathos. This is a great lark to her. She's a bright girl and a quick student and she could certainly go professional if she wants to. I think she has inherited both her parents' aptitude.'

Even so, he wasn't all that sure that things would work out well. As he later said, he was frightened for Liza. But she took it so easily.

Saul Chaplin, one of the great men of the Hollywood music scene, was in on this undoubted moment of showbiz history, accompanying the couple. 'She was absolutely remarkable,' he remembered for me. 'Not just like her mother, but showing the signs of being a star on her own.'

There would be other glimpses of that. She was fourteen when one of the *grande dames* of Hollywood (a polite term for a frequently vicious breed of women gossip columnists who could make and unmake careers of stars at will), Hedda Hopper, invited Liza on to her TV special.

Liza sang – what else? – 'Over the Rainbow' and Hedda smiled and kissed the little ungainly girl, who, nevertheless was beginning to fill out in what were generally accepted to be the right places.

That was not to say that she didn't have a weight problem. It was a family trait, and it occurred at about the same time as others in the household were battling with the scales. More seriously, her home was hardly one of uninterrupted domestic bliss.

In fact, her mother's marriage to Sid was becoming more fraught by the day – and as Judy's unhappiness increased, so did her own weight. At times, she seemed to resemble one of the fat ladies in a circus who look as though they could be punctured by a strategically-pointed pin.

By the time she was thirteen, Liza herself had tipped the scales at 165 pounds. Psychiatrists would have a field day with that one. It was a problem heightened by the clothes she had to wear. A little girl who had once postponed going to an ice show because she didn't like the dress she was given to wear would worry about a thing like that and Liza was true to form.

Sid was equally worried about his own weight problems. So he decided to take matters into his own hands. He dragged his wife and step-daughter off to a health farm. A diet of carrot juice would be the ideal way of ensuring a weight loss, he was told. It worked – for Sid who lost ten pounds and Liza who shed fifteen as easily as she could by now perform one of Judy's dance routines. Judy, however, didn't drop an ounce. This didn't help her mental state and soon afterwards she suffered her biggest breakdown to date. She was carted off to hospital in New York, while Liza went back to school in Los Angeles. Sid Luft's greatest problem was warning his step-daughter that her mother was seriously ill without suggesting the fact that she might be dying. As it was, Judy pulled through and Liza had learned once more that she, too, could survive the almost unendurable.

If these were not – to say the least – the happiest of moments for Liza, she has tried to deal with the results of what happened then. As she once said: 'I live for the present, but I've spent my life building memories.'

And there would always be changes for the better, when Judy would improve and behave as though nothing had ever been wrong. Those were the real high spots, the times when Judy would plan a future in which there would equally always be a place for her daughter.

Judy's latest idea was more exciting to her than most. She revealed the details to Liza as the two sat in the shadow of a mountain on the French Alps. Judy was on holiday. Liza was at yet another school, which Judy and Sid hoped would be more suitable than any of the other educational establishments she had attended in the States.

Judy told her that Pop and she were moving to London. They had just rented a delightful house in the King's Road, shortly to become second only to Carnaby Street as the fashion centre of the Swinging Sixties capital, but at the time just a rather nice and fashionable thoroughfare cutting its way through Chelsea.

'It was perhaps the happiest time of our lives together,' said Sid Luft. Judy was happy – she loved the Palladium and everything about England – and that radiated to the other members of the family and tended to make them more joyful, too. Apparently, that was infectious as well.

Liza herself was to say: 'London was my warmest memory. We had so much fun and we were all together like a family.'

The house had at one time belonged to Somerset Maugham, a fact that tended only to add to the excitement of being in London.

It was a productive opportunity for Judy and Sid to recharge their batteries. Their marriage seemed to be working out well again and that, too, was infectious. It was an exciting place to be, particularly then, before the mass influx of tourists who were to come when the swinging started. By all accounts, none of them took it for granted for a single day.

For a time, Judy toyed with the idea of making the British capital the Lufts' permanent home. It was a city that loved her; that knew her films as well as any American city did and it was true that perhaps *A Star Is Born* had been even more successful in Britain than it had been in the States. When she starred at the Palladium, London was hers almost as much hers as it had been Danny Kaye's, and that really was saying something.

There was, though, another reason for it: London was a place for only good memories. It was the one spot on the map where she felt she could really consign to the scrapheap of unwanted moments the unhappiness that Hollywood and much of America still represented. There were no ghosts of Louis B. Mayer around to haunt her in Chelsea.

Liza recalls the happiness of London for something else, too. It was a place where both she and her mother could let their hair down. If Liza liked to remember her mother laughing, this was the place where she did so more than almost anywhere else, and that was good enough reason to treasure their associations with the city.

In fact, Liza remembers London for all sorts of reasons –

particularly for her new school (yet another one), this time a tutorial college, the kind which provides lessons for the not-too-bright youngsters who persistently fail examinations which their wealthy fee-paying parents are determined they should pass.

The Misses Eden's and Wolf's School for Young Ladies prided itself on concentrating on the attributes of its students not necessarily previously appreciated by their former houses of learning. This school turned out to be one of the few happy chapters in Liza's educational history. And in so doing proved to be not a bad advertisement for the somewhat chequered reputation of British schooling, both State and private.

'It was almost like private tutoring,' she recalled four or five years later. 'I have friends in their second year of college who are just studying things I learned there.'

She remembers it, too, for the time she first realised she fell in love – with shoes. In fact, she describes it as a shoe fetish which she retains to this day. Other women crave diamonds or furs or expensive perfumes. For Liza it was, is and always will be shoes (and diamonds, furs and expensive perfumes).

The reason she says is clear to her: Judy had a thing about Liza's feet. She was afraid they weren't strong enough and always insisted on her daughter wearing heavy ungainly brown shoes. In London, Liza did the 'Season'. She went to débutante balls, wore stunning couturier dresses – and heavy brown shoes.

That had almost as bad an effect on her as the dress she wore on the way to the ice show. Now, though, she thought she knew the answer. There was and could only be one result: she determined that when she was old enough to be on her own, earning her own money, she would have the most fashionable shoes money could buy. And she did. From the moment of her first sizeable pay cheque, she would have her shoes specially designed and made for her in Paris.

Britain wasn't simply getting to know the British people and their culture, enjoying family life and going to school. There was some professional experience for Liza, too.

Judy had an engagement at the Free Trade Hall in Manchester, which, in spite of its somewhat unartistic name, was a fairly hallowed place for Northern English theatrical spectaculars. More important, it was the scene of some of the greatest concerts by the world-famous Hallé Orchestra.

For this show, Judy was joined by her elder daughter. As Brian

Sale wrote in the *Daily Express*: 'As she sang with her fourteen-year-old daughter Liza, it could almost have been the Garland Sisters. Off stage, they look like mother and daughter. But on stage with the new slim Judy dancing around in drain-pipe slacks, they look like sisters.'

They weren't merely complementing (or complimenting) each other. They were quite clearly rivals. When Liza sang 'The Travellin' Life' and 'Gypsy In My Soul', the audience went crazy. Judy was not happy.

Their most stunning number together was another from the Jolson/Garland catalogue, 'After You've Gone'. Liza was dynamic, throwing everything into the song the way she had seen her mother do a thousand times before.

Mr Sale was enthralled: 'A start in show business for Liza, who looks so like her mother did twenty years ago.'

By now, that wasn't such an original or perceptive suggestion. Of course, Liza was going to follow those footsteps, steps that had themselves walked in the trail of some of the greatest names in entertainment history. As for Liza, she confined herself to thinking about being a dancer. An actress and a singer were not yet on her list of ambitions.

Soon after this time, the family moved back to America. It wasn't that the climate of London or anything else about the city had taken its toll, but their declining bank balance had – and whatever else Judy could say about the Americans, when they paid to have Judy Garland starring in one of their shows, they did so with more money than the London Palladium management or any other British theatrical organisation could then muster. The Lufts were fairly close to being broke.

Sid decided that the best chance of Judy making any serious money was in New York. That wouldn't be bad for Liza either. She was immediately enrolled in another school – this time, the New York School for the Performing Arts, later to become an established part of kids' knowledge the world over, thanks to the movie and TV show *Fame*.

In May 1961, Judy made a triumphant return to American show business with a concert at Carnegie Hall. In terms of major occasions in theatrical history, this one is near the top. It was recorded for posterity and became one of Judy's finest albums. But Liza's memory of the occasion is much more personal. She sat in the front row of the great concert hall – and Judy leaned over the footlights on all-fours to give her a huge kiss. At that moment, the entire audience was doing the same thing – in spirit, at least – to them both.

But for Liza, Lorna and Joey as well as for the two senior Lufts, it meant a return to Los Angeles. The children couldn't have been more unhappy, but one of the lessons which they had learned only too well by now was that permanence was for other people. And their nomadic lifestyle might have made other people unsettled, but not this family of theatrical gypsies. Presumably, if you were born in a trunk, you were inclined to want to lug it around from place to place.

Liza certainly had learned how to cope with it. It did not mean, however, that she necessarily had to like it. Much, much more, she liked what was happening to her professional abilities. By the time she was fifiteen, it became apparent to everyone who knew her that she was a very talented dancer indeed.

By July 1961, she danced in a summer stock performance of the show *Wish You Were Here* in the theatre-in-the-round used for the Melody Tent at Hyannis Port, Massachusetts, immortalised as the family home of the Kennedy clan. She worked as an apprentice there, mainly doing things like painting scenery. But she appeared in other productions, too.

On one of the few occasions in which Judy and Vincente had been together since their divorce, they both went to see Liza in *Take Me Along*. The two still tried to talk when it came to their daughter's affairs. They now discussed the notion of Liza being allowed to work in the company during the summer and both came to the conclusion that it would be a very good idea indeed. Judy could hardly watch the show for the tears that seemingly cascaded in a constant flow down her cheeks. Later, both parents and daughter all had dinner together.

Vincente was to say how impressed he was by it all. It was the first time he, for one, realised how serious his daughter was about having a real career in the theatre.

He personally was also excited for another reason – going to the tent for the show brought back memories of his own beginnings at the Minnelli Brothers Tent Theater.

Liza appeared, too, in the chorus of *Flower Drum Song*, the Rodgers and Hammerstein show about the life of Chinese families in San Francisco. This was a conventional way for youngsters who didn't have the kind of pedigree that Liza possessed to enter the profession.

But she appreciated being there as much as any ordinary kid. There was no Judy Garland weight thrown about by Liza Minnelli; in fact she frequently wished that she *was* from an ordinary family. She was excessively embarrassed by all the attention she was being paid, as much as anything by the parents of the other chorus kids.

Judy was proud as any mother would be expected to be. Or were the tears for something else? A year later that would appear to be the case.

'That was about the age that I remember thinking Liza was quite remarkable,' Sid Luft told me.

So undoubtedly did Judy. She would listen to Liza singing – off-key frequently; she shared her husband's belief that the youngster's vocal attributes were not what either would have liked them to be. As often as not, Judy called out regular instructions to her daughter from the bedroom or bathroom: One minute it was, 'Wrong lyrics!'; the next, it was likely to be, 'You're singing flat!'

There couldn't have been a much better professional education for Liza or certainly a more devoted teacher. Sid Luft is the first to recognise this.

'It was incredible how hard she worked at it,' he said, 'but she couldn't sing yet. In fact, I never thought she would be a singer at all because of that lack of voice – her mother had been a great singer from the age of about twelve. I just imagined she would be a pretty good dancer.'

The Lufts moved to Scarsdale, in Westminster County, New York, and Liza had to change schools again. This time, it was the local high school – the community was one of America's richest (the huge house they lived in in Scarsdale was fairly typical of the surroundings) and Liza hated every minute there. There were, however, to be redeeming moments, as we shall see.

But at first, Liza loathed Scarsdale. 'I've never seen such a snobby town in my whole life,' she said a few years later, at a time when she could afford to speak her mind. 'I can get along with anybody, really. I like people so much and I figure that everybody in the world has something interesting to say, right? So why should I not listen? But when I marched into school that first day, which is a terrifying experience for any kid, nobody would talk to me.'

She stayed in the tenth grade at Scarsdale for six months; because of her fellow students, hardly the happiest six months of her life. A couple of years later, she would say of the young people of

Scarsdale: 'They all go to grade school together, and then to high school together, and then they go off to college together and everything's fine. But then *boing*...! They get a knock from life and they don't know how to handle it. And you're going to get knocks sooner or later, right?'

The inference was that Liza had already had her ration of knocks. That was true, although there were still more on the way. Among her current ones was the sheer loneliness of the new school at Scarsdale. She was finding it harder to be cushioned simply by being a celebrity. The tight community of this extremely wealthy and fashionable suburb seemed to be, if not ganging up on her, then building its own kind of protective chrysalis around themselves, one that they were not allowing her to penetrate in any way. Knowing that was as hard as the experience of trying to knock down the walls and break in.

If Judy had known all that, she might have adjusted her life so as to make those frequent changes unnecessary. But she didn't and the strain on her elder daughter was such that it was a wonder she didn't bear even deeper scars for the rest of her life than actually were cut into her psyche.

It was all part of Judy's lack of security. She might have been sensational in another *Star Is Born* if only one were offered – and there was always talk that one would come. Her latest pictures had revealed a talent for serious acting for which few had given her credit – yet the grass looked greener at the other end of the country. Other parents changed jobs that resulted in their children having to change schools; why was her case so special?

It might have been easier for Judy to understand the problems of her children – and for Liza in particular (she seemed less secure in herself than did the others every time a new school perched itself on her horizon) – if her own childhood had been more conventional. But a woman who went on stage as soon as she was able to look a spotlight in the face, who then became a child star of unimaginable magnitude and who had had to battle with Louis B. Mayer and his empire, perhaps couldn't be expected to begin to understand why it was so hard for others not to go to an ordinary school in an ordinary neighbourhood and not to want ordinary things.

She couldn't really understand why Liza had felt deprived when she had had Humphrey Bogart and Lana Turner popping in for her tea parties and when 'dressing up' clothes meant model dresses handmade for her and based on the creations prepared for Cyd Charisse. And she couldn't understand her daughter any more now that she was in adolescence and thinking of her professional future.

Yet these were the thoughts that ran through Liza's mind as she contemplated the first loneliness at Scarsdale High School.

Life was not all torture, however. In their home itself it could be very pleasant indeed. The family Christmas concerts were preserved for posterity on tape. They sang and acted and said slightly unpleasant things about each other, like Lorna being cross-eyed and knock-kneed and Liza resembling a zombie.

The reason that Liza resembled a zombie was that she was suffering from flu at the time – which was why she introduced herself as 'Typhoid Mary' and said she had nothing to say because she felt so rotten.

She also had one of her first boyfriend problems. 'He was too damn attentive,' was how her stepfather now remembers the event.

Judy got Sid to handle that. He remembers the occasion as the only time he and Liza really had cross words with each other.

What he told the boy – who had no idea who Liza's parents were in fact – was 'Judy Garland wants to see you. A car will be over.'

The youngster only realised who Liza was when he saw Judy waiting at the front door. At that moment he learned that Liza was the daughter of Judy Garland and that hell had no fury like this woman's . . .

It turned out that what had really happened was that Sid had been to a place of somewhat shaky reputation – girls were known to perform there without all their clothes – and had seen Liza in the audience with the boy. He might have been embarrassed for her to know that he went to such a place, but more so, he was incensed that she, too, frequented it. The boy would not forget that moment in a hurry.

This problem, though, had nothing on her attendance at school.

'The only thing that really interested her there,' Sid Luft said, 'was the dramatic class. Out of one semester, somewhere in the neighbourhood of 180 days, she was absent forty days. Or late.'

But she was always present in the afternoons – for rehearsals for the school play, *The Diary of Anne Frank*. Liza played the lead. It wasn't a professional performance, but people got to talk about it and for the first time, they got to talk about Liza Minnelli. Word got around quickly how outstanding Liza was. In fact, not just Liza, but all the kids in the production. No one appeared to make anything of the fact that Liza was the daughter of Judy Garland and even if it had registered, it didn't matter very much. What the parents, their friends and the local newspaper critics noted was that this was a very good play, very well performed.

Certainly Judy thought that. She and Sid went to see the production and suddenly they weren't superstar and super-producer, but parents (Sid never thought of himself as simply her stepfather on family occasions) watching their child take the lead in a school production. They knew, just as every other parent knows, that their child was the best.

Of course, that was only part of the story. With all the pride she possessed bursting out of her, Judy also cast her professional eye over what was being offered in the school auditorium.

Afterwards she said: 'I've always known she was a marvellous dancer, but she dazzled Sid and me with her performance . . .'

More than that, she dazzled Judy with the way she treated the job at hand. Judy would have been a very strange mother indeed if she didn't offer all the professional expertise that she had to her daughter who was plainly now in the same business – albeit without getting paid for the privilege. And Liza would have been a very strange daughter indeed if she had taken it. Fortunately for Liza and for the school, Judy accepted her girl's decision.

'She was very professional about rehearsals,' Judy noted, 'took direction only from the director and wouldn't let Mama butt in with free advice.'

Being just parents was, of course, a luxury for people like the adult Lufts – as it was for their children. Lorna, at nine years of age, was brought to tell a journalist: 'We don't call her Judy Garland at home. She's just Mama.'

'Mama' herself was a little concerned about that. She jokingly – but those jokes were usually only half in jest – said that the children never played her records at home. 'They aren't too interested in my career.' That was anything but true. Since she was three years old, Liza had known *everything* about her mother's career and everything she had picked up had come from her – and she loved every bit of it. The same was already true about Lorna, and Joey certainly knew no other life, even though at six he wasn't ready to commit himself on whether or not that was the way he wanted his own life to go.

As far as Liza was concerned, however, there were no doubts. And even if there had been, *Anne Frank* would have put them to rest. It may only have been performed at a school in Scarsdale, but as far as she was concerned, this was Broadway and the party at the end of the play's run was at Sardi's and not the school refectory.

And in truth, it was much more than just an ordinary school play in which she, as the daughter of old pros, carried the entire load.

It had an amazing effect on Liza's career. At fifteen she was enjoying the advantages of being in a strong cast – at a time when no one was yet thinking of a professional career for her.

So good was the production, in fact, that the school was invited to take their play to Israel – a compliment indeed, considering the subject matter of a Jewish girl in hiding from the Nazis. The Israeli Government were enthralled with the performance – at a time when the country considered it dearly needed friends, the publicity value of the tour was not lost on the authorities, although their praise was genuine enough – and described it as one of the best they had seen of a play that had such deep emotional meaning for them. Certainly, the emotional appeal was considerably more there than in other countries, yet the school tour continued in Greece, Italy and other countries in Europe and was highly received wherever it went.

Liza's first overseas 'tour' was a sensation.

'That meant a lot to her,' Sid Luft recalled. 'Her movements were a little too energetic. But you could see the abilities at fifteen.'

That was in a field no one had thought of her being before – a straight actress. If it wasn't a professional company, there are not many school productions invited to travel 6,000 miles with their 'shows'. Even so, that was not the kind of show business she was already yearning for.

At this time she was also spending a considerable time simply coping with that goldfish bowl syndrome. It got out of hand in several diverse ways. She herself was anything but a celebrity, but she couldn't help being treated as one at school, where her fellow students regarded her with the same kind of curiosity as did the professional producers.

It was something over which she quite plainly had no control. She was Liza Minnelli, daughter of Judy Garland, and in that respect her situation was akin to being the child of the Queen of England. Every time her mother got in the news – planning a new film; going on a new diet; rowing with a studio; rowing with Sid – Liza was expected to account for her actions. They were never her fault, nor her responsibility to deal with, but that didn't matter.

It has never been said, but these effects of living in the greedy public eye had a great deal to do with the unsettled state in which Liza lived. Would changing school, for instance, make her feel a little easier? Of course, it never would. And the early days were always the hardest. They were the times when she was more an object of curiosity than later on when people had begun taking her for granted – by which time she had to be ready to up sticks and change schools yet again.

Sometimes, as we have seen, she bore the brunt of the sarcasm that was at times as potent an enemy of her mother as was the studio system. Sometimes, too, she simply had to cope with being in the news for doing the sort of things that others did every day of the year without anyone outside their family circles taking the least bit of notice.

Now, however, the school problems were almost- and almost is an important word here – behind her. But others were not. Being Liza Minnelli meant being public property.

Certainly, everyone in Hollywood knew about her boyfriend Tom Cooper, who went out with Liza for the best part of a year and 'starred' her in an amateur film he made called *An Incidence of Seeking*. It lasted for eight minutes and Liza played a girl who goes mad when her boyfriend finds a new love.

Liza complained that she didn't understand a word of the script, but made the picture just the same. Later she told him she didn't think she looked attractive enough in it and was glad that Judy never saw it.

A happier part of the relationship was that Liza converted Tom into a one-man audience and to him alone sang some of the songs for which she would later become famous. One of these was to be her record hit 'The Travellin' Life'.

There were other events that became better known to the public. In September 1962, for instance, Liza was taken ill with food poisoning – not a serious attack; her health, let alone her life, was never at serious risk. Yet the news was wired all over the country and stories about Liza's stomach condition were published in papers from the West Coast to the East.

Liza Minnelli wasn't yet a star, but she was famous because of her relationship to Judy Garland. But did that mean she didn't want to be a 'second' Judy? The answer was plainly No.

There was no doubt that she wanted to emulate her mother. Family guests would see that as they gathered around the piano for an impromptu Garland concert – with Judy leading and Liza (occasionally with Lorna and Joey joining in, too) trying her best to keep up with her.

It was a charming experience to be part of, but nobody felt they were in at the start of a remarkable career for a second Garland girl. She was not only childish, but she didn't have the range or the seemingly instinctive (that was what everyone thought it was) way of handling a song in a professional manner. That had never been a problem for Judy – which accounted for the value MGM had always put on her.

But Liza wanted to be encouraged, and encouraged she was. Judy and her husband listened attentively and kindly, and advised that she go away and practise. To her credit, Liza didn't regard this as a patronising brush-off and took the advice to heart. Her juvenile warblings – sometimes it sounded a lot worse than that – were as much part of everyday sounds in the Luft household as Sam the dog's barking.

What no one could deny was the certainty – barring some unspoken tragedy – that Liza would follow the family tradition and go into show business. And as her various activities with her mother had proved, she had already begun. Now, however, she was going to be paid for it. For being Judy's daughter, that is, as much as for being a potential actress or singer and dancer.

As yet it was not clear how strong the pattern would be, but inevitably she was being retained as much for her parentage as for herself. Why else, for instance, would she be booked to be the voice of Dorothy in a cartoon sequel to her mother's biggest adolescent success, to be called *Return to The Land of Oz*.

It was both a great experience – to say nothing of a marvellous opportunity for the production office's publicity department – not least of all because she played with a group of big stars voicing superb roles. Ethel Merman was the voice of the Wicked Witch, Danny Thomas was the Tin Man's voice, Peter Lawford the sounds for the Straw Man and Milton Berle was the Lion.

For this, the score was provided by her old friend and neighbour Sammy Cahn, working with his eminent partner Jimmy Van Heusen. Liza's numbers included 'A Faraway Land' and 'Keep a Happy Thought'. And even when the connection with Judy was somewhat less tenuous, the publicity was still as great.

Even having Liza painting the scenery had not been lost on the summer stock company's PR department.

But the most important thing about her which everyone had to admit was that Liza was developing as a great talent of her own. Her stepfather told me he could see this very clearly. 'She could move very well and the ambition was there,' he recalled. 'She was really a very nice little dancer. She could move with great rhythm. But later, I could see the change.' It became obvious about 1962. The Lufts had moved back to California.

Judy was working once more in Hollywood in a totally different kind of rôle; no singing, no dancing, no colour, no glamour. In *A Child Is Waiting*, described as a 'semi-documentary', Judy played a somewhat do-gooding teacher in a school for the mentally handicapped. Semi-documentary meant that actors were working with children, most of whom really were mentally handicapped.

Liza went to the studio to see her at work. It was good for her. She not only learnt about 'straight' acting, but also about children who had the curse of mental deficiency. She discovered that they were friendly and she liked them. Some of them became her friends in a real, unvarnished, unpatronising sort of way. They neither knew nor cared who her mother was. They wanted her for herself and she wanted them for themselves. It was good for them both.

There was no doubt that she was striving, even at that age, to be a second Judy Garland – although the first Judy was still there seemingly at the top of her second career, with her childhood and juvenile work now safely locked away in the archives of people's memories and affections. The current, but still original, Judy was fixed firmly – or as firmly as the often shaky Garland could make it – on the entertainment scene and was plainly established as one of the Greats. This was the kind of Judy Garland her daughter was trying to emulate. Liza had no ambitions to be in Andy Hardy-type movies or even to prance down the Yellow Brick Road with the Tin Man, the Straw Man or the cowardly Lion.

'She was a show business child,' said Sid Luft to me in our interview. 'She had been exposed, not just to her mother, but to her father's considerable talents as a director. We were all show business people involved in her life.'

At sixteen, the voice made its first somewhat tentative appearance. Privately, and in class, she started to realise that when she sang everyone around didn't run away. Not only was there a distinctive voice there –

with not a little of a Garland-like tremulous touch obvious – but those who heard it could recognise a pleasant sound they wanted to be repeated. If that was so, she reasoned, why should she not be paid for doing it, too?

The idea became firmly implanted in her mind when she heard her mother and stepfather talking about another new school – another new school to which she would be sent. Now, she decided she was putting her ungainly brown shoes down and was not going to go – to any school anywhere.

She would have ample opportunities to prove that fact, for this is when the tour to Israel and Europe was due to begin. It came when Judy and Sid were having one of their periodic rows. Only this one seemed more serious than most. Judy was threatening to take her two young children to England (which she did) while Liza was living with Vincente.

Both Judy and Liza were in New York, Liza with friends, Judy a few blocks away when the crunch came. It was then that Sid decided to take Lorna and Joey away from their mother. He locked them in a hotel room.

Judy was distraught. All she could think of was that her eldest daughter would have to intercede. Such was the power of the sixteen-year-old, and the authority she had with both sides, that she was regarded as a suitable intermediary.

Liza arrived to find the hotel lobby ringed with police and Judy's lawyers. Judy had called them all. It was a moment of high drama as Liza prepared to fight her stepfather through the bedroom door, rather like a priest trying to prevent a convict jumping from the top of the prison roof. It was much easier than that. Sid simply and immediately opened the door of the room and Liza found her half-brother and sister happily watching television. He agreed that he wouldn't take the children away from their mother without her consent. It pleased Liza, at least. Happy now, she sauntered down to the lobby where she nonchalantly told Judy (hinting at the pain, anguish and difficulty with which she had solved the problem) that everyone was OK.

But the children still weren't out. When, later, Judy discovered that Lorna and Joey had somehow got out of the hotel and were walking in Central Park, she again told Liza to act. She was to bring them to the back door of the building where she herself would be waiting in a limousine that would whisk them to 'freedom' – and

Europe, a continent both Lorna and Joey had indicated they had no desire to visit again.

In the meantime, Sid had got them back into his room. This time, Judy forced her own way in and once inside proceeded to scream: 'He's hitting me! He's hitting me!'

Her bodyguards raced in after her and pinned Sid to the wall, while Judy rushed out, the two younger children with her. They all jumped into the waiting limousine.

Next stop was London – where Lorna and Joey were made wards of court and were prohibited from leaving the country; particularly with their father. Her marriage, Judy declared, was over.

Liza didn't stay in London with the rest of the brood. She went off to Israel at what proved a very suitable moment. When the tour was over, she went to Paris. It had been her mother's and her stepfather's idea.

Liza had been sent off to Paris for 'finishing', as was considered the thing for well brought-up young daughters of the stars – a few years earlier Jane Fonda had had the same experience.

'She was a very clever girl and we all thought that half a year at the Sorbonne would do her the world of good,' Luft recalled for me.

The idea was that she would learn the history of France at the Sorbonne. She stayed a term – which, as she was to say, was about as long as she remained at any of her schools. But that wasn't the main purpose of being in France. It was the 'done' thing for someone of her age, sex and status to do and if in the course of being in the country she could learn French as well as something of the country and its more reputable citizens, so much the better.

Judy had the idea that it made more sense to pick up the language that way than to go to a Berlitz school. She was undoubtedly right. Unlike a number of other young people sent on a similar expedition, Liza did learn to speak French fluently – if not always grammatically correctly. Even so, as she told *Good Housekeeping*, her most memorable experience on the trip was meeting Bobby Darin, who was every young girl's heart-throb in the early 1960s (and who was to die tragically young from heart failure a decade later). She said it was her first crush on an older man, but, as she said in the magazine piece, he probably never knew.

Actually, Liza was not alone on the trip. There was definitely a case for Judy's thinking that there was safety in numbers.

A woman friend of Judy's went along with her to act as

companion chaperone. But there were six other girls with Liza, too, one of whom was a daughter of the chaperone. Paris was a wonderful place for a young girl to be, but the Lufts were not unaware of what she could get up to there alone and unescorted and were not prepared to take any unnecessary risks.

The course was under the generic heading 'La civilisation française', but Liza didn't find it particularly civilised. 'I was bored,' she was to say. 'I knew what I wanted to do and I had it out with myself' – which might have been considered easier than having it out with Judy.

Liza said that living in Paris did two things. It introduced her to those Paris shoes that were to become an obsession – even though she would still have to wear the brown Oxfords much of the time – and finally convinced her that she wanted to go into show business as a career – as if it hadn't been an idea running through her brain all her young life to date.

Why, she couldn't be sure – except that she was fed up with all the parental attempts to educate her which she was experiencing. Paris had been one of them, and it didn't compare with some of the other schools they had suggested. Certainly it was one of the best.

They wanted all the 'good' things about Paris for Liza without any of the complications. On the whole, it seems to have been a wise move and one without any spanners thrown into the works. Of course, it all contributed to the 'gypsy' feel about her life, but there appear to have been no ill effects – which is precisely what the Lufts had in mind.

Liza was determined on two things: she was not going to go to any more schools and she was coming home. So she sent her mother a telegram and then determined that, for a time when she got back, she would go and live with Vincente.

She took advantage of this situation. Daddy wouldn't object to her striking out into the family business. Would he? She was almost certain of the answer.

Even if Vincente had any objections, Liza would have a ready answer. She was going to use this new talent coming to the fore.

Liza decided to take matters into her own hands. She was going into a show. And if necessary – and she was convinced it would be necessary – she would do so without her mother's approval.

Chapter Seven

THERE WAS a strange ambivalence in the way Judy Garland looked on her eldest child. She loved Liza – some might say too much; allowing her to take on roles in the house and the family that were clearly beyond her years. She admired her and could see there was a burgeoning talent there yearning to be allowed to express itself.

As Sid Luft recalled for me: 'She certainly didn't drive her, but I must say that Judy encouraged Liza. And they used to love to sing together, move together and invent things together around the house. Lorna came into the same fold. The three girls more or less loved to sing and invent show business characters between them.'

Yet Judy had at the back of her mind the torments to which she had been subjected at Culver City, both by Louis B. Mayer and his henchmen and by her own stage mother, an *eminence grise* in her life she would have hated to emulate; and so, as far as Liza was concerned, she held back.

'Judy certainly told both Liza and Lorna about the other side of show business and its pitfalls,' Sid Luft said.

She actually did more that that on the day Liza came to her mother and said that she had the chance to go into a show. Judy was not pleased.

Judy Garland was not allowing her child to face the kind of world she herself had had to experience. There were those who detected in this hostility to a showbiz career for her daughter an element of insecurity, even perhaps of jealousy for a gawky young girl who was about to emerge if not as a great beauty, then as a pretty actress.

Yet it can be fairly safely assumed that that was not Judy's idea at all. She genuinely knew better than almost anyone how hard it would be for a youngster going into one of the toughest professions in the world. She also knew that opening this first door for her own daughter could lead to the next one being slammed even more firmly in her face.

The world would love to see a 'second Judy Garland'. It would appreciate even more seeing that second Judy fall flat on her face – and would take full advantage of every opportunity that presented itself to ensure that that would happen.

The rôle of the stage mother had spun around in an unimaginably wide circle. Mrs Ethel Gumm had worked her tail off to make Judy Garland a star. Now Judy Garland was going to do her damndest to be certain that Liza Minnelli knew what the problems were and if that meant discouraging her from going into the business, that was all right, too – for the moment, at least.

Liza, for her part, knew that she had to have parental approval before she set about embarking on a professional career. There were laws that could be invoked to stop her.

Her first move was to get Vincente's consent. That, she reasoned, would be the easy part. He genuinely couldn't have been more pleased. Her mother, she knew, would be totally against it.

In that, apparently, she was wrong. Judy wasn't *totally* against the notion of Liza going into showbiz. She just wasn't for it. And now she put it into words for the first time: she told her she wouldn't stop her, but neither was she going to help her. Those words that she used, Liza later recalled in the *Good Housekeeping* piece, amounted to an instruction that her daughter should never again come to her for a cent.

Discussing it herself, Judy remembered thinking: 'What would I say – all sorts of motherly things about going back to school?'

No, she knew that wouldn't work. What she actually claimed she did say was: 'Watch me, learn from me and learn from my mistakes.'

Considering both Judy's triumphs *and* her mistakes, that was quite a course of instruction she was recommending.

Judy was playing in Las Vegas when she first got wind of what was happening. Liza's telegram from Paris read: 'DEAR MAMA . . . I WANT TO TALK TO YOU.

Later, Judy told a reporter: 'I think she decided to go into show business when she was an embryo. But I wanted her so much to get the best education. When the wire arrived, all I could think about was this child flying half way around the world, all of the time rehearsing what she would say. Then I started rehearsing what I would say . . . off the plane practically before the door was opened. She charged right up to me; I shot the works.'

What Judy claimed to have said may not quite have been the unvarnished truth: 'Liza, darling, why don't you go into show business?' Could anything be more encouraging?

Having delivered herself of that bombshell blessing, she said, they both dissolved into tears.

A few years later, Liza related the story somewhat slightly less romantically. Judy, she remembered, was nothing like as sympathetic: 'She had that cold, dispassionate look in her eyes that told me she knew, although she was against it, there was nothing she could do about it.

'"All right," she said, "you do as you please. I can't stop you. I won't try. But you're going to have to make it on your own. I know it's been bothering you for a long time. I hope you make it, baby, I really hope you do.

'"But you might as well know something else now, so you won't expect it later. There will be no money from me. When you leave, you leave me and everything I have. It's got to be that way. You can't have me to fall back on every time you fail or you'll do nothing but fail, knowing I'm waiting. Do you understand what I mean?"'

As Liza later reflected: 'I don't think that I did. I was sure she'd soften up sooner or later. That time I was wrong.' Judy wasn't in any mood to contemplate softening up. She had made her pitch and the order of the day was to be cruel to be kind. There was another factor – Judy was jealous of a young girl whom she knew could make it.

Liza, though, wasn't worried about blessings, guarded or otherwise. She simply opened the frame Sid had made, took the five dollars she had 'earned' dancing at the Palace, and set off. Judy showed no signs of softening up.

Indeed, she took a long time before those signs did appear and when they did, Liza felt good reason to suspect the motives. The truth of the matter is that Judy had been against her daughter going into show business from that first 'embryo' stage she had referred to in that interview.

She didn't want Liza to follow her for all the reasons anyone sitting in a psychiatrist's chair could start to contemplate. One day, a learned institution will devote a whole course of study to 'Judy Garland And Her Problems'. This was certainly one of them.

Liza, meanwhile, couldn't allow herself to worry about that at that time any more than she could have done before. Nothing would be allowed to curb her ambition. Sensibly, she made for New York and, equally sensibly, for a dancing school. These establishments were not difficult to find. It is impossible to walk round the environs of Broadway without bumping into a hundred signs offering the kind of lessons she was seeking. You could then and can still hold your breath between dance schools and not feel any exertion. The problem was finding one that was really suitable. She wanted to do ballet – except that she was told (also wisely) that her legs were too long for that kind of activity; they would be uncontrollable. Jazz dancing was more her field. She found her school and went to work.

Liza also thought of taking singing lessons – until she realised that her own voice had now arrived and if her mother could do as well as she had without a single singing lesson in her life, why did she need them? She concluded that she didn't. This attitude did not, however, result in floods of offers of work.

She booked herself into the Barbizon Hotel for Women and hoped that there would be sufficient work to allow her to pay her bill. It would be nice to speculate that the clerk writing down her name on the hotel register wondered whether he was in on one of the great momentous events in modern entertainment history – the moment Liza Minnelli checked in at the beginning of everything.

There was a much more significant event soon after. Liza could no longer pay for the room and was unceremoniously thrown out. Her luggage meanwhile was confiscated.

They say that problems improve the mind and help one to appreciate the good things in life. Her mind might have been improved and she may have filled herself with sufficient confidence to determine to 'show' the people who had inflicted such an indignity on her, but there is no evidence to suggest that she felt any better for the experience.

In the 'Born In a Trunk' number, Judy sings about 'haunting all the agents' offices'. That was now precisely what her daughter was doing and the only thing she had to show for her trouble was the chance to sleep on the steps of the fountain fronting the Plaza Hotel.

She couldn't afford a hotel room – but plainly had enough sense and sufficient good taste to choose the right part of town in which to lie down in the open; a better class of people than in The Bowery where one couldn't walk either at night or during the day without tripping over one of the sleeping bodies covering the pavements.

Things did, though, get a little better. There was a little work modelling for magazines like *Seventeen*, and she broadened her academic experience by taking drama lessons in the one corner of the world that had more unemployed actors and actresses per square feet of street space than anywhere else on earth – Greenwich Village. At the Herbert Berghof Studio in the Village, she showed just enough talent for people to talk about her for occasional jobs.

Sometimes, these resulted in her having sufficient funds to spend on the smallest rooms in the tiniest, cheapest hotel in the neighbourhood, but these could make the steps of the Plaza fountain seem a lot more inviting.

She wasn't going to ask Judy for money. For one thing, she knew she wouldn't get it. For another, she knew, too, how she would feel when the request was turned down.

Her father, of course, *would* have bailed her out, but there would have been no satisfaction in that. So she had to see more agents, suffer the indignity of more refusals, all in the hope that she would before long be introduced to a producer.

At one agent's office, she heard a man say sarcastically: 'God! that's just what we need – Judy Garland's daughter!'

It was the confirmation of an earlier thought she had allowed herself. If *Judy Garland* couldn't get a job merely because she was Judy Garland, how could Judy Garland's daughter? She said that she was depressed for weeks after that notion seemed to be confirmed. But she was lucky. Others might have been upset for years about the remark she overheard – without any obvious signs of things changing. But for Liza things did change – and it was because of Judy.

The work came – once the word got out that there was gold in them thar publicity hills. This was especially so at a time when there were more stories circulating about the state of her mother's marriage – by most accounts, now floundering on the rocks and unlikely to be rescued – and even worse, people were saying that she had once again attempted suicide.

None of that was easy for Liza who was experiencing the joint strain of looking for work in the most overcrowded business known to humanity – while at the same time knowing that the interest was entirely in her ancestry – and worrying at the same time about her mother's physical state.

On the one hand, she felt she wanted to be with Judy – which was precisely what her mother herself wanted – and on the other, if she didn't start building on her shaky professional foundations now, it would later on be much too late. So she took the opportunities that began to open for her – and decided to hang the motives. The point was to get work. Let the producers worry about their reasons themselves.

And if Judy were able to think about anything but her own health, she was not interfering. As Liza put it, her mother was 'smart enough to stay out of it – she never made calls.' Judy justified what may have appeared to have been a lack of interest in her daughter's progress by saying: 'I never want to be guilty of getting you a job'. And as Liza noted: 'She's not.'

But if it wasn't Judy's direct influence, the indirect help was enough.

On the other hand, Liza would deny that it was *all* through Judy that she began to get the odd job. She said afterwards: 'Producers are tough. They don't care who your parents are. They're out there to make a buck and if you're not good, you're not going to get a job. If someone allows you an audition, that's one thing but you have to come through and perform.'

Part of the problem was that although she looked very much like her father, so much of her was also Judy. At five foot four and a half, Liza was three inches taller than Judy. Nevertheless, she was built like her. There was not much in the way of hips, but her bust was reminiscent of Judy's; in another branch of showbiz it would have been called voluptuous. And the voice, now maturing into a full-throated dynamic sound, was so like hers. There was the same call to an invisible, unknown public that said 'Come and love me . . . and if I make you cry, you'll love me more.'

Liza may have worried about the 'Rainbow' strain of pathos in what her mother did, but she had it, too. When she sang in the minor key of love and lost chances, she was at her best. When there was a call to be raucous, she was already doing it the way Mama did – with an arm held high. It was not copying Judy. It was instinctive. It was talent – and that was what was about to be recognised. It was also Liza's principal strength. But at the moment, it seemed people *were* only interested in the novelty value of having Judy Garland's daughter in a possible bit part or perhaps dancing in a chorus – and Liza accepted.

She didn't begin to ask herself why, if that were the only reason, Judy herself still sometimes hit the low periods when *she* couldn't get work. But when you are young and depressed, you don't always rationalise things. So she took the work and only wished someone would forget who her mother was. Or if they did still remember, that they would have the guts to say: 'You're good enough to be anybody.' Never had she wanted to be a nobody more. But this 'somebody' did get work. In quick succession, Liza appeared in *The Fantasticks* and *The Pajama Game* (a show in which an understudy named Shirley MacLaine was discovered), all in repertory.

She said that she knew how all the reviews would begin – all of them would use the words 'Judy Garland's . . . ' She was of course, right. But the criticisms nevertheless were generally good.

Indeed, most of the critics were a lot kinder than was Judy herself. For some reason that no one could possibly explain – certainly the two people alive who were mainly involved cannot – Judy was letting everyone know that she had a daughter who was going to be marvellous in show business and her name was Lorna.

To one journalist, she confided: 'What I live for is to see that my children grow up to be honest, hard-working people. I don't care if they go into show business, but Liza is already on her way and if that's what she wants, super.'

Nice and slightly begrudging. But there was a sting and it came straight from the tail: 'Lorna, however, has a much better voice than Liza and will probably overtake her if she decides to go into the business.'

Lorna, of course, *would* decide to go into the business.

Nevertheless, Judy was plainly trying to tell Liza something. The message, out in public and in very clear black and white, was hardly one of appreciation – either for her talent or for the kindness she had been extended over the years by her eldest child.

Was Judy now playing the woman spurned? Was she simply bitter? Or was she displaying signs of her mental imbalance which failed to recognise that Liza was a pretty unusual daughter? Whatever the reason, it was fairly obvious that these were not nice things to say about the girl who had been confidante, companion and friend as well as little daughter.

Liza, however, knew one thing and knew it well: if she were going to succeed in that business, she had to do it in spite of her mother and not because of her. And that went, too, for all the unpleasant things that other people would say about her.

The sad thing was that Liza really did mind. She would mind a little less if more work came in. Liza knew it would come – if she didn't know that, she would have packed up. Show business is all about optimism.

What she needed was simply the break – wasn't that what everybody wanted? The kind of break that came when a man tapped Liza on the shoulder as she stood at the kerb where Broadway meets 46th Street. It was the sort of thing that no decent writer would dare put in a novel and which, Liza later commented, only happened in the worst movies, but she swears it happened. The man said: 'Danny Daniels is looking for you for a show.'

It turned out that Mr Daniels was a producer who had seen Liza at work and had concluded that there might be something more in her than the shows in which she had appeared had brought out – in which case, he had something more he could offer her: third lead in an off-Broadway show.

It also had to be admitted – but he didn't dare do so to Liza herself – that he was worried about getting enough coverage for his show. Having Judy Garland's daughter around could do no harm at all.

It is quite possible that, no matter how broke or depressed she was, had she known the real reason, Liza would have turned him down flat.

It is also true that she never regretted taking the bait. How could she? That tap on the shoulder as she was trying to make her way through the crowds to her dancing class was the sort of break that usually only happened to chorus girls in *42nd Street*. Nobody had to tell her that she was going in as a nobody but was going to have to come out a star. Events spoke for themselves.

Liza would play a girl with the extraordinarily glamorous name of Ethel Hoflinger.

The show was a revival of a hit that had been big on Broadway itself twenty-two years earlier; it was called *Best Foot Forward*, and was all about a young girl from a small town whose excitement becomes overwhelming when a big star comes to call.

Actually, the idea for choosing Liza had come from the twenty-three-year-old producer Arthur Whitelaw, for whom the whole thing was an article of faith – two articles of faith actually: one, that he was old enough and mature enough to raise the money to put on his own show and, two, that he was perceptive enough to choose the right cast.

Once having got Liza to agree – agree? She was ready to kiss his feet – he went through the process of making sure his initial hunch had been correct. He auditioned her – toughly.

The day before the audition, Liza rang Judy, who now seemed conciliatory. She told Liza to watch her poise, to relax, not to be nervous. Actually, it was Judy who was nervous. 'She was a nervous wreck!' Liza later recalled. 'Wow! Was she funny!'

It is a story that Liza seems to have changed somewhat as the years have gone by. Judy may well have been nervous, but mainly because she hated the idea of Liza going into the business at all – especially without her.

If Judy *had* told her daughter to relax, the instruction and the inherent warnings that went with the order had no great impact. Liza was shaking from the top of her elfin-cut hair to her rehearsal shoes.

What was more, she arrived for that audition twenty minutes late. For what looked like her first big break, she was breaking the first rule – arrive on time. As things turned out, it didn't make a great deal of difference.

Whitelaw asked her to perform two numbers. Liza chose 'The Way You Look Tonight' and 'They Can't Take That Away From Me'. She was making a vital point – when important matters are at stake, play it safe; choose standards and don't try to be too clever.

The producer was sufficiently impressed. 'I decided right on the spot that she was the girl I needed,' he later said.

Liza was as excited as the girl she was to play – except that just as things were about to get going, Liza broke a bone in her left ankle during a run through and her foot had to be put in a plaster cast.

The accident happened on the eve of her 17th birthday – she caught the foot in a floorboard, tripped over and snapped the bone. Her birthday was spent with her leg suspended above a hospital bed.

But she was back in time for the next rehearsal – endeavouring to kick the plaster cast in time with the music. She had the sense – and the humour – to realise that out of the disaster could just be snatched the germ of a plus factor. Certainly, the publicity department thought so. If she wasn't that good at dancing with a foot in plaster, being photographed in her present condition was not lost on either the PR people or the newspapermen who were delighted to co-operate. Once more, being Judy Garland's daughter was no handicap. Being Judy Garland's daughter with a leg in plaster starring in – and being photographed dancing in – a show called *Best Foot Forward* seemed like an opportunity straight from heaven. Especially since the injury wasn't diagnosed to be all that serious.

As a result of Judy's influence – the strange ambivalent Judy; up one minute, down the next; at once angry that Liza should contemplate following her into show business and determined that nothing should stop her from succeeding – Liza found herself appearing in the media, performing songs from her show on national television, an advantage no other off-Broadway production could possibly boast. Mr Whitelaw was glad indeed that he had had the foresight to book Liza for the duration of the show.

If truth be told, he was even more glad that Liza had broken her foot. Just before the plaster was to be removed, Liza appeared on the Jack Paar *Tonight* show, which was just about the biggest thing on television. Again, Judy had arranged it. She told Liza to make sure that she showed her plaster cast. She hadn't for nothing seen the way the publicity men from MGM operated. Liza co-operated and Paar was happy to go along. After all, the best kind of publicity is that which both sides – the seller and the buyer – want equally much. It was a good item for him.

It looked as though the foot would be mended in time for the final rehearsals and opening night. In fact, after all the publicity, the management were ready, if necessary, to put the opening off until she was ready. Or else it was quite prepared to open there and then, with Liza's best foot going forward as though it had just hobbled out of the ambulance, but the worry and the anxiety were enough to drive both her and those around her insane. So once again, Judy decided to help.

She turned up for a party wearing sequins, rhinestones and feathers and sang and danced with the young performers as though this was going to be her own show. Liza was thrilled. Judy told her she knew she would be as good as the people in the original production, which she remembered so well.

That one had starred Nancy Walker and a youngster about to become a Hollywood sensation called June Allyson. It was subsequently filmed, with Miss Allyson sharing most of the honours with Lucille Ball, who played the Big Hollywood Star who

accepts an invitation to the college ball. The most notable scene was
the huge walk through town by the girl and her hundreds of friends
singing the college song, 'Buckle Down, Winsocki.'

Liza was taking advantage of an opportunity for which many
another girl would have given five years of her life. This girl was
going to buckle down herself now and make it the start of a
remarkable career.

But because of her foot, the opening was finally postponed for
three weeks. It was worth it.

She succeeded immediately. The show was a huge hit on its first
night and Liza Minnelli was almost a star. Almost.

Like every other member of the cast, she worked for the Equity
minimum of $35 a week – which, it must be confessed, seemed like
riches unimaginable for the performers for whom unemployment
had simply been a way of life. But for Liza the rewards of *Best Foot
Forward* could not be quantified in monetary terms. She might never
have been able to take her enthusiasm to a bank for a loan, but her
talent was certainly sufficient collateral. As far as she was concerned,
this was an investment with dividends to come.

She could not possibily have known how quickly their arrival
would be.

The show was at the Stage 73 Playhouse, but as Lewis Funke
mentioned in the *New York Times*, it was 'an Off-Broadway opening
[turned] into a Broadway première.' And that was precisely what it
was.

The mystery had been heightened by Judy's rôle in the first-night
proceedings. She didn't turn up. Perhaps that could have been
predicted. What was not so predictable was the effect it had on
almost everyone else involved. To calm the people in the audience,
an announcement had to be made from the stage.

People speculated that the reasons could have something to do
with Judy's health and possibly her marital difficulties. Except that
her last bout with illness had been reasonably short-lived and she
and her husband now seemed to have climbed off the rocks and
were back outwardly as a happily married couple. In fact, it was now
Liza's stepfather who was acting as her spokesman.

Sid Luft explained the reasons for Judy's absence to the Press:
'My wife said it was best not to let anything detract from the girl's
début.' And he added: 'We are extremely delighted that Liza and the
show seem to have made a hit.'

Judy had been on holiday in the Bahamas and it looked as though she were deliberately extending her stay. In fact, she was in New York but was resolutely not going to the theatre. Liza tried to explain things away: 'She made a big thing about somebody telling her the opening was the next night. But I know the real reason she didn't come was because she didn't want to draw any of the attention away from me. You know, the Press would have cared more about who Mama was with and all that jazz.'

Liza was, in truth, a lot less understanding. During the intermission, she could be heard shouting into the telephone, her eyes red and smudged with mascara: 'But Mama, you knew it was tonight!' Vincente had no inhibitions about being there. He was at the theatre to give Liza every encouragement and then plant a huge kiss on her cheek, as she basked in the excitement of the occasion, not really totally sure where she was or how she had got there.

'I thought she was wonderful,' said Minnelli's *père*, 'and I must admit I was more emotionally involved during her performance than I had expected to be.'

And so were members of the audience who delighted in her performance which, by almost all accounts, was remarkable. Whatever the reason for Judy's absence, in the end, Liza was probably better for her not being there.

At the time, however, she was bitter. A bottle of champagne bearing Judy's name awaited her daughter at the traditional after-the-opening party at Sardi's – when theatre companies try to pretend they don't care what the critics say and demonstrate the fact by eating and boozing at the famous restaurant opposite Shubert Alley. Liza looked at the bottle with disdain.

It was a time for nail-biting and saying terrible things about the critics, the 'Butchers of Broadway' who could consign their work to instant oblivion.

Normally, it wouldn't have mattered very much to an off-Broadway show. There were no off-Broadway butchers, at least none with any recognisable clout. But this was different. Everyone involved knew that the critics were there and they cared a great deal what they would write. As things turned out, no one need have worried. They liked the show and loved Liza – even if much of the attention seemed to have been devoted to the absence of the star's mother.

Mr Funke, of the *New York Times*, noted that Judy ought to have attended the opening: 'She would have been pleased because Liza

did very nicely indeed. It was what you could call an auspicious
début.'

And he added: 'She acted, she sang and she danced and never
for a moment did she give any indication that she knew the
spotlight was on her every movement; that out front, the tiny
theatre was filled with friends of her mother and father...She
conducted herself with grave and attractive presence and all the
way she gave indications of her breeding.'

Mr Funke was plainly aware that he was present at the beginning
of something big – or if he wasn't, it was a good hunch. So good a
hunch, in fact, that everything about it seemed to indicate a degree
of history being made.

Inevitably – and this probably did not over-please Liza – the
comparisons with Judy were there in every glowing, excited report
about this momentous début.

As the *Times* critic said: 'There is a little of Judy in Liza. She's
even perhaps a mite shorter, the curve of her nose is a definite
reminder and there is the same quality to be noted at times. Her
voice has some of the touching quality that has been the trade mark
of Judy Garland and, like her mother, Liza seems capable of letting
that voice go all out in a crescendo of emotion.'

Liza was remarkable in a number specially written for the show
and for its new star by the team of Hugh Martin and Ralph Blane:
'You Are For Loving' was a sensation. So, too, was 'Just a Little Joint
with a Jukebox'.

As for the show, Mr Funke said: 'Back in 1941 when it was
launched under the brilliant direction of George Abbott, it was one
of the season's main hits. It had a vibrant freshness and innocence
and a carload of talent.

'The revival is not that blessed, though all the youngsters are fresh
and vibrant and generally simulate a kind of high-school innocence.
Under Danny Daniels' direction, action seeks to inject life into a
tepid book that in spite of revisions...remains tepid...'

Somehow, though, that didn't seem to matter, and as the critic
pointed out, the show was only of passing interest to his readers,
compared with the début of the star.

'The major interest is Liza – who does put her best foot forward
and helps keep *Best Foot Forward* from limping home a loser.'

They were words that did not have to be written. Now was the
time for the sour grapes – those words about Liza only jumping on

her mother's bandwagon and that she should have saved herself and everyone else the journey. Why didn't she find herself a nice job as a children's nurse or a shorthand typist? Someone was bound to say that.

But those words were not written and nobody, it seemed, wanted to say them.

In the *Los Angeles Times*, William Glover reported: 'A wide-eyed singing-dancing image of her stellar mother [all right, it would not be avoided, presumably], the seventeen-year-old lass arrived at the Stage 73 theatre in a revival of *Best Foot Forward*.

'For her New York professional bow, the hefty hopeful relies mostly on the vocal, visual and performing style perfected by Miss Garland. So that's bad?

'Her chief opportunity comes late in the production when she does a brace of numbers that afford a display of lively rhythm and sentimental crooning. They come off fine. As an actress, though, there is lots of room for improvement.

'The show, which was a big hit back in 1941, is a pretty tough job for Miss Minnelli and a lot of other energetic young aspirants to put over. They all work hard but the story and lines are against them. Without Liza's presence to whet audience interest, it is all rather dim fare.'

But Liza was not dim fare by the standards of Mr Glover or of the paying members of the audience. Liza did not let them down and that was the remarkable part of it all.

Somehow it *was* difficult for everyone to accept that a second edition of a best-seller could be worth buying. But they looked and they bought and they were ready to book again for more of the same.

They had braved police lines – there to curb the enthusiasm of the people who had come to see Judy – to get into the theatre and they all pronounced it worthwhile.

Later, Judy posed for pictures hugging her daughter and congratulating her on an evening she plainly might not have minded having herself.

Was professional jealousy involved? No one would admit that was so and neither Judy nor Liza certainly would have said it was, but occasionally the most loving of parents experiences a dense of 'I-wish-I-could-have-done-it' after a child's triumph.

The second night, Judy did appear in the audience, and cheered and cried with the people around her.

She said afterwards: 'Oh, did I cry! I cried and I cried. I was so proud of my baby. She had worked so hard and all alone. And you know Liza's the first one of us to do this. I never had a Broadway show. All I had were variety shows.' In that, too, perhaps Judy was betraying more than she was admitting: possibly, she was just a little jealous that Liza was achieving so much, not just without her, but in a medium in which she herself had not had the opportunity to make any impact. It may sound absurd, but professional jealousy can be a deadly thing.

The police barricades were brought out again and this time the people behind them were satisfied. The interesting thing is that they would have been equally quelled if Judy hadn't turned up. That night, it was getting a glimpse of Liza that proved exciting enough.

The UPI wire service echoed most people's feelings when it joined in the clamour. 'Miss Minnelli . . . was outstanding in a cast of extremely personable and talented youngsters. She proved to be a natural comedienne, a fine dancer (despite a recently broken foot bone that kept her slightly under wraps) and a singer with an appealing voice that reminded one of her mother's singing at times.'

Liza must have forgiven the writers for harping on that. Everyone else did. She might have got the initial attention because of who she was – or rather who she was related to – but the applause was all for her. That was nothing she could afford to sneer at and nobody would have expected her to do so.

Judy was careful not to allow her daughter to think that all was perfection in what she did – and that she had nothing more to learn. This time, it was her daughter's own good she had in mind and nothing less than that.

Time and again, she gave her instruction in both the way to sing and dance and how to project herself to the audience. She told her to respect the words she was singing and not content herself with reaching a high note and holding on to it. Without the words, there was no point in having the notes. There was a psychological message there.

Liza did not merely get reviews in the posh columns of the posh papers – that might have been expected – but seeing the way America reacted to the show and its discovery of a young star, the treatment was now of the kind reserved for a top personality everyone had been talking about for years (and they didn't mean Judy).

Liza was talked about and interviewed on television and radio. She was the subject of conversation at the Algonquin – the kind that with almost anyone else would have started out nice and flattering but ended up in a flood of catty laughter that would have called for drinks to be served in a saucer.

But that was not how they spoke of Liza. It was now plainly the fashionable thing to say you had been off-Broadway and had had a stunning experience.

They invited Liza to parties, the fashionable people who a few months ago would have scorned such thoughts as beneath their dignity. To one, Liza summoned up the courage to say: 'You don't want me. You want Judy Garland's daughter.' Now, though, people were wanting her for herself. It was quite possible that it didn't matter about her mother. Alas, possible but unlikely.

Liza was always aware of her situation. She said: 'When you're seven or eight or nine, you don't really care who your Mama and Poppa are. Just so you have them and they love you. And when you're ten, you go around telling everybody, "I'm Judy Garland's daughter" because you want everybody to love you. I know I used to. And then when you're about fourteen, you want everybody to love you because you're *you* and *not* Judy Garland's daughter. So you keep it quiet. You don't tell anybody who you are. Well, I guess you grow out of that stage, too.'

She remembered the actor Walter Slezak who had had a famous father, telling her to beware of the pitfalls of being Judy's child. As he told her – very tellingly indeed – 'A famous mama can open a lot of doors for you, but there's nothing she can do for you between 8.30 and 11.'

As Liza said: 'That's very true. And it's the *important* time, right? Between 8.30 and 11. I mean, they may come to see me because I'm Judy Garland's daughter, at first, but if they go away liking me, that's me, right?'

It really was right – and by all accounts they were going out liking Liza, for being Liza.

Look magazine treated the whole thing as an event of mammoth importance. They produced a massive spread headed (in small type) 'Liza Minnelli' and then underneath (in much bigger letters) 'Judy's Daughter Bows In'.

Well, it wasn't quite a bow into the big magazines – she had done that at the age of five with her dancing classes – but it certainly was a big, big bow into American show business.

The spread was full of pictures, Liza dancing in front of the chorus, Liza singing solo and Liza – of course, with Mama, who, it has to be admitted, *did* look slightly wistful at the attention being paid not to herself but to her daughter. That was not a usual experience for a woman of forty. But then Judy was not every mother – stage or otherwise.

'Where did the vivacious seventeen-year-old daughter of Judy Garland and film director Vincente Minnelli get the talent that aroused unanimous praise?' asked Sam Gastan in the *Look* article.

'Perhaps it was born in her and nurtured during years on the periphery of her mother's spotlight. Or it may have been spurred by the mortification of her very first appearance.'

He was referring to Liza's appearance in *The Good Old Summertime* and her failure to put on her pants for the film. She probably enjoyed that one as much as all the comments about her relationship with her mother.

How long would it be before people would just accept her for herself? Longer than she might have hoped. The *Look* piece certainly dwelt on the future at length.

'Ahead are television guest spots, more musical comedy and motion pictures. Liza Minnelli is determined to get ahead on her own merits in a demanding craft. And she is learning as her mother did before her, that there is no short way over the rainbow.'

That line was as inevitable as the comparisons with Mama. When Liza told another reporter: 'I don't want to become another Judy Garland,' it was a cry from the heart. The association with her mother might have opened the doors for her, but now she was beginning to almost wish that they hadn't. It would have been a lot more pleasant for her if all the comments were restricted to just how good Liza was.

'I realise that all my professional and personal life I'll never be able to be disassociated with my mother,' she told Vernon Scott for his piece in the *Milwaukee Journal* in July 1963. 'I really want to be. I guess someday I'd like to be thought of as Liza Minnelli, who happens to be Judy Garland's daughter, but who also happens to be Liza Minnelli.'

Liza and Judy were now doing a TV special together – not Judy's show in which Liza appeared as a guest, but their own show together.

Liza knew of the comparisons that would be made; indeed they were already being made in rehearsal. 'I know I sound like mother when I sing, but I don't intend to do it. It just happens.'

Liza's showbiz debut: on the set of In the Good Old Summertime *(1949) watched over by her mama, the star of the picture, Judy Garland.*

Liza bids farewell to Daddy in 1951. Vincente Minnelli stayed at home while Liza joined Judy on board the Queen Elizabeth *for her European singing tour. (Keystone Press Agency)*

Liza the ingénue: thinking about her first screen role in Charlie Bubbles *(1967).*

Enjoying life: with Albert Finney in Charlie Bubbles *(1967).*

Love and rivalry: Liza and Judy rehearse their show at the London Palladium in November 1964.

The applause she wanted most – from Mama: an offstage moment during Flora the Red Menace *in 1965.*

Husbands: left *Peter Allen (1965),* above *Jack Haley Jnr (1974), and Mark Gero (1979).*

Liza with David: it all looked so good – but, as usual, it wasn't! (Rune Hellestad/Corbis)

Real fame at last: Liza being measured for a wax model at Madam Tussauds in London in 1974.

Liza in command at the London Palladium.

*A wistful look as Liza leaves the Savoy Hotel – and Peter Sellers –
on the night their romance went sour in 1973.*

With two of her biggest influences, husband Jack and sometime mentor Gene Kelly, in 1974.

With Joel Grey in Cabaret *(1972): they made a marvellous team.*

The Liza her fans remember best – in Cabaret *(1972).*

With Michael York in Cabaret – *the screen romance that was not to be.*

The sophisticated Forties look in New York, New York *(1977).*

The saxophone was her principal rival for the affections of Robert De Niro in New York, New York *(1977).*

Love with Dudley Moore – in Arthur *(1981).*

'Liza's Back,' said the posters. *She looked good from the front, too. (Rune Hellestad/Corbis)*

That similarity would not be mentioned very often in years to come. Nobody would later accuse Liza of copying her mother. But those accusations came often enough while she was complaining of the need to be her own girl. She was not however rejecting opportunities for work which only heightened the link between Judy and Liza.

Liza would have been an idiot to turn down the exposure of the nationally-networked TV show, one that would be likely to be seen overseas, too, even if it only heightened those comparisons. She did not turn it down, because Liza was a very intelligent girl – with equally intelligent agents and other advisers, not least of all her mother Judy Garland.

The much-respected show business writer, Bob Thomas, noted: 'If she comes across on television as well as in person, Liza might make it. She has the same elfin charm and ingenuous manner of her Ma.'

That was a prescient judgement if ever there was one. Mr Thomas was being cautious because it was against all the odds, even now, that the daughter of a superstar could really succeed on her own – and on her own would be the only way she could succeed. He knew as well as she did that riding on her mother's skirts would be a gimmick that would last only so long. Already, there were those who were praying she would trip over while they were still around to see it.

His judgement, however, was perfectly correct. Liza was more of a hit on the show than was her mother – and Judy was generous enough on that occasion to enjoy it and let her daughter take the spotlight.

Liza had to admit that she was worried about the perils and problems of stardom, should it come.

She told Bob Thomas for his piece in September 1963: 'I suppose I want to be a star – if being a star means acceptance in the profession.' That, too, was a judgement that showed not just considerable maturity on Liza's part, but admitted to one of the facts of showbiz life. For all the devotion of an audience, there is nothing to compare with the admiration of one's peers. Al Jolson used to hold Sunday concerts at the Winter Garden Theatre on Broadway, which he regarded as virtually his own house, just so that other people in the entertainment industry who worked the rest of the week, could see for themselves how great he was.

When stars are called that by fellow entertainers, they know they have finally arrived.

Even so, Liza wanted something that her mother had never achieved. Along with the adulation went – as Judy had discovered – the ownership of that individual by the public. It was inevitable. Great entertainers don't merely play to audiences, they make love to them. In exchange for that love being returned, they surrender their own lives. Liza recognised that. 'I would like to avoid some of the things that go with stardom, especially the lack of privacy,' she said. The seventeen-year-old wished that. The more adult Liza Minnelli would know it was mere wishful thinking.

Judy would later give Vincente a lot of the credit for Liza's success. She said: 'The kid knew exactly who to get to help her. I guess she kept her eyes open whenever she was on her old man's sets.'

But Judy's influence was what everyone else saw – and she saw it herself. It was obvious that some of Liza's own success was rubbing off on her mother. She saw it as a way of making Judy feel happy – and that made her happy, too. For no matter how much the maudlin and the pathetic side of Judy's act provided her with an extra dimension, there could be no doubt that she was at heart a discontented person. As Liza was to put it herself years later: 'There was in her a very deep wound, somewhere far down, which she could never close up because she had to use it when she sang and when she acted. She needed that pain there because it was her work.'

Now Liza was glad to have found a means of easing that pain – and letting its effects move over to her, to give herself that extra dimension that was so vital.

Liza stayed in the show for five months. She left because Judy wanted her to. She said that she needed her back home in California with her. There was a new TV series on the way and she couldn't possibly undertake it without her rock and her right arm at her side.

In 1963, all the Garland clan took part in a Christmas edition of *The Judy Garland Show*, Liza, Lorna and Joey performing one of the old Gumm Sisters routines, a particularly nostalgic moment for Judy.

For once Liza was inclined to take the view that if she were not now thinking of herself, no one would do so for her. But Judy was sometimes not the most generous of people and now she was demonstrating her selfish streak.

But she was a clever, sometimes crafty lady. When Liza told her she had a boyfriend in New York whom she didn't want to leave, Judy made inquiries and put matters right in her own way. This time, she wasn't going to discourage her daughter's romantic entanglements; no question of sinister telephone calls and car rides to secret destinations or unpleasantness of any other kind (at least, not the way she saw it). On the contrary, she rang the boy, a dancer called Tracy Everitt who was in a Broadway show, *How to Succeed in Business Without Really Trying* (he was trying to succeed in rising from the chorus). The next thing that Liza knew was that Tracy told her he was leaving New York and flying out to the West Coast. Judy had offered him a job dancing in her show and he was in no mind to decline that offer.

It had the result Judy anticipated. She didn't want Tracy particularly, but she did want Liza. Absolutely according to plan, Liza quit the show and flew to California herself.

Her life had changed in those five months. They were five months of people sitting up and noticing the young girl who everyone knew had a famous mother. So the success was even now somewhat muted in Liza's eyes. But it was there, just the same. She was the talk of *Variety* and Sardi's, where the people in the know about the world of theatres chatted about her talent. And talk about her talent was the sweetest she could possibly hear. When details of those words filtered back to her, she thought there was a future and she felt content.

Even more so was the notion that perhaps, some day, she would not be spoken of as simply Judy's daughter.

Liza was making records now – of a couple of numbers from the show. And she admitted they did have the smack of a certain sense of *déjà vu* about them. 'When I hear my voice on a record or something, I'm really surprised at how much it resembles hers,' she said. 'It's kind of, well, spooky.'

Chapter Eight

WHAT NO one could doubt was that Liza had put her best Paris-shod foot forward and marched ahead of all the predictions of the direst of consequences that should now be awaiting her.

As a result of *Best Foot Forward*, Liza won the Daniel Blum Theater Award for the most promising young actress of the year.

The award gave the critics reason enough to keep on rhapsodising about it. 'We Dig a Rising Start in *Best Foot Foward*,' trumpeted the *Daily News* of New York. 'Miss Minnelli, a shapely lass in her late teens . . . is no May basket beauty-wise, but in addition to a splendid singing voice (a lucky heritage) she has a wonderful flair of comedy,' wrote James Davis.

The *New York Morning Telegraph*'s Whitney Bolton knew it had been all Liza's show: 'She can belt it out in barrel house or jazz, can bring a tender moment in a ballad. Her one spectacular dance with three young men is superbly arrived at . . . a brand-new, bright new star had risen in the theatrical heavens and I'm not one to diminish its light forthwith.'

The *New Yorker*, in its more sedate way, reflected on the situation and came to much the same conclusion: 'Miss Minnelli, who is Judy Garland's daughter . . . is a lovely singer and a passable clown and her natural wistfulness is effective and touching when she has the opportunity to show it,' wrote Edith Oliver.

Among those who had seen the show was Ed Sullivan, then the most potent force in US entertainment. A kind word from him on one of his variety shows was an endorsement that could make a star overnight. Now he had done that for Liza. The off-Broadway musical actress was about to become a national star, appearing on his show just before she left for the Coast.

She said that she was so nervous – 'scared knock-kneed' was how she graphically put it – that it wasn't easy to hide her fright. In fact, she maintains, it was all pretty disastrous. Not too disastrous, however, to stop her getting new work, the best of which was the TV show she did with Judy. The series has gone into popular mythology as an outstanding flop. On the contrary, it kept running for an entire season – and probably would have done better had it not been scheduled opposite the immensly popular Western series *Bonanza* – and provided millions of Garland fans who normally never had a chance of seeing her in anything but her movies with an opportunity to appreciate her at her best. And, some of the time, she really was at her best.

In November that year she was better than ever, because she was with Liza Minnelli, a seventeen-year-old who a few months before had been unknown but who now was making a little name for herself.

As a result of that appearance, Liza Minnelli became very well known indeed. She did her own thing, singing some of the songs she enjoyed most and did a series of duets in a medley that – had there been such things as video recorders at the time – would have been taped all over the land. As it was, those who saw the programmes enjoyed them thoroughly. The edition with Liza – unlike most of the others – was shown all over the world.

The romance that had brought her from New York was now over. But her career had barely begun.

Liza was now in demand – to her satisfaction the *Saturday Evening Post* seemed to appreciate that. Not once did an article they published call her 'Judy Garland's daughter'. That was indeed something.

Nevertheless, the Judy influence was stronger than she would ever want to admit. Just as she had felt sorry for her mother, had wanted to do what she could to make her as 'normal' as possible – considering everything a really forlorn hope – so she also craved her approval.

So much of what she did was with Judy in mind. When Liza went back to New York, while Judy remained at home, they talked on the telephone daily. Not so surprising. Liza was only seventeen. But it was the mother telling the daughter *her* problems, the child offering the consolation.

Judy would phone at the least opportune moments – when Liza was with friends, with boys, giving interviews.

'Mama, I'm so glad you called . . . I love you, too.'

Her visitors heard it all. She gave Judy an expurgated daily diary. She told her of the offers she had had, the ones she had accepted, the ones she had turned down. It was nothing new for her. She had heard her mother talk of such things for fourteen years. The only difference was that now she was dealing with these matters for herself and by herself.

She told her about the fashion show at which she sang in New York the previous night.

'What did you do?' Judy asked her.

Liza told her the song. Judy didn't know it. 'Sing it for me,' she said. So Liza did sing it. She had to – even though there was an audience of journalists in the room.

Judy liked it. Liza admitted that she had had a standing ovation among the gilt chairs. Judy said she could understand why. 'Really Mama,' she said. 'You're wonderful to say that, Mama.'

Liza appreciated the Judy Garland who was now watching from the sidelines of her life. 'What a morale booster she is,' she said. 'Wow!'

Liza was plainly a very intelligent young lady as well as a potential star. Of course, that word was being used about her. But she couldn't accept it just like that. In fact, for years afterwards she would express her doubts. In 1965 for instance, in a revealing interview with Jean Sprain Wilson for the AP news agency she declared: 'I'm not a star – not yet. But I'm on my way.'

That was a fact that had been recognised since *Best Foot Forward* and was certainly obvious to the people at that 1963 fashion show.

There was not much about Liza that wasn't star-like – apart, that is, from the schoolgirl excitement that she showed to strangers and possibly also the way in which she spoke to journalists.

Very little about Liza resembled a later generation of young pop singers who, clutched from obscurity, believed that the world owed them not just a very good living but a form of worship. That wasn't Liza at all.

Norman Poirier noted in his piece: 'Only when she speaks of Hollywood does her easy laughter give way to cold rancour.' 'Hollywood is the rattiest place in the world,' she told him. And she meant it.

And she wanted to get the record straight about her mother, too. 'They say Mama is hard to work with,' she told him, 'and temperamental and all. But I've been with her and listened to her to try to explain how you couldn't do a song such and such a way because it didn't make sense. But they had to do it their way every time. Well, she'd just walk off to her dressing room and wait there till they saw it her way.'

Liza seemed as if she were now giving notice that she was going to do things Her Way. Frank Sinatra had not yet given the world a new *cri-de-coeur* called 'My Way', so the significance of the remark was somewhat lost on both her and her interviewer, but it was there just the same and she meant it every bit as much as did Ol' Blue Eyes and his lyricist.

She was also glad that she hadn't gone into full-time show business much earlier, as her mother had. 'I think a career robs youngsters of too many things. It's too competitive. They should have poems and football games and all the fun of growing up...It's a very lonesome life.' And she said she was speaking as someone who had made her début – of sorts – at two.

With respect to Jean Sprain Wilson, that was fairly evident from the TV show with her mother. But it was establishing the fact, just in case it had escaped other people's notice.

She was once again saying that she didn't want fame to alter her feelings of wanting, almost craving, privacy. As she said: 'I keep real, on the ground, by keeping my private life separated from show business.'

Her friends were, on the whole, not in show business. Most were executives in corporations whose only link with TV was studying the economic results of commercials on bulk sales.

Nevertheless, she wanted to make sure that people knew her name – and how to pronounce it. This was the first recorded public declaration that her name was not pronounced, 'Leesa', but 'Ly-z-er'.

There was another declaration that people had heard before: Please not to call her Judy Garland's daughter – all the time.

'It's kind of an advantage,' she conceded. 'I know why people come to see me. I hear them in the lobby talking. They expect a carbon copy or they expect me to be no good. Originality is the one thing they don't expect.'

In a long interview with me in 1963, Judy spoke of her worries and concerns over that. She was going through one of her own introspective periods – and looked it. Her marriage had finally collapsed and so, it seemed, had her health. 'I think Liza has a problem – and it's me. I am not really good for her because everyone who goes to see her expects to see me. In fact, those who do go are so taken in by her that when they see me, they expect to see Liza. But that isn't a consolation to my daughter. She isn't helped either because I still think of her as my baby. But she's doing brilliantly just the same and I'm very proud of her.' I believed Judy in 1963 and have no reason to change my mind now. She was proud – and occasionally jealous.

Sometimes, however, the jealousy was overpowering and suppressed all other emotions. She loved Liza, wished her success, yet could do seemingly impossible things.

One moment she could be photographed hugging and kissing her daughter, the next she was going to court against her.

That happened in September 1963. Judy impounded her earnings. A judge decided then that Liza couldn't spend a cent she earned unless Judy gave her approval.

Probate Judge Joseph A. Cox formalised the relationship between mother and daughter – to her daughter's evident chagrin. He declared Judy her official guardian – 'limited guardian' was the term used – and said that nothing Liza earned could be spent without Judy's say-so, and the approval, too, of the court.

When Judy signed a contract on Liza's behalf with the famous Creative Management Associates to act as the seventeen-year-old's agents, the judge approved. He decided that Liza's affairs needed to be put in order. But the fact that it took a judge to do it gives some hint of how pleased with the idea Liza was.

The agency would deduct ten per cent from everything Liza earned – and then hand over the balance to Judy. The money, however, had to be deposited in Liza's name in New York banks. If Liza wanted to get her hand on any of it, it would take an order from the Judge.

Liza wasn't happy, but she was willing to compromise. 'Please may I keep half of it?' she asked in effect. She was told no. The order would stay in force until she was twenty-one.

This was a hard time for Judy. John F. Kennedy had recently been assassinated, an event which she took as though it were her own brother who had been gunned down. Indeed, she regarded her contemporary, the President, with the same affection as she would have felt for a brother. They spoke regularly on the phone – the attractive, vibrant President and the star whom he remembered adoring in *The Wizard of Oz*. One of the perks of the White House was being able to speak to her whenever he wanted to do so – and even to ask her to sing 'Over the Rainbow' to him. When he died, Judy was inconsolable. There were more illnesses, more dependence on drugs.

And then Liza herself was taken ill. In January 1964, she awoke on what she has come to call a 'black morning', unable to get out of bed. She had a temperature that looked as though it were going to send the mercury racing out of the thermometer. Her legs, she said, felt like 'wet noodles'. She called a doctor friend and within an hour, she was rushed to Mount Sinai Hospital in New York. They diagnosed a kidney stone. She was seriously ill for eight days, receiving treatment for an ailment which doctors had decided was probably hereditary – indeed, her father was to die from kidney disease more than twenty years later.

Judy was with her when she was taken into hospital, but then, assured that she was all right, flew off to Los Angeles. When Liza eventually left her hospital room almost a month after being admitted – a room which was full of the peanut butter sandwiches she had been avidly consuming – she declared: 'I feel fine. I just have to take it easy and not belt around too terribly much.'

Judy took note of that and ordered it put into effect. Her daughter would not be allowed to belt around at all.

The one thing she was not going to allow was Liza going back to work – without her permission. Liza protested that she knew what she was capable of doing. 'I've had a good long rest. I'm tired of resting and ready to go back to work,' she complained.

And indeed she did have work to go back to. She was signed to take the lead in a musical show called *Carnival*.

In fact, her agent had come to see her in hospital and asked if she felt well enough to do the show. She signed the contract there and then.

The show wasn't an important one and it certainly was not playing at a prestige theatre – the Mineola Playhouse and at the Paper Mill Playhouse at Milburn, Long Island, a fortnight later.

Judy said 'No.' In fact, Judy was determined that she wouldn't do the show. But Liza said 'yes' – and the lawyers were called in again.

The producers, Frank Carrington and Laurence Feldman, received a telegram from Judy's attorneys. It was very much to the point, if not exactly brief:

'JUDY GARLAND MOTHER AND LEGAL GUARDIAN OF LIZA MINNELLI A MINOR HEREBY INFORMS YOU THAT BECAUSE OF CONCERN FOR HER DAUGHTER'S HEALTH SHE HAS NOT CONSENTED AND WILL NOT CONSENT TO MISS MINNELLI ENTERING INTO AN AGREEMENT WITH YOU FOR THE PERFORMANCES OF SERVICES BY MISS MINNELLI STOP

IF YOU EMPLOY MISS MINNELLI YOU DO SO WITHOUT MISS GARLAND'S
CONSENT AND AT YOUR OWN RISK STOP MISS GARLAND WILL TAKE
ALL LEGAL STEPS NECESSARY IN CIRCUMSTANCES TO PROTECT HER
DAUGHTER'S HEALTH STOP.

The producers decided to be conciliatory – but that did not mean
they were going to oblige. 'The last thing that we want to do is
endanger Miss Minnelli's health,' they declared. 'If it serves her
interest we will tear up her contract. In fact, that is precisely what we
offered to do but Miss Minnelli insisted that she is in perfect health
and will do the show.'

Judy determined to do all she could to stop her. 'I shall do
everything in my power,' she declared.

Her power was not exercised to the full, however. Liza did the
show. It was the first time in her life she had said 'No' to Judy. It
proved to be a heady experience. With all sorts of repercussions, few
of which either of them could have anticipated.

It was during the first-night performance at Mineola, with Liza on
stage, that the phone rang. A stagehand took the call, complaining
that no one ought to have been ringing at that time – the phone
could be heard in the auditorium and had already caused a few
laughs where none should have been. The man at the other end was
insistent. He needed to talk to Liza. The stagehand was equally
insistent. Liza was on stage and nothing would drag her off.
Eventually, he compromised on leaving a message: her mother had
attempted suicide.

Liza got the message during the interval, made her own call and
satisfied herself that her mother would get better. Incredibly, the
shock was not severe enough to spoil Liza's act – it is said that she was
even better in the second half of the show than she had been during
the first.

The show itself would turn out to be an invaluable contribution
towards Liza's career. It was based on the film *Lili* in which Leslie
Caron had played a circus waif. Now this was Liza's role, a lost girl
who contemplates suicide because no one in the circus company
among whom she lives seems to care – until a puppet tells her that he
cares, he really does. And so do all the other puppets in the company.

Writing in the Long Island newspaper, *Newsday*, Mike Grady
began with the usual phrase: 'The comparisons to Judy are
inevitable – the tremulous voice, the respect for the lyric, the wide

eyes, the clenching hands, eyebrows never still.' But having got that off his chest, he wrote what his readers mostly wanted to know – and Liza to have confirmed: 'Yet by the time she sings her second number "Yes My Heart" the applause belongs to her alone.'

That was indeed success. Nevertheless, it was, Liza was to say, the beginning of 'a bad period for me'. Depending on where you stood in the Judy-Liza conflict that was either a gross under-estimate of the situation or an overstatement. Things certainly were fraught between the two Garland girls, a term that seemed appropriate now that they were not merely matching talent with each other, but temperament, too.

At seventeen, Liza was $3,000 in debt and her creditors were threatening to instigate bankruptcy proceedings – which she was to say was practically a record. It probably was. She decided not to go to either of her parents for help, but gave her lawyers power of attorney to sort things out for her. Somehow they managed it without invoking Judy's guardianship or that of the courts, and the creditors were paid.

Relations remained strained – although Judy knew about Liza's attempts to get herself out of trouble and seemingly admired her for it. Before long, it was Judy who made the big gesture. She was about to go to London to star once more at the Palladium. 'How would you like to come with me?' she asked her daughter. Liza said yes. A big, big yes.

And that was roughly how London took to her. Judy's reputation was unsullied in the British capital. Liza was an unknown quantity apart, that is, from appearing on Judy's TV show, which had been a big success in Britain.

But in the next few weeks, she was a 'name'. She appeared on British television and there were pictures in the papers.

The Palladium trip didn't exactly make Liza as big a star as her mother in London, although the reviews were, on the whole, encouraging. But English people were no longer asking, 'Liza . . . who?' And if there was a lingering affection for Judy, it was rubbing off on to her too. Certainly, it did prove that everything the theatre's patrons had said about her mother in the 1950s still held. And if Judy thought Liza was good enough to appear with her, London wasn't going to argue.

As Liza remembered in the *Good Housekeeping* interview: 'It was terrifying for a couple of reasons. First of all, Mama is so adored. In a way, a Judy Garland concert is a revival meeting. My mother's fans are totally idolatrous. No matter what age they are, she holds them in thrall. Anyone else on the stage just cannot buck that orgy of emotion. [On the whole, Liza was proved right in that respect; but, and this was a great tribute to her, it really didn't matter.] Secondly, Mama at this point suddenly realised that she had a grown-up daughter; that she wasn't a kid herself any more.'

And that was not funny. As Liza pointed out, Judy now knew that she had to be competitive. That, too, was a different feeling from the jealousy she had previously felt. Being jealous of a member of the family who was working in a different medium was one thing with its own connotations. Being competitive with your own daughter, working in the same show, appearing on stage at the same time, was something very different.

Now, somehow, Judy was trying to score from her own daughter. Had this been a film in which both were appearing, she would have hogged the camera, made sure that *she* got the best angles. She probably would have had it written into her contract. Now, though, she was saying to her daughter: 'You're not as good as I am and I'm going to prove that to you.'

It was not lost on the staff of the Palladium. One member of the crew there told me: 'It was strange to see. I could tell from Judy's face, beneath the make-up and the sweat pouring down her face, that she was eyeing Liza all the time. She almost looked bitter.'

Liza herself was to put it like this: 'I wasn't Liza. I was another woman in the same spotlight. It was just too hard for me to try to cope.'

So she tried not to cope. Except that it was Liza's spotlight, too. She was, as she had said, 'on the way' to being a star. And even if she wanted to let her mother have all the glory, it wasn't an easy thing to do. Instinctively, she fought against it. So Liza was competitive, too.

She felt she had to be that from the time that Judy stopped the show, ordered the band to cease playing and told them that she had an announcement. They were going to see a brand new talent. 'Ladies and gentlemen,' she declared, 'Liza Minnelli.'

Liza said: 'I was just trying to hang in there and sing along with her. I was used to Mama always being Mama. But when I started to sing . . .'

'It was her night,' Liza conceded. 'I *wanted* it to be her night. I'm sure that happens with almost any mother and daughter. It happened to my mother in front of 8,000 people [an exaggeration; the Palladium holds just over 2,000]. I'm sure that people were overjoyed that I wasn't just rotten.'

If she had been 'just rotten' she wouldn't have lived – professionally speaking – to tell the tale. If nothing succeeds like success, nothing fails as much as failure at the London Palladium. More than one top international star was to leave that theatre with his or her reputation in tatters, the news crossing the Atlantic as quickly as if it were bounced off a satellite. Liza, as she stood on stage and sang to her new audience – even though Judy was constantly taking the microphone out of Liza's hands during the performance, as though trying to teach her how to use it – had no real worries.

In truth, Liza really didn't give any impression of nerves or anxiety. She sang 'Pass That Peace Pipe' and there were those in the audience who felt like passing her a big magnum of champagne.

One Palladium employee remembered for me: 'I could swear I went home that night convinced that I had seen history in the making, really. Liza was better than Judy and Judy knew it.'

She knew it to the point of abandoning any further thoughts of going into business 'against' Liza. She told everyone – said it, in fact, at every one of her Press conferences – that she was just proud, too proud to put it into words.

As Liza said: 'Mama's competitiveness disappeared immediately after the Palladium performance and she fell into a period of unparalleled motherhood with me.'

Twenty years later, Liza described it all like this: 'We went through what women go through for years in literally two hours. It was like Mama suddenly realised I was good, that she didn't have to apologise for me. It was the strangest feeling. One minute I was on stage with my mother, the next moment I was on stage with Judy Garland. One minute she smiled at me, and the next minute she was like the lioness that owned the stage and suddenly found somebody invading her territory. We were singing and I looked at her and the killer instinct of a performer had come out in her. For some reason, it made me laugh because I knew the imitation of her I was going to do for her afterward and we both howled.'

Judy for her part said afterwards: 'Liza, I thought you'd be so cute out there and so darling – my little baby girl. And then you put one foot forward and one hip went back just on the right beat and the hand went out and I thought, "Oh my God, I've got to be good now – this kid ain't fooling around".'

It certainly was a moment of adjustment for Judy. She realised not only that her daughter was no longer a little girl who needed her support – even if the support had mostly been the other way for much of her life – but that she was capable of a separate existence in her own business. The umbilical cord had been cut and the baby was thriving.

People were able to see that for themselves. When they went into record stores, staring them in the face was the picture of a wide-eyed gamine with a slightly wistful look. Her lips looked ready to declare that she had walked across her own rainbow and was not totally unscarred from the experience.

Capitol had released her first album. The LP was called *Liza! Liza!* and if it were slightly reminiscent of the song that had given her her name, it proved once again that she was her own woman.

The album included titles like 'The Travellin' Life', 'Try To Remember', 'Don't Ever Leave Me' and a Liza standard 'Maybe This Time'. The fact that this had turned out to be a Liza standard showed the impact she was now making.

It wasn't a Judy standard. It was a Liza song.

'No one deserves to sing so brilliantly on a début album,' wrote one critic. Peter Matz's Orchestra did her credit. In fact, Mr Matz deserves the sort of credit widely given ten years earlier to Nelson Riddle for his contribution to the rebirth of the Frank Sinatra career.

Meanwhile, the Palladium management decided that the original Judy–Liza visit had been so successful that they were called back for a reprise the following November.

Now Judy felt a proud, protective mother again. It wasn't competition, she could conclude, simply the watching care of a parent for her child. Friends could see, in fact, that Judy was hovering over Liza as though her daughter was a newly-hatched chick and she herself the mother hen. It was as though she finally realised that for some time their roles had been reversed and now, with the two of them in the public spotlight together more than ever before, she wasn't allowing anyone to think that she wasn't doing her job perfectly.

When Liza had a straight role in the TV series *Ben Casey*, Judy was her self-appointed drama coach.

She was to tell Tom Burke in *The New York Times*, just how much help Judy was in dealing with the part of a girl suffering the effects of a mishandled abortion. 'I knew how I wanted to see it,' she told him. 'But not how to *be* it. So I sort of gingerly took the script to Mom and said, you know, "Mama, help me".' In effect, it was the best appeal she could have made to Judy.

Her mother sat her down on the floor and then joined her there. Judy told her: 'Now read me your lines, and the doctor's lines, both.'

The doctor was supposed to say: 'Did you want to have the baby?'

Judy told her: 'All right, he's a doctor, he isn't getting personal. But how *dare* he intrude on you, how *dare* he ask you that, how *dare* you be in the hospital, if only you could have married the father, if only he'd loved you, which he *didn't*. Now, *did* you want to have the baby?'

As Liza underlined it now, Judy was a bigger help than she might have realised. Her mother-cum-coach asked her the question and Liza replied, 'No'.

'All I had to say was "No", but it came out right. Because she had given me the thoughts – the pause, not the line. Then she said, "Read me his line again", and I did, and she said, "Now, this time you are going to concentrate on *not crying*. That's all you have to worry about, not letting him see you cry. Your baby is dead, your life is ruined, but you're not gonna cry, you're a strong girl, your parents have told you, your teachers have told you, *you know it, you're not going to cry!*"' That was effective because, as Liza said, 'My "No" came out even better. She taught me how to fill in the pauses. And if there's a way I act, that's the way. From that day on the floor. And now, if maybe another actor will say, "What are you using in that scene?" I'll say, "Well, I'm playing that I'm not gonna cry." They'll say, "Whaaat?" But I know.'

She will also remember that it was her mother who taught her, after all her singing and dancing and notwithstanding Anne Frank, how to act. Judy's motherhood role took on new dimensions now that she was convinced that Liza was not just going into showbiz but was about to be a huge success. She may have preferred it had her daughter not turned into a second Judy Garland, but provided it was just a 'second' and that people still said the first was the better of the two, she wasn't going to argue.

What happened next might have been better explained had Judy

been a Jewish mother, but perhaps Sid Luft's influence had been
stronger than one has been led to believe – although they were now
in the midst of an acrimonious divorce action. According to Liza,
Judy turned to a young man she knew and said, 'Boy, have I got a
girl for you.'

Chapter Nine

THE 'BOY' was Peter Allen.

Peter was part of the Australian singing duo, Chris and Peter Allen and it gives some idea of Judy's current situation that she met them at all.

She was touring the Far East with her current lover Mark Herron – they would marry later and then divorce after Judy complained that the marriage was never consummated; if that is so, did they just sleep when they shared hotel rooms in Australia, Japan and Hong Kong and then in London? More to the point was that Judy was grabbing what work she could get. In Melbourne, a place not usually considered to be on the itinerary of superstars, she was so affected by the pills she was taking, that she was unable to either sing or talk coherently. She left the stage and didn't go back.

Instead, she and Herron went on to Hong Kong – where Judy collapsed and was for a time pronounced dead. But she recovered enough certainly to make a tour of the local nightclubs.

At one of them, she saw the pair who called themselves the Allen Brothers – although they were not that. Chris Bell was Peter Allen's best friend and they worked well together.

If working in the Far East was for Judy a come-down, for the Allens, it was different. Coming from Australia, Hong Kong was almost their back yard. And it was 'abroad'. It meant status beyond anything they could achieve at home.

Herron told everyone he was marrying Judy, even though she was still legally tied to Sid Luft (later they claimed that they were married at sea). He may have thought Judy had eyes only for him, but she eyed Peter Allen and thought him an attractive, personable young man. She didn't want him for herself though, but for Liza.

She was now going to embark on what the business knows as 'agenting', although she would say that the only form of commission she had in mind was her daughter's happiness. She wasn't after work for Liza, she was seeking a husband for her. Liza may have started out later in show business than she had herself, but she was going to catch her up on the domestic front. Incredibly, despite all her own unhappiness, she felt that marriage was just what Liza wanted. It would certainly bring to an end – or so she thought – the stories she was hearing of boyfriends of whom she would never have approved. (She was plainly not looking in the mirror at her own crazy marital situation when she thought that.)

Liza's romantic situation provided her with a new challenge and she was going to act on it in an old-fashioned way. After years of being manipulated herself, Judy was something of a wily bird. She handled the matter of introductions so discreetly that they might have gone totally over the heads of the people concerned had they not been so cleverly targeted.

The way she dealt with it was so subtle that she made it all look like a business arrangement – which makes it sound a lot more like *The Godfather* than it really was. But it was Machiavellian and Judy did make Peter Allen an offer he could not refuse.

She invited Peter, who was then twenty-one, and his partner, a year younger, to join her own act – in Toronto, Las Vegas and Miami. Since the real name of the game was getting them to meet Liza she also arranged that they should meet influential people in London. She told them she was acting as their sort of unofficial agent. Not a bad one for a group starting up in the business to have – especially in London where Judy seemingly could do no wrong, even if she wasn't in as good a voice now as once had been the case.

Liza was still there, soaking up the atmosphere of the city where she had done so well.

For once, Judy really did know the mind of her daughter. She introduced Liza to Peter and they instantly got on well. To say it was love at first sight is no doubt stretching matters too far, although Liza was saying the right things to the people she thought mattered, and even to the inevitable reporters.

She said that she was attracted to Peter from their first meeting. They spent a great deal of time with each other in London. The visit extended way beyond its originally planned duration, largely because it was a good place for them both to be.

One night they were in a party at the Trader Vic's night spot at London's Hilton Hotel when Peter made his proposal – with an audience. The party had consisted of Peter and Chris, Judy and Mark Herron and Liza. Judy went to the ladies' room and Chris Allen left to make a telephone call and for a brief moment there were just three of them – Liza and Peter and Herron, whose place in the story is more significant than might now, in the light of subsequent events, be thought likely.

As they sat in the dark, smoke-laden atmosphere of what was not the most fashionable haunt in the 1960s, but the sort of place where businessmen on expense accounts would be with women to whom they were not married, Peter leaned over their third companion, looked Liza as closely in the eyes as the curtain of smoke would allow and asked her not to go out with anyone else.

Herron did the almost unforgivable. He joined in a private, very private conversation – and told Peter that the only way he could demand such a thing was by asking Liza to become engaged to him.

Peter didn't take the time to think that one out. He simply said, 'All right, let's be engaged then.'

In her *Good Housekeeping* interview, Liza said: 'I was so stunned, I just shrugged.'

But later she admitted that she thought it was a joke. She was not sure however how to go along with it. Only a few minutes later did she realise he was quite serious.

Herron told his own fiancée the news when she came back to the table. Judy – of course – burst into tears. Sometimes, she made those tears seem like something she had learned from Louis B. Mayer. They could be very effective. But now she was just a mother doing what most mothers did when they heard that their children were going to be wed.

Liza was still stunned, still just sat, not realising quite what had happened, but looked happy. Peter was stunned in a totally different way. He danced around the room as though the developments of the past few minutes had turned a clockwork key and he was one of the dancing teddy bears sold on trays in Oxford Street, a mile or so away. Total strangers were told that he and Liza Minnelli were now engaged.

Naturally enough, at least one of these strangers was either a newspaperman or had a friend who was, and the news was not long restricted to the patrons of Trader Vic's. Especially after Peter returned from his flat with a diamond ring of his own, which he used to wear on what Americans called their 'pinky' finger. Now it was Liza's engagement ring.

Judy was delirious with happiness. Liza wasn't so sure how she herself felt. 'I was uncertain and afraid,' was how she subsequently put it.

But she tried to explain the almost inexplicable: 'He's as nutty and crazy as I am. I mean by that he is funny. We kick up our legs, run around, laugh and talk to strangers. We're uninhibited.'

And more important, Mama loved him.

And that was the news that had to be flashed across the Atlantic. Before Mama could wipe her eyes, Liza was talking to Hedda Hopper. Yes, she was in love and they would marry in America.

Miss Hopper was extravagant in her assessment of the importance of Liza's fiancé. 'He and his brother Chris have a singing group that hit London like The Beatles hit America.' That may have been wishful thinking on the brothers' part, or perhaps simply on Judy's or Liza's or whoever it was who made the original call to La Hedda, then at the tail end of her role as a one-woman Californian earthquake. The truth is that they didn't amount to anything very much at all.

Judy though, of course, reckoned that they did. She also had a designer ready to produce her daughter's trousseau. Ray Aghayan would make The Dress. That had been one of the duties of mothers of the bride for as long as anyone could remember. Now, she was entering into the operation at full pelt. No one had yet asked who was going to pay for it all.

In the meantime, Liza had to get her father's permission. So she flew to Paris where he was then working.

Vincente, who always did have his feet somewhat more firmly planted on the soil than did his former wife, wasn't so sure. It was, one now supposes, partly due to the usual reluctance of a father to part with his little girl. But he also questioned Liza's choice.

Liza was taken aback by that. 'It scared me,' she said. The main reason for her fear was that it was the first time she could remember that he had said 'No' to her for anything.

Despite what Hedda Hopper had said, no one was offering Peter and Chris together, or even Peter on his own, any work. That was no way to start married life. Vincente's wife, Liza's newest stepmother, Denise, came to a similar conclusion and asked, 'Who is Peter Allen?'

Liza said she was 'torn apart' and recalled Peter telling her: 'The only thing your parents have in common is you. They did something very good together when you were born and they did it with love. But now I'm your family. If you really love me, we'll get married now and to hell with everyone else.'

But that was easier said than done.

Liza went from Paris to New York, because she had professional obligations to fulfil.

Actually, she hoped she would have professional obligations. What she had was a professional opportunity that *could* lead to obligations. She was due to audition for a new George Abbott show for Broadway as the lead.

The very fact that this man was considering her was the biggest compliment of all. 'Mister' Abbott – he was never known as anything else; no one would dare to call him 'George' – had made more Broadway careers than any other man. At the age of 106, he would still be producing shows. That was his age when I met him and we began talking about Liza. 'That was some gal,' he said. 'What a talent – and what a waste.' She may have become a superstar, but she could have done much more.

Back in the early '60s, it was Abbott's hunch that set her on the road to success. But even this man, who had a built-in meter that told him whether a thing would work out or not, was not convinced.

She had auditioned four times already and although Abbott had liked her, he wasn't sure.

The show was called *Flora, the Red Menace* and was partly intended to be a satire and partly to demonstrate just how far America had gone since the age of Senator Joe McCarthy and his various witchhunts. At last, thought Abbott, America could laugh at Communism. The story was of a young innocent girl in the days of the Depression of the 1930s, who, without realising it, gets involved with a Communist cell – and with a man – and sings about it all. The girl is actually a fashion illustrator. Her love is another anarchist who is more politically aware than she. When he joins the party, she sees no reason not to join, too. Whoever got the part had to prove she could sing better than she could think about politics.

That was the rôle that Liza wanted. Now when the opportunity arrived to show how much she did want it, her mind was divided between the project in hand and the question of her romantic life.

She decided that, no matter what, she was going to work to get the job. If she lost it, there might be no other chance of reaching Broadway on her own. She didn't say so, but there *were* always other men who were after her. If it didn't work out with Peter, she probably could get over it.

As she said, 'This was always my ambition. To do a George Abbott show on Broadway. This is all I ever wanted and I guess that all my life I've been preparing for it.'

So if Mr Abbott wanted five auditions to be sure, five auditions he would get.

After the fifth one, she was told that the part was hers. It had not a little to do with Fred Ebb, who with his long-time partner John Kander, wrote the songs. Liza admitted she had been 'clubbing' Ebb to persuade Abbott to give her the rôle.

Liza was arguing from a degree of strength. She was no longer the young girl who slept in the street because she was thrown, bag and baggage, out of hotels for ladies. Her track record after *Best Foot Forward* and the Palladium was formidable.

She already had two apartments. The reason was that she decided to share homes with her friend Tanya Everett, who was in *Fiddler On The Roof* on Broadway – and both signed different leases on the same day. So rather than split up their friendship, they decided to share them both.

Liza explained that one: 'The point is that we each need an apartment and if I'm working it's a hassle to get from the East Side to Broadway on matinee days... the traffic is incredible. So I sleep in the West Side apartment the nights before matinée days.'

Tanya would do the same thing or would reverse the procedure when necessary. Each stayed where it was most convenient for them. 'And the best thing of all is that you don't get sick of your room-mate.' You could do that sort of thing in 1965 if you were nineteen and had the money.

But she wanted something more to go with the money. Her romance was unconventional but she had that. Work was an ongoing process. She couldn't afford just to bask in what had already happened. She had wanted the *Flora* part for two years, ever since, in fact, she had first heard some of the songs. That was, of course, before even *Best Foot Forward*, but the producer Hal Prince had said she was then too young. Yet Prince had other projects in mind – including his Sherlock Holmes show *Baker Street* – and couldn't get straight on with it. Now, though, he was determined to close the deal. Thanks to a little influence from Mr Ebb he did.

His faith in her proved right. So did hers in him. She was to say that, 'Probably my biggest talent is the way I choose people. I have good instincts for who belongs in my life. Maybe when you grow up with Ira Gershwin around the house playing piano . . . But no, it isn't just that. I automatically surround myself with people who are *smarter* than me and I learn. Fred Ebb always says how scared we were at the beginning but it was Fred who was scared. Because he was in charge. For years, I just did what smart people told me to do.'

When her agent phoned the next day to tell her the part was hers, she was convinced it had been smart to do what Fred told her to do, in handling the audition. She and Tanya 'just went crazy'. She said that the two girls 'tore around the room, jumping and laughing'.

This was plainly going to be a good time for her. At six, it had been a case of 'Judy and the Kid'. Then before she knew it, she was thirteen and, 'thirteen was a dog. I tripped over everything . . . Sixteen is when you've been in twenty schools. Eighteen is great, but nineteen is best of all. That's when you're opening in your first Broadway show.'

In all sorts of ways, it was refreshing to hear a nineteen-year-old saying just that and not pretending she was weighted down with the cares of the world and full of experiences way beyond her years.

The show had its try-out in New Haven. There was a so-so sort of reaction from the audiences who went to see it, but George Abbott and his company felt encouraged – until, that is, Liza crashed into a set, fell over and was convinced that, for a second time, she had smashed an ankle. She was a girl who liked to live up to promises but when someone said, 'Break a leg' it was asking too much for that to be honoured, too. As things turned out, this time her foot, though bruised, stayed intact.

At first, she was racked with nerves. She stood in the wings, knowing that she had forgotten everything. She wouldn't remember. She couldn't remember. There was nothing to persuade her she would recall what she had to do. Until, that is, her cue came and she danced on stage, word perfect. Ten minutes later she was having a ball. That was one of the great advantages of being a star. You are on long enough to have a ball. Poor little bit players only have the nerves – so a lot of them never become any more than bit players. No one knows that, given ten minutes on stage, they could be as good as Liza Minnelli. Of course, that was not saying it all. She also needed the talent that would make Liza Minnelli, Liza Minnelli.

She had a great deal to be grateful for and a lot of that gratitude was centred on the songwriter who had ensured her getting the role. Perhaps it was only to be expected that she was now calling Fred Ebb her only real friend – next to Peter – as he helped her try to resolve her relationship problems during the four months that the show ran.

As one gathers from the short run, *Flora* was no huge smash. But Liza was. She was awarded a Tony for her part in the show. She was the youngest-ever recipient of an award which Broadway actors and actresses treated with the same respect as their brothers and sisters in Hollywood regarded the Oscars. In a way, it was a more important award. The Oscar has been frequently treated as a thank-you gift for past services. Sometimes acting plays only a small part in the considerations of the judges. That was not, however, the way the Tony was regarded.

Liza was treated, meanwhile, as a prize exhibit at a new kind of flower show where half the people inspecting the blooms had expected them to wilt and half of those hoped to have those expectations fulfilled.

Eyes and mouths opened as Liza came on stage and the audience waited to see just how like Judy she was – and if she wasn't, they were ready to work out why.

Life magazine featured the phenomenon extensively. 'Soon,' it reported, 'Judy's image faded and Liza's came into focus.'

Her voice quivered and people loved her for it. Sometimes, said *Life*, it got out of control, but that didn't matter. It 'only added to her likeability'.

The theatre itself seemed to quiver a bit at the end of the evening and the audience got out of control a little in the ovation it gave Liza. Judy herself would have had reason enough to have been very satisfied with the shouts, whistles, claps and stamping of feet that was the public reaction to it all.

Afterwards, George Abbott gave Liza a big hug and they went out in to the warmish spring Broadway air and looked up at her name in lights before going into Sardi's for the traditional first night party.

On the whole the critics didn't like the show. Certainly, they didn't think it was anything like as good as its star.

The critic Bone (such were the ways of his newspaper) saw the show at its New Haven, Connecticut, try-out and reported for *Variety* that he liked what he saw.

Variety wasn't called the showbiz Bible for nothing – theatre people didn't get out of bed in the morning if *Variety* told them that things looked bad for the business.

'*Flora*,' declared Bone, 'has enough good points about it to rate consideration as a potential hit. Shy on name values [which gives some idea of Liza's place in the industry at this stage, despite all that had gone before it] it is going to have to rely strictly on its entertainment merit for solid acceptance. The merit is there, however, and needs only skilled nursing to cash in.'

Bone was not unaware of the main attraction offered, despite the 'shyness' about existing stars:

'Buyers who expect just to ogle "Judy Garland's daughter" should leave applauding an excellent on-her-own performance by the girl. Miss Minnelli has intriguing stage presence, a good voice and a captivating manner in her portrayal of a young girl mistakenly swept by romance into Commie party membership, but she emerges as an individual at the final curtain.'

Leonard Hoffman took himself along to the Alvin Theater and wrote in the *Hollywood Reporter*:

'The whole show has a precious quality about it,' (Mr Hoffman imagined the show was aimed at the supposedly 'In' set.) 'I guess I'm an "outer", because although the audience response was generally warm, I felt only lukewarm about this new musical comedy starring Liza Minnelli.

'I suppose the root of my reaction is due to the fact that there's too much caricature and too little character to the book by George Abbott and Robert Russell.'

Liza was perhaps different. 'In a kind of a button-down gamine way, Liza Minnelli as the somewhat confused Flora radiates charm. She doesn't come across the way her mother Judy Garland does [we were waiting for that] either as a personality or as a singer. Miss Minnelli has undeniable stage presence as well as a voice; but neither have reached full maturity yet. She's young, more than promising and has a strong following à la Barbra Streisand.'

He thought she did particularly well in the number 'Not Every Day in the Week', which was a duet she sang with Bob Dishy.

All this seemed to echo what other critics said. *Time* magazine thought the show was 'strangely plotless'. Liza, though, 'puts vocal muscle and wistful appeal into her spindling rôle. She has the wide famished eyes of a waif, that vulnerable little-child look of hunger and wonder.'

Newsweek was not over the moon about Liza's performances but made the same comparisons with different conclusions. 'The musical marks Miss Minnelli's Broadway début and the impulse is to bend over backwards to judge her on her own. While correctly insisting that Liza is no replica of Judy, they have boomed her as an engaging, accomplished performer. She is engaging but far from accomplished and it is unpleasant to see her rushed into a big Broadway show at nineteen as though she were another Barbra Streisand.'

The *Los Angeles Times* coined the phrase, 'Liza Goes Over the Rainbow'.

And the eminent critic Walter Kerr told his readers in the *New York Herald Tribune*: 'Liza Minnelli, who no longer needs to be identified as Judy Garland's daughter and I apologise for just having done so, has many a fetching way about her. Her smile, for instance, is marvellously unsteady, always eager to shoot for the moon, always on the verge of wrinkling down to half-mast. Her profile, which seems to be made of what children call funny putty, rumbles upward nobly like a crocus asserting itself before the weather has quite turned . . . Actually the girl's urgency occasionally produces a faint rasp in her voice that she'll do well to get rid of. She can hang on to the blaze in her dark eyes though and to a perky independence that exactly fits the lilt of Kander's best tune, a ballad called "Dear Love".'

But he really had said it all. Liza was an exciting crocus.

The New York *Daily News* said it all with its headline: 'Liza Minnelli puts needed zing in songs of *Flora, the Red Menace*.'

Joanne Stang wrote in the *New York Times*: 'Watching Liza Minnelli is like picking up a seashell to listen for the ocean. The mature adult knows that no water rushes through the convolutions of each limpet, but old memories of warm sand and the hum of other pearly fragments prove irresistible. He hears the roar.

'Seeing Miss Minnelli in *Flora, the Red Menace*, provides a similar delusion. You know it cannot be Judy Garland up there . . . You know for many reasons – notably because she said, publicly and plaintively, 'If people want to see my mother in me, they're going to. If they so desperately want to find her, they will," and added, "but I am myself".'

Miss Stang had found the right course to take. She had discovered Liza's sensitive spot. She herself couldn't see a great physical resemblance. But when she went to a Boston try-out, she saw *something*.

'Onstage in Boston, though, the roar was there. A singing of hearts and valentines, hands at her side and her spaniel eyes wide, she is so similar in gesture and especially in a particular constricted nervous energy, a subdued trembling, an odd vibrato of the body as well as of the voice that... although such comparisons may ultimately drive her to despair – they are inevitable. Indubitably, she is Judy Garland's little girl.'

The hope was that she could survive without Judy's tragedies.

George Abbott was more inclined to see Liza for the 'myself' person she craved to be. 'I'm afraid you'll think I'm sounding off because of *Flora* but I think she is the most wonderful girl, very vital and devoid of any pettiness. She's always on the job, she has an unnerving instinct for what's true and right and she's a quick learner. I find her a delight.'

When the show finished, Judy entered the picture again. She discovered that no close-of-play party had been arranged – which to her was sacrilege. Plays closed but that didn't mean people couldn't continue to enjoy being together.

So Judy took charge. She made all the arrangements. It would be at the Waldorf Astoria, which was just about up to her standards, and selected the right vintage champagne, ordered the caviar and the *hors d'oeuvres*, which she specified to the finest detail.

Liza was amused by it all. When it was all over, she said, 'It got to me. Mama didn't have any money. But she got her party' – by charging the bill to Liza.

In fact, Liza could afford it – although she was still restricted by the court order, holding her mother responsible for her purse strings.

She didn't try to play older than she was – her age and the way she carried it was very much part of her charm – but she dressed in a much more sophisticated way than Flora had. Instead of the tartan dress and tam o' shanter favoured by her stage alter-ego, she wore a mink-lined leather coat, which she said was a present from her stepmother. She liked hats – but found them difficult to come by.

Most difficult of all was still the problem of being recognised for herself. 'There goes Judy Garland's daughter,' would call passers-by on Fifth Avenue. She had to accept it as a compliment.

The reaction to her first album was another compliment. It was followed soon afterwards with an album recorded by Liza and Judy at the London Palladium.

Judy and Liza at the Palladium was an instant best-seller, grabbed instinctively by two different generations.

Now, when Hollywood producers talked about film rôles for Liza – and several were being spoken of – they were not thinking about linking mother and daughter. They wanted her for herself. Liza was hedging her bets. She only wanted parts that would be good for her.

The same appeal of Liza alone struck the TV networks. Now they were offering her her own specials.

At Christmas 1965, she was the star of ABC TV's *The Dangerous Christmas of Red Riding Hood or 'Oh Wolf, Peter Wolf.'* Liza played Red Riding Hood in this musical spoof of the familiar story. Cyril Ritchard played the wolf.

And she was now playing to a different, more sophisticated audience. Liza was going into cabaret. It turned out to be a very wise decision. A new Liza was playing to a new group of people, mostly middle-aged, mostly those who knew Judy in her *Andy Hardy* and *Meet Me in St Louis* days. She had to show them more than any other audience she had faced before that she wasn't just a carbon copy of her mother.

She succeeded brilliantly, playing to, singing to, even teasing customers who could break an entertainer simply by making a lot of noise with their bottles or cutlery.

At the Coconut Grove in Los Angeles, still a fashionable rendezvous for what remained of the Hollywood set, she was thrown in at the deep end.

John L. Scott wrote in the *Los Angeles Times*: 'The dark-eyed lithe girl dances extremely well, boasts the gift of comedy and a vibrant stage personality.'

Others could see that vibrant personality as well. She went back to London, this time to the Talk of the Town nightspot, which liked to call itself a theatre restaurant.

It was London's answer to Las Vegas, although they didn't gamble at the 'Talk'. But the original was ready for her now as well.

There is nothing that the industry likes better than the smashing of records. In 1965, she broke all the attendance statistics at the Shoreham Hotel in Washington DC with an act that proved especially popular with the Government and diplomatic community in the city.

Meanwhile, her LP, *There Is a Time* received the magazine *Hi-Fi Stereo Review*'s 'Best Album of the Year' Award. In June 1966, she signed a contract for the Sahara Hotel at Las Vegas – for a reputed $30,000 a week. There, she would repeat the act she had played in Los Angeles and London and, most recently, at the Olympia Music Hall in Paris, which remembered Maurice Chevalier at the zenith of his career. The French fans invoked the name of one of their most honoured entertainers. To them, Liza was '*La Petite Piaf Americaine.*' Compliments did not come much higher than that.

But there were even more select audiences awaiting her. When, that year, Prince Rainier and Princess Grace of Monaco celebrated the centenary of Monte Carlo at a huge shindig that rivalled the proceedings at their own wedding party, Liza was asked to be the star guest. Naturally, she jumped at the chance and equally naturally she was superb.

The *New York Herald Tribune* reported: 'Liza Minnelli is not pretty but she is startlingly beautiful. She never acts...she is always natural, herself, uninhibited, in full control.'

Perhaps, even so, her most appreciative audiences were her fellow New Yorkers.

Liza opened at the Plaza Hotel's plush Persian Room and was a huge success. One reviewer said that at last she was a performer in her own right. There was one exception, however – the writer who said that she had not experienced enough of life to sing the torch songs that had attached themselves to her now, and with considerable effect. 'Honey,' declared Liza, 'really! If she has seen half the life I've seen...I mean really.' Yes, showbiz was already a great educator for Liza and not just because of all the things she had picked up in the Luft household.

She explained for those who needed an explanation: 'I've supported myself since I was sixteen...Life could not possibly be boring ever. There is so much to see and do in this world.' And that would keep her happy – just so long as people didn't try to make her a 'swinger'.

Part of the trouble was perhaps that Liza didn't look as though she were going to sing torch songs. She wore a pony tail and her pale blue dress had a Peter Pan collar. It was another demonstration of enjoying being nineteen and not pretending to be anything else. Well, if showmanship was being different, Liza was already a showman.

In fact, the whole performance rang with a kind of class that was rarely seen. It was more strident than Streisand, more powerful in many ways than Judy and more sophisticated than practically any contemporary entertainer who wasn't old enough to be one of her grandparents. All in all, not an experience to forget in a hurry.

Newsweek magazine told its readers: 'She is letter perfect, right down to her exaggerated consonants, as if she had written fifty times on the blackboard: "Take care of the consonants and the vowels will take care of themselves."'

She changed her dress half way through the show and her new outfit was dominated by tights that showed quite the most magnificent legs seen in the Plaza since Betty Grable stayed there. 'But underneath, there is no metamorphosis,' said *Newsweek*. 'She is still a wide-eyed sweet sixteen, showing off for company, evoking more than anything else, imperishable memories of a glorious American entertainer.'

All right, so if one couldn't get away from the comparisons with Judy, there was a lot to be said for them being in Liza's favour, and they certainly were – which also set her apart from most other entertainers of her generation.

Recording his appreciation of the performance at the Persian Room, John S Wilson in the *New York Times* noted that this was a 'new' Liza (the fact that he could allude to such a thing when talking about a nineteen-year-old showed that Liza was no ingénue).

'The transformation of Liza Minnelli begins after she has made her way through two songs and a medley in her performance in the Persian Room . . . ,' he noted. 'The dark-eyed, black-haired nineteen-year-old daughter of Vincente Minnelli and Judy Garland [nobody could yet avoid making the connection, although Vincente should have been pleased that he was at last included in the relationship] making her New York nightclub début, indicates in these initial songs that her scope as a vocalist is limited to an attractive, half-spoken intimate style and belted, all-out climaxes that thin out to raw shouting.' So far not so good.

It was one of those reviews where you had to be patient enough to read on before coming to the conclusion what the writer was intending. He really thought more of her than he was saying – and he was saying a lot.

He went on to say, if one reads between the lines, that her material gave the impression of her being a fairly ordinary sort of gal.

'Her opening numbers suggest we are in for the slick but relatively anonymous kind of performance that often turns up when a singer has had an act created for her.'

But wait. There was more – and it was encouraging.

'Miss Minnelli starts to remove herself from this rut with an amusing song on the pronunciation of her name (It's "Lie-za", not "Lee-sa") in which she shows a delightful comic flair.'

What Mr Wilson should have considered was that this was a début as startling and as important in the Liza Minnelli story as the opening itself. It was the first time that she had sung 'Liza With a "Z"' in public. A notable event indeed.

Once more, people were talking about a 'new' find. Her manipulation of letters of the alphabet, her quick-witted response to the words she was offered, the way she related to her audience were all significant in themselves. If Judy had mastered the London Palladium audience in the shadow of Danny Kaye, her daughter was doing something very similar. The song was straight out of Kaye. But she managed to make it sound like Minnelli. That was both showmanship and stardom.

There was no doubt that for all the similarity between mother and daughter, and the familiarity of a great deal of Liza's material, there was something new and even original here.

Here was a young woman with the confidence of a politician, the suppleness of a ballet dancer, the voice of a female stevedore. She had the gift of singing one minute as though powered by a steam engine and the next of lulling her audiences close to a stupor with a song that sounded as though it were encased in velvet. Finally, her audiences would be made to feel as though they were sitting on some hidden Jack-in-the-Box.

You couldn't hear 'Liza With a "Z"' without wanting to jump up yourself. The floors of the Persian Room vibrated with the tapping feet not just of Liza but of the people watching her, too.

Of course, one couldn't get over the fact that her name was still linked with those of her parents, but even she could realise that by now it no longer mattered that much. People knew that Liza Minnelli was a good entertainer in her own right. And if Judy's or Vincente's name was mentioned, chances now were that it was done for journalistic professionalism. A reviewer would not have been doing his job if he didn't provide every bit of information considered necessary. And saying that Liza was Judy's daughter was indeed necessary.

It didn't matter now because Liza was a success. 'Liza With a "Z"'
was a big success. Big successes needed big numbers. It turned out to
be her 'Singin' in The Rain', 'Mammy', her 'My Way', her 'Rainbow'.

Perhaps even more important, it showed the cementing of her link
with the song's writers Fred Ebb and John Kander. She could not
have hoped for more.

Someone shouted: 'Sing "Over the Rainbow".' 'It's been sung,' she
replied.

Mr Wilson detected the excitement, for all his initial reservations:

'A couple of songs later, she wistfully imagines herself at a dance,
singing "All I Need is the Boy", when suddenly she is confronted by
a boy – a short, round, well-scrubbed prototypical product of
Saturday morning dancing classes who declares himself to be Neal J.
Schwartz.

'Mr Schwartz, it quickly becomes apparent, has been to more
advanced dancing classes. Assisted by a tall thin colleague, Bob Fitch,
he puts Miss Minnelli through a swirling series of turns and lifts that
make it startlingly clear that she is an uncommonly good dancer.'

The 'relatively anonymous' singer was an uncommonly good
dancer. 'From there on, Miss Minnelli's act is a buoyant blend of
dancing, comedy and song. As a singer, she is at her best in subdued
settings that permit her acting ability to supplement her vocalising.'

Wilson concluded: 'Her talents as a comedienne are well served at
the Persian Room by special material written for her by Fred Ebb and
John Kander.'

The people who were really well served were those who paid to go
to the show at the Persian Room and the readers of *The New York
Times*. They were told that Liza had signed to make her first movie. It
would be called *Charlie Bubbles* in which she would play the secretary
of her co-star and director Albert Finney in a Shelagh Delaney story
that she said she loved.

It was news that registered with the people at the Plaza and made
them look forward to it. They knew they were in close to the start of
something really big. History had happened and was being recorded.

One woman stopped her in the lobby. 'You sing better than your
mother,' she said.

Chapter Ten

THE YEAR 1965 was a good one for Liza. She won a Tony for *Flora*, making her the youngest ever recipient of the award. There was just one doubt in Liza's mind now – how Peter fitted into her life.

If there had been love at first sight, love on second consideration was not so easy. They quarrelled a great deal. Peter wanted to get married straight away, and straight away lasted for two years. He constantly asked her to marry him and she was constantly putting it off.

She didn't want to prejudice her career. Liza may also have wondered whether she was going to place her fiancé in a situation that was even worse than her own. As tough as it had been for her to be Judy Garland's daughter, it would be even harder on him to be the husband of Judy Garland's daughter. She didn't want him to be Mr Liza Minnelli.

Judy was upset now because Peter turned down a chance for Chris and him to work with her. He wanted to stay in New York so that he could be near Liza, rather than tour with her mother.

The 'brothers' found it difficult to get work. What was more, Peter was jealous. He didn't like the closeness Liza felt for Fred Ebb. She, for her part, thoroughly disliked his friends, with whom she had nothing in common and thought they were pulling him down.

If this was what marriage to Peter would be like, it didn't augur at all well for their future.

But then things got better. Peter and Chris found work. They appeared on television, including a spot on the Johnny Carson show that was to bring them closer attention.

The rumours about them multiplied. That Liza had broken off her engagement was one. Then that was compounded by suggestions that she had transferred her allegiances from Peter to Chris – or that she was now dating Bob Dishy, who had been her leading man in *Flora*.

Vincente was aware of it all and told Liza not to worry. 'He said,' Liza later recalled, 'that people have to write something and they get bored and sometimes make up things and the fact that they write about you at all should please you in some way even if it isn't true.'

As Liza noted, showbiz could be a dirty biz.

She worried a great deal about that. Even the fans weren't an unmitigated delight. There was always some old lady who would tap her on the shoulder and say, 'Turn around – and let me look at ya, honey.'

'You feel like an idiot,' Liza said.

Finally, the to-ing and fro-ing was over. On 3 March, 1967, Liza and Peter were married at a private ceremony in New York. It was held at the Park Avenue home of Stevie Phillips, Liza's agent.

Both Judy and Vincente were there. So were Peter's parents and his sister Lynn, who came over from Australia especially for the ceremony.

They made an attractive couple, the bride of twenty-one and the bridegroom of twenty-two. Liza wore a Victorian wedding dress.

Judy was content with it all, except that she was so broke she couldn't afford to buy them a wedding present. Like many another young bride, Liza had picked out her idea of the perfect gift – an Irish linen tablecloth. This was totally beyond Judy's pocket. Liza had to decide that it didn't matter. There were more important things to consider, especially a husband she was convinced she loved.

Also like many another young couple, they were both determined that this was for keeps.

Peter would tease her. Whatever it was that appealed to him, it certainly wasn't her looks. 'Your nose is too big,' he taunted. 'Your mouth is too full. Your eyes are too big.'

Liza seemed to take it all very seriously. 'Sometimes,' she declared, 'my ugliness overwhelms me. At least, I don't have to stay beautiful for my fans.' One of those fans painted a picture of her – she looked as if she had just been pulled through a rain forest. If she could laugh at that, there wasn't a lot wrong.

One of her great strengths was just that – her strength. She could be as tough as a pair of studio electrician's old boots and as carefree as a teenager who suddenly realised nobody was going to shout when she got home from the disco after midnight. The sense of release was tremendous. Someone described her as being twenty-three going on sixteen. That just about said it all.

But not the way Liza saw it. 'If I read one more article where I'm described as being perky, I'll puke,' she declared. Reading that – and yet another reference to being Judy Garland's daughter. She was beginning to feel that, at last, she was quite capable of standing on her own – and that all the things she had been saying for so long about having that capability were finally being recognised by other people, too.

In fact, Liza said she had never been happier. They took an apartment and did what most other newly-weds did, went from shop to shop, looking for furniture, curtains and the other essentials of married life.

She would say that she loved nothing more than coming home at night or, if she weren't working, having a quiet evening in – an evening of silence which would suddenly be broken by the noise of her hi-fi at full strength.

Peter, she said, she loved. 'Oh, he's beautiful. I'm so in love.'

Liza and Peter took on a new rôle – as surrogate parents for Lorna and Joey. Their mother was in the midst of a series of rants and raves and the children couldn't get out of their home quickly enough. Peter, says Lorna now, was like her big brother. He only agreed to 'surrender' the youngsters when Judy rang demanding it.

They had their dog Ocho, which they illegally smuggled into New York from a trip to Puerto Rico. They had found it outside a bar called Ocho Puertos, hence his name, and decided that getting the required papers was an unnecessary formality. Fortunately, it didn't have rabies. But it did bite. After a couple of altercations with Liza's wardrobe mistress and a doorman, she reluctantly decided to have the animal's teeth pulled out.

Vincente took one look at the mongrel and declared: 'That's the best imitation of a dog I've ever seen.' Imitation or not, Ocho was happy with its lot – and with good reason.

It was, their friends noted – and Liza and Peter had to agree – the most spoiled mutt in the United States. It lived on a daily diet of the best steak, chicken livers and caviar. After his biting exploits, the best sirloin had to be finely chopped up, but he found no trouble with the caviar and chicken livers.

Nothing would be allowed to spoil their own happiness either – even if the fact that they had single beds, pushed close together, but single nevertheless, did make friends shown round the premises wonder.

When they were separated for a short time, as when Liza had a nightclub engagement far away from home, she gave the impression of being distraught. She couldn't wait for them to get together again. But the fun didn't last. In fact, the honeymoon was very brief – literally. And it wasn't difficult to see why.

Whereas other young brides regard this all as the most exciting time of their lives, for Liza it was an anti-climax. Being a housewife – or as the American women's libbers liked to term it, a homemaker – didn't really begin to compare with opening on Broadway or at the Persian Room or the Palladium and Liza didn't try to pretend that it did.

She said: 'I couldn't adjust to normality.' She explained in her *Good Housekeeping* interview: 'All my days had been crammed with high periods and low periods. There were no middles, no times when I was just tranquil. I was used only to screaming attacks or excessive love bouts, rivers of money or no money at all, seeing my mother constantly or not seeing her for weeks at a time when she was away on location. Now it was breakfast, lunch and dinner, shopping . . . consistency.'

Now she was depressed – the kind of depression other women experienced after having given birth. So far, there was no sign that Liza was ready to have a baby, but she was suffering from post-natal depression. She had given birth to a new life and craved the old.

She didn't blame Peter for this. In fact, she said he convinced her that she now had absolutely everything she had ever wanted and was ready to enjoy and appreciate it.

And, she could add, he did appreciate how different she was from the wives of most of the people he knew. They sat down often and contemplated their existence. 'You've got to realise you're not an ordinary wife,' he told her in the kind of understatement that said as much as she could have wished. 'I don't expect you to make three meals a day, wash my shirts and things like that. I don't want you to put yourself in that rôle, because you'll fail. I love you . . . so don't do this stuff. All right? Quit bugging me and stop burning up the kitchen.'

He helped her with her singing practice and he charmed Lorna and became a pal of Joey. She really didn't have much more to ask for. There was also a tranquillity with her mother – and that had never been easy to achieve.

Liza had long known how to deal with Judy. She knew when

things were good for her and when they were bad by a kind of telepathy that could not readily be explained. When Judy was in a low state, Liza simply didn't answer the phone to her. It wasn't that she was not sympathetic, but it simply didn't do any good to treat matters any differently.

Peter was there to answer the phone, as he was to deal with the bills and the other things husbands were supposed to take care of.

But Liza was a star and nothing could stop that. As she was to say, when she went to Sardi's, they knew her. She didn't have to wait for a table.

Most people knew her. 'The Liza Minnelli Look' – a jacket and sweater over a pleated skirt – stood out from the pages of *TV Guide* and was instantly copied. That was also stardom.

She was making money now – and keeping it. Debbie Reynolds noted the difference. As she told me: 'Liza became a star at a time when she could be rich – which her mother could not.'

In fact, Judy began to think she was having a rough ride from her daughter. She said that Liza owed her money. There was talk of a law suit for $1 million, but if it ever reached lawyers' offices, it certainly did not get to court.

Mother and daughter were back on their roller-coaster again except that this was the adult part of the ride, where the highs were very high indeed and the lows made one feel as though the bottom was falling out of one's stomach. They didn't talk for weeks on end, and then would spend hours on the phone. But from about now and for the next two years, they would hardly ever see each other. Liza had a problem which even Judy, who seemed to collect crises the way little boys collected stamps, did not. As Liza got richer and more successful, so Peter seemed to achieve less and less. At the time, she made statements saying how well he was doing. Well, he wasn't and he wouldn't – until he made it big as a songwriter; but by then their marriage was over. At this stage, they were competing with each other more strongly than Liza ever had with Judy.

'The competition nearly killed us both,' she said. What it did kill was their marriage. But it was a slow process. The marriage lingered rather as her mother's had with Sid Luft.

There had been stories of sexual problems circulating. Years after their marriage ended, she would say nothing to confirm or deny them. But Peter's greatest success has been entertaining on the gay club circuit.

Liza had never held back in admitting that they were basically incompatible, especially because of her own income. 'Women's success,' she says 'embarrasses men. A woman's afraid he'll leave because he's embarrassed.'

In this case, there was embarrassment all round. The marriage, she has since decided, was 'horrible'. Peter 'almost broke up' when Liza really started making it big.

The marriage actually came to an end when Peter told Liza he was in love again – with another man.

She decided: 'I'll never marry another actor. Ever. Ever.' But she went out with other men, too, and because Peter knew that she did, there were further strains on her marriage. The biggest strain on her own life, however, still continued to be Judy. 'For all the people who want to help me because I am Judy Garland's daughter, there are just as many who won't help me for the same reason,' she declared. There was also the niggling feeling that perhaps her mother had rather too often shared the latter sentiment. To make things worse, that belief was not restricted to their private telephone conversations or the now infrequent moments when they were together.

Indeed, there were new problems with Judy. The woman who was always coupled with Liza's name and who had been such a powerful influence now seemed to be sitting in her daughter's shadow. She made her own theatre and nightclub appearances, but the great days were plainly over, while her own marriages came and went.

People were saying that Liza, having made it so that she could stand up on her own, had neglected Judy. Liza didn't entirely deny that. But neither did she seem calm, warm, and all that sympathetic to what was spoken of as the Garland plight.

'My mother,' Liza told one reporter, 'needs someone to convince her that she does not have to be a living legend. All her life, since she was a girl, all the time she was growing up, she felt she had to prove herself and how can you be happy that way?'

Nevertheless, she told Sheilah Graham, the British-born Hollywood gossip, 'My mother is a strong woman. She's not the tragic figure people make her out to be.'

In one respect, she was right. 'When things get hard,' said Liza, 'she gets upset, then it's over and she's back on her feet. She's built up resilience.'

Liza found words as easy to formulate in her mind and then to speak as to sing. But she wasn't happy about her mother and it was all too easy to see between the lines, hers and Judy's.

Her father knew about all that and he took his daughter's part. 'Liza finally came to realise,' he said, 'that she could conquer Judy's giant shadow simply by being herself. And as she started achieving her success, her confidence grew.'

It all sounded like the perfect success story. On the other hand, if you were one of Judy's close friends, it had the mark of smugness about it. Perhaps Liza wasn't quite as mature as she wanted people to think and possibly her father was a little more generous than he should have been. Was this Vincente's 1960s way of spoiling her?

Kay Thompson loved Liza and knew her faults – and how she got over them. 'Liza always makes the right mistakes,' she said. 'She goes just so far and then she pulls back from the abyss.'

Now Liza's job was not merely to pull back from the abyss, but to make sure that she didn't go near any such yawning chasms again. She would, because she was capable, because she had the right advice and she took it and because there was nothing to match her ambition.

She had always seemed to know the right time to act. A friend told the story of when Liza was a baby and crawled. 'Johnny walks,' said the older woman. 'Why don't you?' The next day Liza did – because she was ready. Now Liza was ready for her next stage. She made *Charlie Bubbles*.

More than anything else, the picture provided a new dimension to the Liza Minnelli career. *Charlie Bubbles* itself would not have made Liza a star. But in a small part, it established a definitive Minnelli personality; no longer just the gamine or the girl who sang songs that made people jump out of their seats, but the youngster who really didn't care about the mores of society, who when trodden on, would get up and dust herself off. The flattened body would somehow puff itself up again like the cat in the Tom and Jerry cartoons who had got splattered against a wall or fallen under a steamroller. And that was the real Liza, too. Nobody could flatten her for long. Not even a review like that of John Simon: 'The supreme deadweight is Liza Minnelli, whose screen début proves easily the most inauspicious since Turhan Bey's.'

Certainly, her part wasn't big and she wasn't exactly brilliant in it. But not everyone shared Mr Simon's view, eminent critic though he was. Al Cohn – who knew something about showbiz himself – wrote in *Newsday*; 'Liza Minnelli's breezy role in *Charlie Bubbles* leaves her as bubbly as ever.' Liza knew her limitations as a screen actress, as she faced the cameras for the first time. But she wasn't going to let them make any difference.

Even the scene in which it looked as though she was posing in the nude. 'It's not sensational,' said Liza. 'I only have to look nude from the back. I insisted on wearing tights and panties and pasties while filming that scene.'

Albert Finney had chosen her himself because he thought she was right for a segment of a picture about a successful British novelist who yearns to leave London for his roots in northern England. The film was shot on location in Manchester as well as in the capital.

She was in Britain for three months. 'Nothing is as crazy as London is now,' she said. It was Swinging London in the Swinging Sixties and anyone who was young and could afford the price of a dress in Carnaby Street that would fall to pieces after being taken off the hanger knew that this was the place to be. Liza showed every sign of loving every minute of it – possibly because of the way she had first become involved in the project. Finney wanted an American girl for the secretary who never allowed anything to worry her very much for very long.

Finney, she said, had never seen her in his life before she walked into his office. But he knew that she was what he was looking for. And to make things even better, he didn't mention Judy once.

'He's terribly self-sufficient. It's all terribly interesting. Everyone is terribly enthusiastic,' Liza later said.

And if the critics weren't all terribly keen, that didn't mean that Liza was terribly worried. Somehow, neither were the producers who were happy enough to make her new offers of new work. Some she considered, others she rejected out of hand.

She was now established in four media – the cinema, TV, the nightclub circuit and recording. The *Liza! Liza!* album had sold half a million records by the end of 1967 and on its strength she had signed a new contract with Herb Alpert's A & M Records.

She made singles like 'You Are For Loving' and 'His Woman' that sold well enough, including one that was written by Peter, 'Middle Of The Street'.

When she did a concert, it became an album, like *Liza Live at the Olympia Music Hall In Paris*. Albums like *It Amazes Me* and *There Was a Time* were followed by *Liza Minnelli*. When that appeared in 1967, the title spoke as well as played for itself as far as Liza's status in the business was concerned. There was no need for fancy names on her records. But the surname was superfluous. The name 'Liza' was enough. Everyone knew who it was – and that would stay the case for the next two decades.

She liked what she was doing. 'Modern music is talking about things that really happen. There was a period when there was no lyric in songs. They were so boring – yah, yah.' But although she loved the Beatles – particularly their song, 'When I'm 64' – contemporary songs were 'disjointed thoughts,' she said. As she explained: 'They don't necessarily use the best grammar, but, they're getting their point across.' Which was exactly what Liza was doing all the time now.

At least, most of the time. In 1967, Broadway audiences were enchanted by a new show called *Cabaret*, based on Christopher Isherwood's story of life in Berlin, just before the Nazis took over. The book had been adapted – very excessively adapted, some thought – into a play and then a film called *I Am a Camera*. *Cabaret* was not going to be a remake of the *Camera* play or film, but based more closely on the original book, *Goodbye To Berlin*.

Liza craved the part of the English girl Sally Bowles caught up in what she believed to be the divine depravity of the German capital, depicted so brilliantly in the George Grosz cartoons. Craved it? She was obsessed by it. Fourteen times she auditioned for the rôle, only to be beaten at the end by Jill Haworth. The producers had told Liza right at the beginning that they had built the show around her – and then worried whether an American could play the part. Sally Bowles was English, wasn't she? Despite the fact that Julie Harris had played her in the film version of *I Am a Camera* (and she had played her as a *sort of* Englishwoman at that) they agreed that it ought to go to an English girl. So Jill Haworth got the part and Liza Minnelli learned to cope with the disappointment. Other exciting things were clearly on the way.

When she appeared in real live cabaret (if there could be such a thing) Liza was its embodiment; she made the artificiality of it all seem real because somehow it didn't matter that there was a spotlight shielding her from the world outside and that the drapes and the ceiling plaster were mere coverings for pipes, wires and girders – she was already, at twenty, in charge. She had good manners, this young nightclub entertainer. Always, there were thanks for her orchestra, her conductor and the writers of her material – she didn't pretend that all the clever things she said were the product of her own brain. But said *Newsweek* magazine, 'they didn't really deserve thanks. Their frills only obscured the real magnetism of a born entertainer who, especially when she danced, peeped out fresh and perky from the shroud of paint, the nurtured mannerisms that can't be inherited...songs her mother never taught her.'

There was, however, a somewhat strange dichotomy about her. On the one hand, she was very young – twenty-one going on twenty-two – and still had an elfin quality that made her giggle a little too often; on the other, she wasn't one of those young stars who automatically are chosen to represent their generation. Like many of the songs she sang, she was almost a throwback to a previous generation, the owner of an old head on delicately curving young shoulders. 'I was born old,' she said.

Chapter Eleven

EARL WILSON, a columnist who isn't always the most popular with the big names in entertainment – a book he wrote on Frank Sinatra kept lawyers busy for years – said in January 1968: 'Liza Minnelli became a truly great star.'

He was referring to Liza's opening the previous night at the Waldorf Astoria's Empire Room, which was roughly on the same peak as the Persian Room where she had triumphed just over a year before.

This time – as last time – she did it, said Wilson, 'without the assistance of her mother; Judy Garland was suffering from a virus and didn't get there.' So even if it were still necessary to mention Judy in reviews of Liza's work, it was recognised that she was not an essential factor in her daughter's super success.

One demonstration of just how far Liza had come was in the people who had also made it. A society show in a society place brought a high-society audience, not just from people in the social register, who were there in force, but from showbiz, too. Among them, Faye Dunaway, Ethel Merman, Arlene Dahl, Hal Prince and – highly significantly – Joel Grey, who had been starring in that little thing on Broadway called *Cabaret*.

They were demonstrating once again that the most sought-after praise and support is that from one's own peers, the people who were themselves working earlier in the evening. Once they like you, there's no bigger kick for an entertainer. And that was indeed what Liza was now – a somewhat overworked term perhaps, but it fitted Liza Minnelli precisely, in every sense of the word. Liza Minnelli, Entertainer.

As Mr Wilson noted: 'Liza, who will be twenty-two in March, had a turnout that would have been flattering even to her mother. She had an enchanting frankness and freshness and an unexpected versatility.'

He explained the sort of thing that struck home to him: 'When she sang "Mammy", she got down on one knee in the Jolson pattern.'

That itself was more significant than at first met the eye. The things they were saying about Liza now were those they had said about Jolson forty years before. 'I always wanted to do that,' Liza said, about the knee routine. 'I never had the nerve before.'

She even attempted her own version of Gypsy Rose Lee's strip-tease act.

Earl Wilson liked it all. He thought the strip demonstrated Liza's ballet experience. 'Now she has about everything – voice, charm, overwhelming enthusiasm, deepset eyes . . .'

And, Liza told her audience, her name was Minnelli. 'Not Liza Minola'. The chances of finding anyone who didn't already know that – especially in New York – were by now slim in the extreme.

The real significance of the occasion was not that the fancy people came to pay their fancy prices or even that Mr Wilson noted it so fulsomely. Celebrities always find something exciting to see and Mr Wilson was always writing about them and the shows they saw. What was really unusual was that *Time* magazine took a whole page to record what was, after all, just a cabaret performance; a showbiz event that was usually ignored and would be considered too boring to attract people who weren't within a half hour's journey of the venue.

But this was in no way usual. It was a highly different kind of show from a highly different sort of artist. *Time* described it as 'a knockout, non-stop show that had everybody – including Liza – gasping for breath . . . She can belt out a song with the best of them, Judy Garland [it had to come up] included. Her dancing is spirited and ceaseless . . . She can move people to laughter and to tears with equal ease – sometimes simultaneously.'

It wasn't just those who could afford the Waldorf prices who would be showing their knowledge about her. She linked up with her old 'flame' – the one who never knew about it – in a TV special about vaudeville. Bobby Darin played George M. Cohan, and together they sang Cohan's 'Give My Regards To Broadway'. After TV, Liza was making another movie.

And she was telling everyone that her marriage was working, no matter what they may have read. Peter, she said, 'is my rock. I love him. In fact, I like him. I really like him.' The extra emphasis betrayed doubts that she could not admit to having.

When in 1967, he suggested taking her to meet his family in Australia, Liza took up the invitation avidly – and, like all good troupers who needed audiences the way most people need to eat and drink – she worked there, too.

That would present her with a few difficulties she hadn't contemplated. Certainly, she couldn't have suspected there was anything less than glory awaiting her after she entertained Australia's Prime Minister, John Gorton, in her dressing room – with her mother-in-law dancing attendance. Mrs Allen's presence was to prove highly significant, although at the time all Liza could think of was that it was the equivalent of the President popping in back home.

In fact, she quite liked most things about entertaining in Australia. She broke all records at the clubs where she played and, as she deserved, the audiences treated her like visiting royalty. But backstage, conditions were more like the slums of Hong Kong. Workers were cleaning chickens outside her dressing room and the smell was overpowering. Worse was the reaction of the Press. One thing struck home – a story headed: 'Liza Minnelli jeered'. That was what appeared on the front page. The story itself was on the inside. Liza was ready to ring her lawyers. There had been no jeering at any of her performances, particularly in Sydney where the reaction had been one of unsuppressed adoration. The inside story, however, included the line: 'Sometimes, she was jeered at school.' If there was any way of incurring Liza's anger, it was to recall her days at school(s). However, that too would pale to insignificance before long.

Nevertheless, being with Peter, she seemed to be saying, made up for everything. They were clearly on a high. He was with his own people. He had his own work and Liza's success rubbed off on him at the right time and in the right place.

Liza liked to say that she needed to have people she loved around her. In fact, she needed people. People told her that she was alive. People were reassuring. But sometimes, people were downright worrying. 'I'm afraid of things. When I'm on a plane I look around at people's faces to see if they look like the faces of people who're gonna die. And I'm afraid of open spaces, of being exposed. Like when they ride off into the sunset on a horse in the movies? Ugh! I'd drop right off the horse. Dead! All that emptiness. Nothing to touch.'

On the whole, however, she seemed to like most things about the life she lived, even going on the road, 'although it's a kind of a crappy thing for a girl to do – sing in a bar.' There were the proprietors of a few thousand bars who would have lined up to have Liza singing behind their pumps.

That was an undoubted fact. Liza Minnelli was now top of her field and she liked the feel of it.

She had been singing and doing her thing in Monte Carlo again. Her tribute to the centenary of the capital of the principality of Monaco was such a success that Princess Grace asked her back for the 1967 Red Cross Ball there. It was a good move. More select than the 'bars' she joked about, this was society's crème-de-la-crème and she left them all with the impression that in her business she was much the same.

And yet there was reason to wonder whether she wasn't resting too much on her laurels now. Not because she was doing so well and her mother was doing so badly. But because she had a set routine – 'Liza With a "Z"' and 'Mammy' and 'There's No Business Like Show Business' – which no matter how good ought to have been refreshed now and again. But now she was like the vaudeville entertainers of old who sometimes kept the same acts going for thirty or forty years without change – and no one ever questioned it. Liza, however, thought there was no reason to pose any questions. The next trip on her list would be to Puerto Rico, where she was likely to make another fortune. The 'bar' shows were going to prove of much greater significance to her career than *Charlie Bubbles*. As she planned her future, she fancied a part for herself as Joan of Arc. Liza as Joan of Arc? Yes, but she wasn't thinking of involving any of the studying she had not done at the Sorbonne. No, this would be a different sort of Joan – a Joan of Arc in love. Presumably before she got to the stake. Fortunately, no one's ever asked her any more about that idea. They took *The Sterile Cuckoo* more seriously.

In this, she *was* very much the star, playing a college girl not quite sure of herself, who nevertheless manages more than a few sexual adventures.

This movie, too, was not great, but Liza was. In *The Sterile Cuckoo* she was good enough to get an Oscar nomination and especially good enough to enjoy the respect of those with whom she was working.

She knew it was going to be right for her. Liza had read the novel, by John Nichols, on which it was based and when she heard that Alan Pakula was going to direct the film of the book, she hounded him for the part, much as she had driven George Abbott close to distraction about *Flora*.

She had come across the book by accident at an airport. She immediately decided that she and Pookie Adams, the main female character in the novel, had a great deal in common. Pookie was like the kid she herself had been at school. 'I understand Pookie's desperation,' she told the director, determined not to leave such an important matter to her agents.

She sat on Pakula's doorstep until he at least promised he would give her every consideration. He took some persuading. Liza made a screen test but he still wasn't sure straightaway. Besides which, he was under contract to a production company, National General, who had someone else in mind as their idea of the perfect Pookie.

In fact, one executive of National General spelled it out to him: 'You've got a deal,' he said, 'providing you drop Minnelli. The kid just doesn't have it.' Those were words that would later be eaten for breakfast, lunch and dinner. Pakula saw to that. And so did Liza.

The picture, though, couldn't have been more important for Pakula and in going over the head of his producers he was taking more than a conventional risk.

This was going to be his first attempt at directing – although as a producer, he couldn't have had a higher reputation, in particular for what he had achieved with *To Kill a Mockingbird*, which won Gregory Peck his Oscar.

Now, though, he had made the decision that Liza wanted, Pakula knew he had been right to take her.

National General still insisted on their choice. But this time, however, Pakula was declaring that it was Liza or nothing. It was not an insistence he would regret. Nor would Liza, who had turned down a chance to star in the Broadway show, *Promises, Promises*, to take the role. She had also just rejected an offer to star in the film *The Happiest Millionaire*.

As she said, she wasn't doing the picture just to be working. 'For the money? I can go up to Las Vegas for two or three weeks and earn enough to live on for the rest of the year. That's all I need.'

Judy also read the script and told her to 'Go baby, go'. She was ready to go. On the first day's shooting, the schedule had to be changed because of rain. Instead of the planned scene, the crew did an indoor shot. It proved to be the one of which Liza had been most frightened – a scene in which she was seen on the phone, going from laughter to tears in the course of a conversation, with a touch of violence thrown in.

After it, Pakula put his arms around Liza and gave her a huge kiss. Now, directors have a reputation for calling their stars 'darling' and fawning on them. This was not so with Pakula at this moment. It was spontaneous and he meant it. He addressed his comments not to her, but to the rest of the company: 'And it ain't even noon yet and she gives out with an Academy Award performance.'

Unusually, there had been three weeks of rehearsal before an inch of film went through the camera. Pakula thought it would iron out any initial problems and would cure his actors' nerves. Liza didn't seem to have very many of those, although there were a few. It seemed a lot easier to her than playing to a live audience at the Empire Room.

The director later said that Liza had the ability to make anyone she portrayed live. Somehow, for him and for everyone else she became identified with Pookie Adams. 'People thought I *was* Pookie,' she complained afterwards.

Pookie had a tough end in the film. Old ladies would go up to her after seeing the film, touch her gently and ask: 'Are you all right now, then?'

It's fair to say that she was on good terms with the cast during most of the three months that the picture took to film. Wendell Burton, her co-star – there weren't many other actors in it than her and him – told me: 'We were good friends'.

They had first met each other when they showed up for their screen tests in March 1968. 'There was a very special kind of relationship, a very sweet kind of friendship.'

He was moved by her kindness and consideration – 'a very neat person. I learned a lot from Liza, just from her attitude towards people. It was always a surprise to me, because somehow I expected someone like her to be a little more guarded with strangers and people who would walk on and off the set. But she was always willing to talk to whoever was around.'

Once he and Liza went to a small market, not far from the motel where the cast were staying. A stallholder told them, 'I'd like to have you come up to my house.' So Liza, accompanied by Wendell and others in the crew, thought no more. It was a nice invitation, so she accepted and went. That wasn't at all a usual thing for a big star to do. 'My inclination,' said Wendell Burton, 'would have been to make some sort of excuse and beg out of it. But that was not Liza's. She was always willing to do that sort of thing.'

When people asked her for her autograph, she never said no.

What was clear to the people working with her at this time was that, despite her determination – it was almost an obsession – to be finally away from her mother's shadow, she continued to speak of Judy at the drop of a script. And always with affection, despite what she had been telling gossip columnists.

Burton told me: 'After the shooting, we'd go over to her place. She'd be great fun, having a marvellous time.' They played music. 'Harry Neilson was her idol at the time. Then the phone would ring and she would change.' Liza's secretary took the call and gave her the inevitable message: 'It's your mother on the phone.' 'All of a sudden,' said Burton, 'she'd get very sober. She'd go into the other room and talk to her mother on the phone. You could always tell that she was a little bit nervous doing that. But at the same time, she had a tremendous love for her mother.' But there was a reason for the 'sober' look, he believes. As he said: 'I think she was concerned that her mother was trying to exert too strong an influence on her.'

At one stage, Judy said that she was going to come to the location in Rome and Clinton, near Syracuse, small towns in New York State, to watch her at work. Liza knew that if Judy came, she wouldn't just watch and say nice things. She would take over. She would either become her coach and then her director or would end up having a fight with Alan Pakula, who surely wouldn't have tolerated any interference – from Judy Garland, whom he respected, or from anybody.

'She didn't want to have to deal with her mother while she was preparing for her first starring role,' Burton remembered.

This was, of course, crisis time for Judy. They were her last months, although no one could have been sure of that then. 'I detected that when she spoke of her mother it was with both love and concern,' Wendell Burton told me. 'She was also concerned for herself. She was twenty-two-years-old and, despite her success, was still trying to make her own mark. It was an awkward position she was in because she had a great sense of protection of her mother. I could glance over and see how she spoke to her on the phone. I could tell that she was being very careful how she phrased what she said to her. She didn't want to hurt her feelings, while at the same time she intended to do everything she could to prevent her coming there.

Their phone calls were sometimes as hard as ever. Liza knew that Judy was again suffering from severe mental strain – one of the causes of which was the cancelling of plans for her to play a part in the film version of the sex and drugs novel *Valley of the Dolls*. The rôle eventually went to Susan Hayward. Liza liked to say that she was pleased Judy didn't get the part of an arch bitch in the picture because it was beneath her. But losing it resulted in tremendous mental anguish.

Now Liza took on a new rôle as far as her mother was concerned. After years as her adviser and daughter-confessor, she became a sort of unpaid agent. Rightly, she knew that the one thing that would keep Judy on anything approaching an even keel was by working. But, as she saw from the *Valley of the Dolls* experience, it wasn't going to be easy.

Whether she knew it or not, Judy was no longer a good risk for any studio. No matter how hard Liza tried, how many strings she endeavoured to pull, there was nothing her daughter could do. Liza was the one with influence now. However, influence – as Liza herself should have known – can work only so far.

Judy, however, didn't exactly appreciate her daughter's efforts – if she knew about them. In one call, Judy accused Liza of trying to take the other children, Lorna and Joey, away from her. That was not the likely starting point for a rational conversation. All the more reason why Judy had to be kept away from the location for as long as possible – and, if Liza had her way, permanently.

Not so her husband. Peter would come to visit her at Rome when he could – and that helped to put paid for a time to the stories that they were finally separated.

What she was not going to be separated from now was her new career as a movie star.

The *Los Angeles Times* declared: 'Her performance is so strong and so compelling that nothing else about *The Sterile Cuckoo* concerns us very much.'

Sometimes, the nice, charming, 'neat' Liza Minnelli surprised people like Wendell Burton. 'She's a very competitive person. Once we played badminton and I won. She was quite upset. The game had been important to her.' It was as though the game was a show and she wasn't the one getting the good notices.

Said Burton: 'She really wants to win and that's the spark for all her drive.' If she had that, and she nearly always had, she was all right.

Actually, she was not quite all right. She decided to take up a new idea of fun – riding a motor scooter. She became quite good – at falling off. The story got around that it was a motorcycle with which she was playing tricks. Liza gives the impression that she might have preferred the glamour of falling off a 'bike', especially since this was close to the age of *Easy Rider*. But it was just a scooter. Nevertheless, her injuries would have done credit to a big Japanese machine.

The fall came shortly before the Academy Award ceremonies at which she was to hear whether or not she would get her *Cuckoo* Oscar. Her fall resulted in needing twenty-five stitches. Part of a front tooth was broken and a shoulder was severely hurt – 'busted,' she said. She had to have a small hair piece to cover some of the stitches and was on pain killers as she hobbled into the ceremonies on the arm of her father.

She struggled into the hall where the ceremony was about to start. Someone asked her for an autograph. Liza was flustered. 'Would you mind if you waited until the end?' she asked and then smiled sweetly. 'I hope you lose,' said the woman. The wish was granted.

The Award went to Maggie Smith for *The Pride of Miss Jean Brodie*. Liza was to say that she was so much under the influence of painkillers at the time of the presentations that when the envelope was opened and Miss Smith's name read out, she didn't even realise which category was being discussed.

The fact that she was with Vincente and not Peter proved something, too – and seemed to confirm the previous rumours. The Allens had separated, although this time it was just temporary. But on the night of the accident she had been out at a restaurant with actor Tony Bill, who, with his wife, had for a long time been a close friend.

For a couple who had taken two years over an engagement, there was as little rush now for Liza and Peter to make their separation official. For the moment they were not talking about a divorce. Their marriage would linger on.

Peter, meanwhile, had opened a restaurant called 'Prudence' near where Madison Avenue meets 70th Street. The hope was that the advertising people would stop by for lunch among the palms and green lacquer.

Judy's marriage, however, did not linger. But being married did. With Mark Herron cast off, she now wed a New York disco owner named Mickey Deans.

She wanted Liza at the wedding, which they had decided would be in London. Liza, however, was busy – making a new film called *Tell Me That You Love Me, Junie Moon* (The quality of a film is frequently in inverse proportion to the length of its title and this one was no exception!)

Liza told Judy she couldn't make the wedding. 'Sorry, Mama,' she said, 'but I promise I'll come to the next one.'

The wit and wisdom of Liza Minnelli was by now a talking point in most of the New York eateries. She probably thought it was quite amusing herself that March of 1969 because the words swept through the Paramount lot where the film was being shot.

At least that was what people then thought. She soon, however, had second thoughts. Years later, actress Jacqueline Hyde told me about Liza relating the story to her.

'She didn't realise until afterwards what she had said,' recalled Jacqueline Hyde. 'There was no way of getting out of it. She said it very straight, not sarcastically at all.'

Judy, though, did see the funny side. She laughed. Liza said: 'Oh my God! What did I do!' But she did see Judy in New York, shortly afterwards. She wasn't pleased with what she saw. Judy had just celebrated her forty-seventh birthday, but it could have been her sixty-seventh. She seemed old and subdued, not talking the way Judy Garland talked.

Judy used to shock, to scintillate, to make people – not least of them, Liza – laugh. Yet this was a woman who was talking of buying and using non-stick frying pans.

Was it Deans or was it drugs? It was difficult for her daughter to decide. All that she did know was that she was bitterly worried by it. This was not her mother talking, not her mother sitting there. The complete stranger in front of her now was a cause for the greatest possible worry.

She was only too glad she had her own work to think about. Liza certainly was a hot property for television now. In the course of the past couple of years, she had appeared on shows hosted by Danny Kaye, Woody Allen, Perry Como, Carol Burnett and, again, Ed Sullivan – four times between December 1968 and March 1970. And there would be her own first 'Special' on the NBC network. On this she was joined by Anthony Newley, then a big star himself thanks to *Stop The World I Want to Get Off* and *The Roar of the Greasepaint, The Smell of the Crowd*. And if that wasn't enough, he was married to Joan Collins. On this show, it was Liza who was the star. There was no doubt about that.

She and Newley wore matching outfits – he in a check suit and she in a skirt of the same pattern. But the magic of Liza Minnelli was such that somehow eyes moved from the pair to the one star. She should have felt encouraged. Fred Ebb, who provided her material, knew that he had never had his songs put over better. Once more, a huge audience was able to share what was usually restricted to those who could afford to pay for her nightclub appearances.

And yet there were those who thought that she could still have done more with it. In his column in the Los Angeles *Herald-Examiner*, Morton Moss said simply: 'Let Her Do Own Show'. He wondered about the people she had on the set with her – Michael J. Pollard from *Bonnie and Clyde* among them – and decided that they hadn't contributed much. But neither had any of them a lot of what Liza herself had, as she remembered Jolson, Ethel Merman and Eddie Cantor and sang 'There's No Business Like Show Business.'

'Liza only reminisces by proxy,' said Mr Moss, no doubt reminding himself of her tender years and suggesting that most decent lawabiding girls of her age had never heard of Al Jolson, Eddie Cantor, Ethel Merman and 'There's No Business Like Show Business'. As he said: 'Forget the reminiscences. Let the girl do her own show as she did her own film *The Sterile Cuckoo*.' That was, however, a different sort of show and would be a difficult one to repeat.

But the TV special was an important event, nevertheless. If only because it gave her an opportunity to revise her previous views on the medium. 'I've always hated TV,' she said. 'There's no time and I need time to get to know the people I'm working with, and to get to know what I'm doing. You do something on TV and it's over and done with before you have a chance to say, "Hey, what have I done?"' If she asked herself what she had done now, the answer was fairly obviously a very good job indeed.

There was also her new film *Tell Me That You Love Me, Junie Moon*. The picture was proving hard work – as well it might, since it was the story of three sick misfits (a girl who is disfigured; a homosexual in a wheelchair and an epileptic) setting up home together. It becomes a *ménage-à-trois* of almost tasteless proportions.

The director was Otto Preminger, who in his time had directed some great movies, ranging from *Laura* to *The Man With a Golden*

Arm and *Anatomy of a Murder*. But he was now, it would seem, approaching his dotage – even though he would direct two more pictures and live for another seventeen years.

He paid Liza $50,000 for the part, her biggest fee to date, although not yet money that was in the superstar league. Liza didn't find it the easiest rôle in the world to perform – if only because she was required to spend at least two hours in make-up; the scar on her face was very much specialist work. Neither was Mr Preminger himself the most easy person to please.

'Otto is a bit old world,' she said kindly. She didn't totally love him for telling her: 'An actor is paid to act.' And she said: 'It wasn't easy waiting two hours for the lighting to be ready and then working yourself up for an emotional scene.' Preminger was inclined at times like that to instruct her: 'Come on . . . cry.'

He himself admitted that a Preminger film was never free of problems. 'I am not the easiest person in the world to work for,' which was an understatement. 'I do not praise people indiscriminately, but I tell you Liza Minnelli is a professional actress who has more natural acting talent than almost any other young actress I can think of. She did not go to drama school like other young actresses, but obviously, acting is in her blood. She is already great.'

It proved to be a fairer assessment of his knowledge and taste than was his decision to make the film itself, which was crass, uninteresting, and without any sense of subtlety.

Others thought there was a certain amount of indecency in it. The movie was shot in Boston. In one scene, in a local cemetery, Liza appeared nude (she was, in fact, wearing a body stocking). The wife of a man buried there claimed that the cemetery was being desecrated by the scene.

As *Time* noted, 'The film's only redeeming social value is that it has prompted the Massachusetts legislature to ban the filming of nude cemetery scenes.'

Mark Goodman, reviewing the picture, said nothing about Liza herself except to describe her as 'a wild young thing with a penchant for what may be restrainedly described as the wrong kind of guy.' Especially since he was the one who gets her to strip among the gravestones.

No. Mr Goodman reserved his opprobrium for Otto Preminger who 'has always had a certain flair for irrelevant melodrama, but never in his mercurial career has he made anything quite as tacky as *Tell Me That You Love Me, Junie Moon*, which started off as an oddly beguiling novel by Marjorie Kellogg...*Junie Moon* is at base an egregious attempt to exploit both sentimental and kinky appetites.'

The film itself was no great delight to anyone. In *The Illustrated London News* Michael Billington described it all as 'like seeing a venerated senior citizen desperately trying to show he's in love with today by donning see-through clothes.'

For a time, Liza was trying to work out whether she herself liked it or not – even at the stage of things when it would have been expected for her to say it was the best picture ever made and wasn't she lucky to have had anything to do with it? To Liza's everlasting credit, she never said anything of the kind.

'After the first shooting of *Junie Moon* I was in sort of a daze. I didn't know whether it was good or not. But when the lights went up, all the people were wiping their eyes and my father had big tears rolling down his cheeks.'

The good comments were not about the picture itself. Vincente told her: 'I thought you would be good, but I didn't know you knew your craft.'

'Daddy is so sweet,' cooed Liza. Too sweet no doubt to say just how dreadful the movie itself was.

But whatever people said about the picture, it was no longer the topic uppermost in their minds when it came to Liza Minnelli.

This was the time she became involved in one of the most bizarre scandal-that-never-was ever to have been given space in the Press. Too much space, as things would turn out.

The story was being put around that Liza had not just received Australia's Prime Minister while in the country. She and John Gorton, a man old enough to have been her grandfather, were alleged to have had an affair. It was soon accepted as preposterous nonsense, but it lasted long enough to cause a few feathers to fly.

For reasons never adequately explained, the CIA were supposed to have been involved. Vincente, like everyone else, heard about it and decided that the best comfort would be in humour. He sent her a telegram, saying: 'Hi, Ho. Mata Hari. Where's the money?' The story was stupid, but that didn't stop it being painful to both parties. All sorts of allegations flew around – including, the most incredible of all, that Liza had written an article about her affair for the British satirical magazine *Private Eye*. The article – which

Private Eye, normally not reticent about such matters, denied knowing anything about – was then supposed to have been bought for $15,000 by the CIA.

'A pack of lies,' was how Liza dismissed the allegations, which came out after a month-long whispering campaign.

There was a call in the Australian House of Representatives for an inquiry, but this was later rejected.

Meanwhile, Liza said the whole thing was 'vicious'. What was more, her Australian mother-in-law Mrs Maria Woolnough, revealed now for all to read that she was in Liza's dressing room when the star was introduced to Gorton. Nothing happened.

Indeed, when Gorton came to see her, Liza said: 'It was like the President coming back. We were all aflutter...It is so ridiculous that I laughed when I first heard it. I sent a telegram to Mr Gorton and his wife expressing my regrets and assuring them that I was taking legal action to find out who started this lie. I've never written any article. I don't even have time to write letters.'

After all that, *Junie Moon* (which would have been a much better title in the first place) was a walk over. She could even put up with Otto Preminger telling her to cry to order.

But she wasn't crying at being an actress. Now she believed she was established in that rôle at last and accepted for it. She planned to make one film a year. But the pressures and the strains were hard.

She didn't know how much worse things would get. In June 1969 she found out. There was a phone call: Judy was dead.

Chapter Twelve

IT WAS PETER who took the call. By the expression on his face, Liza could tell something was radically wrong. There was a death. 'My father,' she said automatically.

She couldn't conceive it could have been Judy. There had been so many other stories and every time the news of Judy Garland's death had been greatly exaggerated. No, Mama was too resilient, for all her problems, much too vibrant to die.

But it was true. Judy Garland was dead and from an overdose of drugs.

Perhaps it was inevitable that a woman who had been taking all sorts of pills since she was a little girl would die that way. One day, there would be the unavoidable mistake, either the wrong combination of tablets or she would forget she had taken her dose and would repeat it.

Equally inevitably, the stories of suicide would surface – and quicker than Liza was able to contemplate. In virtually every country of the world, there were headlines proclaiming: 'JUDY GARLAND KILLS HERSELF.'

It didn't seem to surprise anyone. A whole coterie of Garland watchers had been waiting for the inevitable suicide attempt which would succeed. For her part, Liza didn't believe it was self-inflicted, despite what the rumours said. The doctors who examined the body assured her that was not the case. So Liza asked for an autopsy. There would have been one in any case, but she wanted people to know as soon as possible that Judy never would have killed herself. There was an inquest. It was not suicide.

Liza saw this as the perfect opportunity to put to rest with her the stories and the clichés – and to emphasise the Judy she knew, the Judy of fun.

'I knew her well enough to know that when she died it was an accident,' Liza declared. 'If all the people who keep a spot in their hearts for my mother's tragedies knew the truth, they would be disappointed. She had a good life, she had fun. Everything was like an enormous party. If there was a calm, she couldn't stand it. She'd make things happen. I loved her for that. She educated me, you know, she educated my initiative. My father gave me my dreams but my mother gave me my drive.'

Now she was driven to deal with death. The words about Judy were all true, but they were the sort of things said by people in a state of shock by which nature has cushioned them from a sad reality.

Judy may have believed life was a party. But that wasn't the way Liza saw her funeral after the body was flown back to New York.

Now she took stock of the situation and realised that she had to be in charge of most of the organisation and at the same time keep an eye on her half-brother and -sister.

Liza herself had needed to be accommodated, too. Kay Thompson helped her sort out some of the essential details, like the place to handle the funeral arrangements. She chose the Frank E. Campbell funeral home. It was the sort of place that was used to handling the mortal remains of international celebrities, and they knew how to accommodate the crowds who would be bound to come. The address alone, near the corner of 85th Street and Fifth Avenue, bespoke its clientèle.

'I was devastated,' Liza said. 'But I was determined that it would be as perfect as could be, exactly as she would have wanted it. We felt we had to appear in control and composed.'

So one of the first people called in was her doctor. He gave her a fairly thorough examination and determined that in addition to her grief, Liza was suffering from severe tension. He prescribed Valium. As Liza said: 'I was so grateful that someone had given me an order, made a decision for me, that I did exactly as I was told.'

She took Valium for the first time – but not the last. She took it the day of the funeral and the day after that. And she took it again and again. But it helped her a little to get through the funeral and the arrangements that had to be made.

Kay Thompson helped her decide other necessary details like the flowers they would have. There was only one hymn Liza wanted played, her mother's favourite, 'The Battle Hymn of the Republic'.

Such thoughts were not uppermost in Liza's mind. But she did feel that there were thousands of Judy Garland fans who would want to go to pay their final respects – millions, even, but there were limits as to how many would go as far as attending the service. But first Liza had to think about herself and her half-sister and -brother.

It wasn't easy for her herself to view the body. She did it in stages, moving a few feet and then sitting down, moving and sitting, before she could reach the coffin. Finally, she and her mother were together. Liza felt weird and was helped away.

The funeral home could deal with what Liza decided was the need for the body to lie in state. For one day only, people would be able to file silently past the bier, as though this was after the death of a queen. In a way, it was.

The fans did as they were expected to do. They came, in one continuous line from morning until night. This was Judy Garland's most loyal audience of all. For once, she 'appeared' in public without someone shouting, 'Sing "Over the Rainbow".' The rainbow had now been crossed.

Liza was asked how she felt. It was a stupid question. But she dealt with it, poetically. 'I think she was just tired, like a flower that blooms and gives joy and beauty to the world and then wilts away. I just want to send her off as she would have wanted to go ... bright and lovely.'

It was a tough rôle for Liza to fill. But she had been fully prepared from the time she wrote her mother's fan-mail replies.

Something was now becoming apparent. By the death of her mother, Liza had taken on the mantle of head of the family. The girl who had amazed audiences by being so strong on stage, now had to be strong within her own family circle. She was.

She was the one who made the telephone calls – very often the hardest of all jobs for the bereaved. She had to call Lorna and Joey, after speaking to Sid. He told me that he opposed Liza's decision to have Judy cremated. He was horrified at this idea, as were the other children. Liza had no difficulty in adapting herself to the wishes of the rest of the family.

There was a further problem in persuading her own father to come to the funeral. He stayed away, because he didn't want to be photographed – as he imagined the newsmen would do – in some grouping of 'Judy's husbands'.

We can speculate that the passing of Judy meant a number of things to Liza, all interrelated, although seemingly contradictory.

She was on her own without having to worry about what Mama would think – and yet at the same time, she now started to ponder more about what Mama would say than ever before. She seemed bubbly, yet she felt broken. Now, she would have to be accepted for herself, without the slightest need for anyone to describe her as 'Judy Garland's daughter' yet, at the same time, because of what had happened, everybody would now mention 'Judy Garland's daughter, Liza Minnelli...'

Liza herself was keeping it all much more personal. She was proud to be spoken of in that way – because the only thing in her mind was the 'lovely, vital and extraordinary woman she was'.

What disturbed her most of all was the talk that she should have known would come. She tried, valiantly but not always successfully, to disabuse people of what was regrettably the truth – that Judy at the time of her death was not the person she once had been. Too many had been in audiences at which a Garland performance was as much an endurance test – for the audiences, not the star – as a show. How long would it be before she forgot the words? Would she stay on her feet for more than a few minutes? What was in the glass from which she drank so frequently? Worst of all were the stories of hecklers – the ones who had no respect for her or her talent or for what she had once been, those who threw bread rolls on the stage, or who shouted out that she was drunk.

The stories stuck and they hurt. Liza was as hurt as her mother, perhaps more because Judy's drugs had had the effect of anaesthetising her.

Liza again and again begged reporters: 'I wish you would mention the joy she had for life. That's what she gave me. If she was the tragic figure they said she was, I would be a wreck, wouldn't I?'

And she tried to analyse the reasons for Judy's dying. It wasn't an overdose, she told herself. 'She lived like a taut wire. I don't think she ever looked for real happiness, because she always thought happiness would mean the end.'

She was also trying to justify the feelings of antipathy she felt for Mickey Deans and for Mark Herron, but gave up.

Instead, she remembered a mother who had a 'joy for life'. And as Liza, Lorna and Joey waited for the funeral services, they remembered some of the laughs. Judy used to joke about her eventual death. That was what they now remembered. 'When I die, I suppose they'll lower all the flags on Fire Island to half mast,' she once joked. Now as they thought about it, they all laughed. 'When you think about it, that's pretty funny,' Liza said. A lot of homosexuals lived on Fire Island and Judy was thinking about her following among the gay community.

And Liza added, her very being filled with pride and glad of the opportunity to say so: 'The middle of the road was never for her. It bored her. She wanted the pinnacle of excitement. If she was happy, she wasn't just happy, she was ecstatic. And when she was sad, she was sadder than anybody.'

And she said about her the things that were customarily said about people who lived to excess – like Jolson or Errol Flynn or Leonard Bernstein: 'She had lived ninety lives in one. And yet I thought she would outlive us all. She was a great star and a great talent and for the rest of my life I will be proud to be Judy Garland's daughter.'

Meanwhile, Vincente had to work out his reactions to what had happened to his daughter. He came to the conclusion that there was much to be proud of in Liza. Despite his reservations about her marriage, he now liked Peter and believed he was good for Liza. As for her career, pride poured out of his very being. He approved of her going into films and the choice of vehicles that she had made.

Liza and Peter flew to California soon after the funeral. There was talk of a film father and daughter would make together, possibly of the story of Scott and Zelda Fitzgerald. But it didn't happen.

The effects on Liza of Judy's death were considerable and they showed in her work. She had other things to think about than a film with Daddy.

At the Sahara in Las Vegas, she didn't quite cut the sensational figure people had begun to expect. *Variety* said the show only had 'okay possibilities for substantial traffic in the Congo Room.

'There is not the liquid flow of presentation during her slightly overlong session (fifty-five minutes) but rather a decided corrugation in mood and material is evident. The black-eyed, angular thrush works very hard – almost too hard in some songs and routines.'

And work hard she did. She believed, rightly, that she had more to do than merely play to her audiences. She went out into the auditorium and found it 'absolutely frightening' that people wanted to touch her. She couldn't understand why they needed to do it. 'People don't touch Barbra Streisand. Something about her says, "Don't touch".'

Once when one woman started to paw her, she replied in kind. The woman had said, 'You're marvellous.' Liza replied: 'But what about you, my dear?' and touched. 'How dare you?' the woman responded.

That was a brittle Liza who should have realised that *she* was the one on display and was inviting all kinds of responses from audiences who had paid for the experience. She was making the woman what she wasn't – part of the show.

Perhaps it was still shock. Having no Judy to talk to on the phone would take some getting used to. She still talked about her mother incessantly, it seemed. 'I'm never sad when I remember Mama,' she told one writer. 'Our home life was not the tragic victim of fate that she presented to the world. That was something she planted there for the public to see. She let everyone else wallow in her misery, while she sailed on through . . . She was not self pitying – except on rare occasions.'

Sometimes Liza pitied herself simply because other people were showing her too much pity of their own. She would go into an elevator and find people looking at her and bursting into tears. Somehow, she was given the responsibility of cheering them up. If she later saw the funny side of that one, the recognition of that fact did not come all at once.

Sometimes, she had a temper and it was in moments like this that she was able to demonstrate it. She did it in a theatrical way which was perhaps what the person at the receiving end might have appreciated. But then she was a theatrical person. Who else could respond to those tears with a yell that said: 'You cried for her when she sang "Over the Rainbow" and "The Man That Got Away". Now at last she's at peace, smile for God's sake.'

She was once asked what it was like singing with her mother. 'Like singing with my mother,' she said. 'I only had one mother, too.'

There was so much about Liza's performance that reminded people of Judy – not least the gays who filled the theatres for their performances.

The relationship between the Garland family and homosexuals went right back to the appeal Judy represented to them. Lorna wrote in her memoir *Me And My Shadows* that any time her mother wanted to hurt her she only had to say that the boys with whom she was going were 'fags'. And yet those gay men were her most devoted audience, as they were for Liza.

They were, she said, 'symbols of love and trust' and offered an emotional openness as well as an artistic sensitivity. Another reason is a more simple fact: had these gays and bisexuals been women, the kind they would have liked to have been were the forceful, strong females that Judy and Liza represented. If they weren't quite sure of their sexuality, the kind of clothes that these two women, senior and junior, wore, suited them perfectly.

Liza had grown up, long before her time. Now she couldn't shelter behind the belief that she was, after all, Judy's little girl. Even at her strongest, this had been an escape mechanism for her. Now it was no longer available. The realisation was quite abrupt and difficult.

Nothing made her feel more that way, it has to be said, than the stories of Judy that came back to haunt her – literally. Late in the summer of 1970, more than a year after Judy's death, Liza discovered that her mother had never been buried.

Now that sounds like something out of a Dracula movie, and when Liza heard about it, her spine ran cold.

It turned out that after the funeral services were held, the body and its ornate coffin was stored in a temporary crypt. A permanent resting place was supposed to have been built, but it never was. Mickey Deans, who had promised to take care of the rest of the proceedings had failed to do so, because he couldn't raise the money.

Liza was so distraught when she heard about that, that she immediately signed the cheque for the body to be properly interred in a new crypt at the Ferncliff Cemetery at Ardsley, New York.

Other things about Judy wouldn't get buried either – particularly those that automatically tied her daughter to her image. For a time it seemed that Liza was escaping from the Judy Garland chains. Judy's death, however, had changed all that. Once more, little Liza Minnelli was poor Judy Garland's daughter.

In December 1969, Liza was complaining, 'Some people will always look for Mama in me.' And that was true, too. Once more, they were asking her to sing 'Over the Rainbow' and were wondering whether hers would be, like her mother's, the Career That Got Away.

Someone once asked her about this attempt to escape from Judy's shadow and the success that she was making of it. An acquaintance, somewhat in awe of being with the girl now spoken of as the new superstar of the forthcoming 1970s, asked her: 'When did you feel you were your own person?'

Liza answered politely. But that wasn't the way she felt. 'I felt like saying,' she told a mutual friend afterwards, 'Hey, there's five foot five of human being here. You're not talking to a ghost.'

But she didn't dismiss the value of the Judy connection or the effect it had on other people. She saw the comfort and appreciated it.

'When I walk outside the theatre and see a lady, someone of another generation, who's been standing there, waiting out in the cold – if I've given her just one touch of anything, because through my mother, through me, she chooses to think "life goes on", that's wonderful. It really is. Things do go on – and on. I guess what I'm trying to be is a good daughter.'

That, too, made Liza different from a number of people who had already achieved success. She did still appreciate it and know there was a duty to her audiences. As James Stewart once told me, 'that's the whole ball-game.'

Sometimes, she seemed to go over the top. Other actresses not only know they are beautiful, they crave people telling them how gorgeous they are – all the time. It feeds the ego and the stomach, making up for all the meals they miss to keep their svelte figures. But Liza, the girl who made herself chocolate ice-cream sodas to help her relax, wasn't in for any of that nonsense.

'It's not that I think I'm ugly. I'm just not pretty. I mean, if somebody is reading a casting list that calls for a beautiful young girl, he doesn't immediately think of Liza Minnelli.'

No, but then anybody looking for a girl who could bring the house down singing tongue-twisters that would tax a Danny Kaye and who could also turn in an Oscar-winning performance in a dramatic role wouldn't expect to be able to cast a beauty queen.

In fact, that was Liza's great achievement. She was both an entertainer and an actress. True, Judy had been that as well, but already Liza was outclassing her mother, and that was no mean achievement. And perhaps one of Liza's greatest talents was being great even when she wasn't being good. Sometimes, particularly in the middle of her nightclub act and occasionally on television, she would miss a note. It didn't matter. Stardom was not about being perfect in putting over a song. It was in the style in which that was done. By now, Liza had it in full measure.

In Paris, they again called her '*La Petite Piaf Americaine*', and treated her as though she were also Princess Grace. Piaf performed in huge smoke-filled rooms in front of audiences that looked as though they contained a fair share of men in striped jerseys with knives in their mouths. Liza had the French Government and the Rothschilds forming part of her public. When she was given a party, she was greeted by a candle-lit staircase overflowing with orchids.

Both her nightclub act and her reputation as an actress had helped secure that sort of attention for her.

As far as she was concerned, that was one of the great values of films like *Sterile Cuckoo*. But she didn't want to take too much credit for that. 'Why should an actor take credit?' she asked. The real tribute should be to the author who provided the book in the first place. In that she was an original. There are very few actors who have gone on record depreciating what they did and saying that the words were written by someone else. She was doing now for her movies what she had been doing in her nightclub act. There was no way on screen that she could come out in front of the curtain and thank all the people listed in the credits, so she did it in interviews. That was generosity that was truly appreciated.

Sometimes, she wasn't all that appreciated – like on the occasions that she behaved like a girl in her early twenties and not like a big movie and Broadway star. She and Peter went to the Tower East restaurant – and were thrown out because they only had forty cents between them. It didn't matter that the head waiter had invited them back a week or so before. This was his night off and his deputy either didn't know who Liza Minnelli was, or if he did thought that she and her husband ought to have known better. Stars occasionally behave like that. To Liza's credit, it wasn't a prank that was repeated.

She wasn't sure either that a lot of the praise heaped on her was always justified. Neither could she understand what people wanted to find out when they asked what she felt 'inside'. She had no illusions that everything worked from the heart. As she told the *New York Times*: 'I've got news for you, pal. I don't think I am all that interesting inside myself, that I could draw everything from there. I would be a pretty limited vision. I'm not allowed. That's one of the great phrases I believe in: I am not allowed. One of the things I'm not allowed is to build a character within my own limitations. You gotta look out, every day, see and watch, or you're going to play the same character over and over. I mean, it's the same as life, right?

Every day has got to be an expansion or ought to be. Every day –
widen the circle, keep widening it.'

People tried to allow her to widen her world, if only to help to
make her feel better. And occasionally they succeeded, not always
realising that was what they were doing. In fact, Liza was to
remember very distinctly one night when she was at home at her
apartment on East 57th Street. Peter came in with a newspaper that
contained a review of her new LP. It was very good. But what she
remembered was that no mention was made of Judy.

She herself couldn't get her mother out of her mind. She didn't
particularly want to, but it was hard.

Liza tried to learn a few lessons about carrying her grief on her
shoulders. She was not going to be self pitying about her marriage
either, although there were now no statements about how much they
liked, let alone loved, each other.

She and Peter were separated now. It was a decision they had
taken, 'mutually and amicably'. In fact, there was no animosity – if
there had been, Liza would have asked herself how she had got into
the marriage in the first place and the first thing one has to realise
about Liza Minnelli is that she never regretted anything. She always
took responsibility for the consequences of her action. It was one of
the adult things she had learned to do as a child and even if, in some
ways, she was still a child, in that she was very much a fully-grown
adult who knew how to look after herself.

Plainly they had grown out of each other – just as teenagers
grow out of friendships or young children grow out of formerly
favourite toys. Both these comparisons applied to Liza Minnelli
and her relationship with Peter Allen. There was affection for each
other, but they were constantly apart and, both had to admit, when
they were, they really didn't miss each other very much. Add that
to all the old problems about her success and his also-ran status
and there was a recipe for an end to their existing status. They
regretted it, but agreed that they really had little alternative. Now
they both had new lives to live.

They didn't need any rows or anything else that would bring
matters to a head. One day, she simply turned to Peter, and said,
'I think we ought to call if off,' and call it off they did. Divorce
would – and did – follow at the same sort of leisurely pace in which
they had begun their marriage. Making any detailed, official-
sounding statement would give the impression of a huge row that

necessitated an immediate – or as close to that as possible – end to their marriage. Neither fancied that; thus the decisions to say that what they had decided was 'mutual and amicable'. That had the sound of both permanence and inevitability about it. They said it was merely a temporary state of affairs, although their friends believed, they knew otherwise – and the friends were right. It was the end, and everyone knew that this time it was going to be for good. And there was no point in denying it, either. In fact, when the Press heard the news, she told reporters all about it.

The marriage to Peter Allen was, in truth, a disaster. To put it slightly delicately, in Sid Luft's words, he was 'not a whole man'. It was an unfair term to use as well as being homophobic. Actually, she conceived during this marriage, which seemed like the answer to all her dreams. But those dreams were shattered when she suffered a miscarriage.

Peter being gay, however, was a serious problem for her. The fact that her most loyal friends were gay men didn't make it any easier for her to be married to one.

'That was devastating to Liza,' Luft recalls. 'When she married him, she didn't know he was gay.'

When she discovered, she was distraught. She flew off from New York to California. At LAX, as the airport in Los Angeles is known – using the same letters as those inscribed on luggage labels – she had rung the man who had virtually adopted her.

'Pop,' she said, 'I'm ready to kill myself.'

He recalled: 'She was so distraught. I said, "Just get into a cab and come here" and we'll . . .' He didn't complete the sentence. It did not need completing. She went to his Los Angeles apartment. 'She was hysterical by the time she got here.'

He called his favourite doctor, Lew Segal, to look her over. She remained hysterical, although the doctor's tranquillisers did the trick. She stayed with her stepfather for two days and then was driven back to her own home – still hysterical.

Peter was out of her life in 1972, five years after they married. (In 1992, he died of AIDS.)

'Peter and I never battled,' she maintained. But there was the battle of the conflicting careers and nothing could quite mend that. Was it sex? She described that as 'one of the demons'.

What was not one of the demons was the desire of so many people to see Liza's career move on. The nightclub engagements continued. So did the offers of shows. (Lorna wasn't doing bad either. After Liza had turned down *Promises, Promises*, Lorna took a part in the show.) But now, it seemed, most people saw her real medium as the movies.

Now there was an offer she was to take up that would make all the difference. The girl with a 'Z' now had the opportunity that would reward her with an 'A'. She was going into *Cabaret*.

Chapter Thirteen

WHEN CHRISTOPHER ISHERWOOD'S story of his days in early Nazi Germany, *Goodbye to Berlin*, first became a film called *I Am a Camera*, *Time* magazine devastated the effort with the words, 'Me No Leica'. They were not to say that of Liza Minnelli in *Cabaret*, which was much more a musical remake of the original play and. film than of the Broadway show, which had made the huge mistake of not employing her in the lead.

There was a totally new score – appropriately by Ebb and Kander – which made it seem like they were making the picture around Liza. Joel Grey would be repeating his Broadway success as the cabaret MC and the musical numbers would all come within the cabaret set-up. No leading man was going to look into the eyes of any leading woman and start to sing and dance. The only 'book songs' used in the picture were featured in part of the background score. Liza's tremendous triumph was in making it all seem as one of those original productions in which she and she alone could have starred. It is not now possible to imagine any other actress in the part of Sally Bowles, the nightclub performer and naïve good-time girl out to make the most of life in Hitler's Berlin.

Not only was she outstanding as the girl befriended by the British author who goes in search of a country about to fall under the spell of the most hideous régime in history, and, though a homosexual, ends up under her spell instead, but she created an image all of her own of those times.

Other stars may become prima donnas and argue over costumes, lines and camera angles; Liza went in search of her part and the times and place that made it.

The film was shot on location in Germany. She didn't like the country. She felt uncomfortable in the place that had supported Hitler and the Holocaust, having to make a movie about the times when the stormtroopers were first assembling for the sport of beating up innocent men, women and children in the streets.

But the film offered one hell of a part – she really had always been convinced that the original show had been written with her in mind and that she had only been rejected because Sally had to be played by an English girl; now Sally was going to be an American, so there could be nothing out of place in it for her – in a marvellous story. If only she didn't have to make it in Germany.

Liza didn't like her costumes either – they made her seem like Joe Nameth, the American footballer, she declared – and she hated the food. After a couple of weeks of sausages and sauerkraut she craved a waffle as much as a Valium (except that the pill she got without any trouble.)

With no chance of finding the kind of American food she needed, she settled on the task of searching for the right costumes – particularly those in use in the nightclub act, the kind the other girls hated because they were expected to grow the hair under their arms (when shooting was finished, Liza threw them a party as well as a selection of razors and soap with which they could shave their armpits).

She wanted things that were silky and slinky and for which she wouldn't have to wear a bra.

Gwen Verdon, who had made a huge name for herself in the stage versions of *Sweet Charity* and *Damn Yankees* (she starred in the film version of that as well), both parts in which an older Liza Minnelli would have excelled, helped in her research. She picked up a stack of clothes in Paris – just as a unique discovery was made: wardrobes full of costumes from German films of the early 1930s found in a locked vault in Munich.

But no one would release them. They reminded the Germans too much of the Nazis. It was a time when they didn't want to remember Hitler. 'I can't find anyone who admits to being German,' said Liza. 'They all say they are Austrians.'

In the end, Liza decided that the most typical and most decadent costumes she could find were the black dresses she had worn for her own cabaret performances at the Waldorf.

Joel Grey had his problems as far as costumes were concerned, too – not those he wore in the picture itself, but in the rehearsals for the film. Bob Fosse who was directing the picture wanted his stars to wear 'approximations' of the costumes they would put on when the cameras actually started to roll. For the 'Money' number, he insisted on Grey wearing a tail coat. So one was hired. 'It came from a costume house and had obviously been on a lot of people before me. Of course. it was cleaned properly, but when someone actually wears it, it sort of revitalises all the other bodies who had ever worn it before. So it was as though Liza was not performing with me – but with a whole chorus line of older Germans.

'That was what she felt and I did, too. We tried to keep ourselves serious about the work. But she kept breaking up when she looked at the tail coat. That was distracting, as you can imagine.'

The art, of course, was to make sure that neither was distracted from the job in hand. And that was where their professionalism came into play. Anyone who has ever been on a movie set will know of the laughs when a leading actor 'fluffs'. No one seems to get at all upset. These laughs are, however, the oil that lubricates the machine of the operation, smooths away the grinding tension. Liza and Joel laughing at the tail coat was an investment in the performances they would actually give on camera.

Just as she had looked for the costumes, so Liza now looked for the real Sally Bowles. The woman had really existed – the real model for the girl she was going to play 'with an element of terrible selfishness and meanness.' As Liza explained, 'She really was a tramp, not just another lovable kook. I understand she was not all that terrific. She wore green fingernails and was full of crap, but she was always working and everybody loved her because she was completely nuts.'

So that was how she would be played. She was hoping that the real Sally would turn up on the set, even if Liza didn't wear dresses with ruffles and carioca sleeves as once she had done, and if her hair was no longer a flaming red.

Sally Bowles didn't turn up. But the old George Grosz cartoons did, as did the Kurt Weil music and the Elizabeth Bergner films that she and Bob Fosse studied night and day for weeks.

And, as for so many other people who go to Germany even today, the biggest impressions were those that were relayed without saying anything. The paving stones and the bricks told their own stories. Everywhere, Liza found herself asking who had been there before, what had they done, what those bricks and paving stones had seen.

The film crew stayed at the Kempinski Hotel where the Nazi hierarchy had wined, dined and slept with women not unlike Sally Bowles. She found it all 'spooky'.

They went to Hamburg and saw the women mud wrestlers and the live sex shows which hadn't changed that much from the days before Hitler. In Munich, they saw neo-Nazi demonstrations. Somehow the spookiness had become even more sinister.

Joel Grey told me he was as infected by it as anyone else working on the movie. 'In fact, for me it was harder. I had my own questions due to my having been Jewish. It made me specifically anxious about it. Everyone had cause to be apprehensive because of the historical aspect of it all. But after a time I had to realise that a whole country of people did disagree with the Nazis. You come to know what goes on in a country. It makes you feel a little more open.'

And they talked about it in the off-duty moments. 'I think we always talked about everything that affected us all and all that we observed. We were a very tight-knit family on that film.'

As for Liza, she might, of course, have been creating a monster for herself – a part which would become so closely identified with her that people would find it difficult imagining her in anything else. That would have been true had she not established that little niche beforehand – she was above all else a cabaret artist; a cabaret artist who had a nice handy line in acting. *Cabaret* would provide her with the opportunity for both.

It was, though, a risk. Every part for every performer is that – make-or-break time. With this, she was out on a limb, having to leave no doubt whatsoever that she was going to come out on top.

But perhaps she had an even greater aim. She had to get rid of Judy's shadow while still doing an act that could have looked as though she was trying to do just that. A shadow had to be cast off in the dark, however. It was never as easy or as simple as deciding she wanted to look different. By so deciding, she was inherently asking of herself a certain disloyalty to her mother's memory. Was it right to cast off the old so soon after her mother's passing? She had to weigh the dictates of her conscience with the needs of her own career. Perhaps Judy might not have approved, but she took the latter course. And this was her real triumph.

In her nightclub act, although there was so much that said, 'This is Liza Minnelli', she would remind people constantly of her mother. She loved to sing 'Mammy', Judy used to sing 'Swanee'. She threw one arm up as she raised her voice. So did Judy. Occasionally, she would go slightly off-key, Judy did it more often than she would admit.

There was also the conflict with the tastes of the audience. Was it wrong to give people what they wanted to hear – especially when you were doing so well at it? She liked to think that perhaps it was, yet she would play it safe. Her act was reminiscent of Judy's.

In addition, there was another factor – the sort of people who came to see her were the sort that Judy had had: the same middle-aged matrons and their husbands who really wanted nothing more than to hear her sing 'Over the Rainbow' – something that she would not do. There were also the homosexuals who adopted Judy as one of their own. Now, they were pouring out their love and devotion to her daughter. Liza knew that. Sometimes, she joked about it. But she didn't always understand it.

Why were they there? There was a sort of strength about her that didn't intimidate the way it would in a man. Liza was beautifully curvy in all the right places and was totally feminine, yet she didn't seem all soft and frilly the way other singers did. Clapping a more conventional woman cabaret artist who came on in long dresses and dripping in jewellery was tantamount to making love to her and that was an idea that turned a homosexual off completely. Liza, though, was different. Because she wore a bowler hat, because she could shout and give out with her numbers, she was the kind of woman many of them secretly wanted to be.

Couple that with her talent and you had a winning formula. She had her feet in several camps at the same time – if one could be forgiven the pun – and that, too, was a recipe for success.

Cabaret was an opportunity to cash in on all that, show her strength, her talents in both acting and nightclub performing and, at the same time, leave no one in any doubt that beneath her outrageous outfits beat the heart of a real woman. Do it right and *Cabaret* could not lose. It didn't.

Stephen Farber noted in the *New York Times* that the picture was ready to shock – as if the whole concept of a musical about pre-Nazi Germany wasn't a shock in itself. Mel Brooks's gag about *Springtime for Hitler* in his brilliant picture and Broadway show *The Producers* only told half of it. *Cabaret* was for real.

For Liza it was the kind of film other actresses – some huge stars among them – crave; the definitive rôle; the one for which they would always be remembered.

Human nature is not like that, but you knew that after seeing and hearing Liza in *Cabaret* (and it was a performance that invaded all the senses and was certainly both a visual and aural delight) she needn't do anything else again. Ever. That was itself creating something of a monster. But for the moment, it was one that others would have been grateful to have share their hours, both sleeping and awake. For Liza Minnelli, the rôle of Sally Bowles was everything she could have wished. As the young woman living a life of depravity in Berlin, she was not just brilliant, she was believable. Her short skirts, the suspendered stockings showing an expanse of thigh to make big strong men start salivating, the low cut dresses, an urchin hair cut, the big, wide, mascara'd eyes were all enticing. The voice was captivating. When Liza sang, the theatres rocked.

Liza couldn't get over how lucky she was to have got the part, particularly after *Junie Moon*. She hoped that it would stop people thinking of her as, so she said, 'a one-dimensional person. No one quite understands why I'm having such a good time – and they give false reasons, "Well she's cynical and she can step out of herself and see everything like it is", which I can do, but I don't very often. Or they make me so full of a need for love that it looks like I'm doing what I'm doing because I have to. It looks like I'm driven. People just don't understand that I go down there and I just have a blast. Maybe they don't want to know. People don't like it too much when you're happy. It's much more interesting when you're driven . . . by demons.'

Was that the Valium talking? At that time, Liza was taking it all for the way it was. There was no doubt, however, that *Cabaret* was the new film that everyone was talking about.

Mr Farber in his *New York Times* piece, wrote: 'At the start, Liza Minnelli's slightly awkward, self-conscious daring seems exactly right for the part. Her first cabaret number by contrast, is genuinely erotic and electrifying; through performance, Sally transforms herself and releases the sensuality that she's still toying with.'

Her performance was one of those rare things – the kind of appearance that made people sitting in front of a screen on which photographic images were projected feel as though they *had* to clap. Somehow, watching Liza Minnelli in *Cabaret*, it didn't seem silly or in the least bit embarrassing.

Liza won an Oscar for *Cabaret*. She was twenty-four. Rarely has an Academy Award been so universally welcomed – especially in this case, where she accepted the Award, saying that she knew it had come to Liza Minnelli and not to Judy Garland's daughter. It was a hard thing for her to say, but it both made sense and was absolutely true.

For what Liza had done was to play a part so outrageously that you knew Sally Bowles was the girl down the street who disappeared into oblivion but who everyone also knew would end up no good. She was the one who was always such fun at school, who did all the things your mother told you no decent girl ever did. She was the one who drank prairie oysters and ate caviar her boyfriends couldn't afford to pay for, but who was at heart so kind, so warm, so friendly, you know men would die for her and have a smile on their faces as they did so.

This was the character Liza created – almost as much as Sally Bowles created Liza Minnelli. A Liza Minnelli who no one now suggested was just Judy Garland's daughter.

Indeed, there was nothing about this rôle that was in the least like anything Judy Garland had ever done. She was no nearer to Esther Blodget in *A Star Is Born* than she was to Dorothy in *The Wizard of Oz*. True, something of the pathos that Judy created could be discerned. Sure, when she hit the high notes and 'gave out' in numbers like 'Money, Money, Money', it was possible to see a resemblance. But you'd have to think about it. There was nothing about her that made you think of anyone else – except perhaps Sally Bowles.

In her bowler hat in the nightclub scenes that seemed to encapsulate so much of the terrors of a city that was about to be bludgeoned by the storm troopers, she was magnificent. It was as though she were on stage at one of the smarter venues at which she had appeared in the last couple of years. It was live. That was why people felt they had to clap.

Joel Grey, who after creating the rôle of the cabaret MC in the original Broadway production, now had to work with a new leading lady, told me that was how he greeted Liza on the set. There was a magnetism about her. From a Broadway star who has about him a great deal of the magnetism of Jolson and George M. Cohan (whom he played in a Broadway show himself) that was some compliment. 'She was a wonder,' was how he put it to me.

'She was generous, very professional and a very funny person. She has a great sense of humour and an ability to find humour and laughter in all kinds of stuff and a great sense of humour about herself. There was a lot about her like the "Liza With a 'Z'" song. She was a wonder.'

That was precisely what she was. And it was a wonder how a still young girl could take charge to the extent that she did in what was only her third film. For with *Cabaret*, Liza Minnelli was herself now spoken of as one of the greats of the industry. She no longer had to sing other people's songs. If anyone now asked her to sing 'Over the Rainbow', they either just wanted to wallow in sentimental nostalgia or had reason to be ashamed of themselves.

Joel Grey told me of some of the problems of working in Germany. 'We just locked ourselves up at this stage and decided to shield ourselves from the outside world. We didn't want to see anyone. It wasn't comfortable being in Germany, but it had to happen there. It couldn't have been made anywhere else.'

The whole crew kept to themselves, in fact. There was a definite antipathy between them and the German film industry who tended to resent that they were there at all, let alone what they were doing with their interpretations fo their pre-Nazi country.

So *Cabaret* was an empire of its own, with Bob Fosse presiding from a throne that was his canvas-backed chair.

Liza knew that she had nothing to be ashamed of herself. She even allowed herself little indulgences, like mixing those large chocolate ice cream sodas. She had a sweet tooth, but if anyone questioned the wisdom of consuming such things, she replied defensively that it was a great cure for bad skin. If Liza had bad skin, no one noticed it.

In fact, she put so much into *Cabaret* that there was little room for anything else. Certainly, no private love affair was going to interrupt her work. There was nothing like that to compete with playing Sally Bowles. One man thought that he could be Sally's rival. Liza put him straight, trying not to hurt but without compromising.

Rex Kramer had been going out with her for a number of months. He was a guitarist and music arranger and looked, someone said, rather like a 'baby-faced Beatle'. He had accompanied her on a number of her nightclub engagements and, as one observer noted, they were like Siamese twins.

Bearing in mind her relationship with Peter, Rex cemented their arrangement with a pair of poodle pups called Lucy and Sophie which he had bought her, although without intending to supplant Ocho.

He sat at her side during the shows as a member of 'Fred's Wire-band'; as her arranger he had put together one of her albums. People said that it was now more than her music he was arranging for her.

She neither denied that this was so nor confirmed it. 'I only think of myself as an observer, a witness, not as a judge. Things happen that I don't understand. I do not judge. I only observe.'

Even so, he was trying to change the kind of thing she sang – to get her into a more 'rock' frame of mind. Off stage, they were still inseparable – although it was noted that Liza still wore her wedding ring on the third finger of the left hand.

People did speculate about that. Was it still Peter's or had Kramer given her his own ring? If he had, were they married or did she wear it for effect?

When you were in the public spotlight as Liza was now, such things were considered important. People wanted to know if Liza was married. She was not. But Kramer was – to someone else. So they were clearly not an 'item', as the journalists in America's popular Press liked to call it.

In Munich, they stayed together in the artists' quarter, Schwabing, where the swastikas on the wall were almost as intimidating as the ever-present Kramer.

They shielded themselves from their surroundings by playing poker and badminton. Other people working on the movie were using their spare time to 'do' the city, take in the historic buildings, the opera house or the countryside. To Liza it was all too redolent of the Nazi era. She wanted no part of it. Partly, of course, it had a lot to do with the film and her rôle in it. No part had ever had that effect on her. To be fair, she never felt herself a hooker, but the ambiance of it all struck home in every possible way.

For that reason, she was glad to have Rex Kramer around. But that feeling wouldn't last. It was while working on *Cabaret* in Germany that she told him it had to end.

Even if things had been different, it would probably not have worked out. Backgrounds did tell and the divergence between their two origins was tremendous. He came from rural beginnings – a farm in Smackover, Arkansas, where Liza had occasionally stayed with his grandparents – who called her 'Liza May', and which she described as 'terrific', but which one couldn't imagine to be more different from New York, Hollywood and London.

Liza May and Rex Kramer really weren't a likely combination and the more that she tried to insist how well they went together, the more those who thought they knew better... did know better.

He professed to hate living in the city, even though playing guitar in shows where Liza appeared meant he saw a number of them. He also was known to see a number of girls and that didn't suggest potential strength of marital harmony.

Liza, though, seemed infatuated. She even toyed with the idea of giving it all up and settling down on his farm. Peter Allen would say however, that he realised she couldn't have meant that when she told him on one of his visits to Ocho – they decided between them that he would always have visiting rights to the dog, while she retained custody – that the animal still lived on its diet of caviar and steak.

When it was all over and Liza moved on to other things, Kramer considered he had certain rights in that direction. She told him to leave Germany. When Kramer refused to do so, she said that she was in love with another – and fabricated a romance rather as she was able to weave words in her nightclub act, full of hand actions, wide looks of her eyes and cries of 'Terrific', 'Right?'.

She had worked that one out when Kramer said he would leave her only if she found someone else.

So Kramer left – and his wife Margaret sued Liza for alienation of her husband's affections. She alleged adultery, which her lawyers delicately termed 'criminal conversation'. She demanded $500,000 in compensation.

Liza's lawyers said they couldn't understand it. 'It's ridiculous they declared. 'There's been no wrong-doing on her part.' To which Kramer's wife countered with a further $50,000 demand for exemplary damages 'in violation of all the rules of society and good morals'. It was an unusual case and Mrs Kramer plainly had good lawyers. Liza confessed that she couldn't face the proceedings. It didn't come to court and after the matter had been settled, Liza confirmed that she had been used all along. Kramer had only gone into the romance, she suggested, because he intended to bring the suit at a convenient moment.

It was a difficult time for her, legally speaking. A few weeks later, Mrs Rose Stander, Liza's former wardrobe mistress, sued her for $27,500, charging that Ocho had bitten her while they were playing at the Deauville Hotel in Miami Beach. She said that, as a result of the bite, she was no longer able to do her job properly, and in particular, couldn't manage the seven-second costume changes she had to perform as a matter of course. The court awarded her $7,500.

That was only part of Liza's problems. The hours she worked, to say nothing of her lifestyle, were beginning to resemble Judy's, but she didn't learn any lessons from her mother. She couldn't sleep so she went for the same course of action that Judy had taken, new versions of the 'downers' that MGM had prescribed all those years before.

It would be many years before the folly of that would strike her. Kramer would claim later that that was one of the reasons he and she split up. He couldn't stand the temper tantrums that resulted from the moods in which she now found herself. The drug problem would get worse; her career would get better and better. Judy might have recognised that situation, too – except that Liza's career was even more successful; if only those comparisons didn't have to be made. Somehow, despite the success, she always felt she was being used.

Liza was being used in *Cabaret*, too. But, as Allied Artists knew when they signed the contract, it would be very much for their mutual benefit. They had a star who had a great opportunity and was in her own turn using it to further not just her own career, but a pretty good movie as well.

When all was said and done – and, as a further credit to the picture and its makers, it took a long time for all to be said and done – the great achievement of *Cabaret* was that Liza could make Sally live without having to identify with her – although she would claim that she did just that. There was nothing of Liza Minnelli in Sally Bowles. Certainly not nearly as much as there had been in Pookie Adams.

This was no ordinary musical – certainly it bore little resemblance to the old-style MGM musicals on which her father had been so important an influence.

'We're trying to show the dirt and the decadence and the perverse atmosphere of Berlin when the Nazis came to power.' And it showed a great deal of Sally Bowles; of her character as well as of her thighs and cleavage. If everything else had been the result of the writers and the director and cameraman, Sally was Liza's creation. She may have been told how to play her, but Liza was the one who had to put their work into practice. Sally was the perfect vehicle and Liza the ideal driver.

She would say of her screen self: 'Sally is a girl who improvises her whole life, and her fantasy of tomorrow is so strong she really can't take a good look at now.'

Well, that wasn't Liza. She had fantasies of tomorrow, but for all her success and the wealth that now attached itself to her, she had been brought up not to forget today. All that she had been responsible for when she was mother to her mother made sure of that. Sally Bowles, on hearing that her mother was seriously ill, would have simply kissed her on the forehead, told her she was a 'darling', offered her a prairie oyster and gone off to spend the night with a man.

She was to say that what attracted her most about Sally was that she was 'eternal'. As she said: 'That's what excited me. There will always be a Sally Bowles somewhere or other. I see her as a reflection of many tragic figures.' But then, as we know, Liza never considered herself or her mother to be tragic figures. Or did she?

She was afforded the real superstar treatment. There were cover stories in the two magazines that counted, *Time* and *Newsweek*. If she had ever doubted that she had arrived before, these were her ports of arrival.

'The real glory of Liza's performance in *Cabaret*,' said *Time*, 'is that it allows her for the first time in movies to do what she does best: a cabaret act. She is one of the finest nightclub performers in the world.' Not only that, she ought to have been investigated by the Justice Department for a flagrant breach of the Government's monopoly rules. 'She is a mini conglomerate,' said the magazine.

Newsweek, which captioned its cover 'A Star Is Born', couldn't help the comparisons. *Time*, too, who described her as 'The New Miss Show Business' at the side of a movie clip showing her wearing hotpants, stockings, black halter top and bowler hat, said that the similarity between mother and daughter was 'more than superficial'.

'*Cabaret*,' said the magazine, 'is a splendidly costumed, beautifully tawdry film, which balances musical comedy and movie drama with admirable vigour.' Not a little to do with this was the music by Liza's own By-Appointment songwriters Kander and Ebb who might have written it all specially for her.

Said *Time*: 'Moviegoers who remember knee-socked Liza as kookie Pookie Adams in *The Sterile Cuckoo* may do a double take as a voluptuous Liza steamily vamps her way through sultry song-and-dance numbers as Sally Bowles.'

The magazine approved of her 'black boots and haltered hotpants cut to the navel' when she appeared at the film's Kit Kat Klub.

Everything about the film was right. You couldn't argue with that. In fact, if you wanted to argue, you were arguing with success. The film was as much a box office as a critical triumph. Joel Grey was brilliant; so was everything else about it. It really did become one of those pictures that are held up as examples of the way movies should be made. It was made in late 1960s Germany, yet it was redolent of a different Germany in a different age. Liza Minnelli could have won an award as Miss 1970 personified, yet no one could think twice about how well she fitted into 1930s Berlin. It wasn't just that she looked a lot sexier than Marlene Deitrich did wearing a not too dissimilar get-up in *The Blue Angel*. In the nightclub scenes, in the rest of the film, in the street, in her apartment, she was like the directrix of a time machine that somehow managed to make her part of the time and the place. You loved her for being so voluptuous, so alluring, you hated her for being so stupid and for throwing away her life.

A few months before his death, Bob Fosse told me: 'I wanted to take the film out of the show format, which had less of Sally Bowles in it and included other characters which I thought extraneous. But the whole point about *Cabaret* was Sally and therefore to play Sally I had to have someone who was strong enough to dominate the picture, both during the cabaret scenes and outside them. Choosing Liza for this was a calculated decision. I knew she could do it. She did not let me down.'

She not only failed to let down the director; she boosted him and his picture. And she plugged it wherever she went. She didn't just coast once the picture was made. Instead, she went on a gruelling theatre and nightclub tour. She was outstanding at Los Angeles's famed outdoor theatre, the Greek. She sang 'Cabaret' as well as 'Liza With a "Z"' and voices in the audience called out, 'We love you Liza'. Then, she turned to 'Mr Bojangles'. There was something appropriate about that – she had a lot in common with the minstrel dancer Bill 'Bojangles' Robinson. Neither of them took their audiences for granted or looked for an easy way of getting across to them. They worked and it showed.

The sweat dripped off her forehead. She apologised to the audience – or rather, she explained: 'I can't help it,' she said. 'God made me a perspirer.' Of course, the people liked that. There was nothing perspiring about watching her, although it was good to see a performer work that hard. It gave people the impression that she cared enough about what she did for that to happen.

They were paying $700 for a table at the Riviera in Las Vegas in the late autumn of 1971 – and giving her a huge standing ovation at the end of the show. It seemed to be $700 well spent, even if most of it went to the head waiter.

She wore her usual outfits, designed specially for her by the house of Halston. No one complained, not least Liza who said they sometimes made her look a little like 'a female Fred Astaire'.

Newsweek said of a Liza performance at the Eden Roc Hotel at Miami Beach the week before the film opened in February 1972: 'She swayed, pranced and rocked in the spotlight like a shapely pressure cooker threatening to explode. She warbled, she bellowed, she ached and enticed with a quivering voice and a quivering body that work together like Nureyev and Fonteyn. Sweat flecked her plum-coloured gown and ran in glistening rivulets down her bare cleavage even before she was well into her gruelling hour-long act.'

The only people who ended up scratching their heads and ringing for their psychiatrists were the producers of the show. How *could* they have allowed Liza to have escaped Broadway? They then settled down and realised that perhaps having her twice would have been greedy.

No one was prouder of how it all turned out than her father. With all the comparisons with Judy and all the stories about her mother and the sympathy and the questions people asked her, too many of them forgot how strong an influence Vincente had been on Liza. Importantly, he was a steadying influence and he provided her with opportunities for happiness that she might not otherwise have had.

She may not have had Judy to call on now, but if *Cabaret* was a success he would have been the one to tell her. If it was a flop, he would have told her so – and why. He would have been sympathetic, but he would have explained why. It was knowing she had Vincente around that gave Liza not just her confidence and her comfort but also kept her in the business.

Now he did not tell her she was wrong. When he kissed her and said it was right, she knew it really was.

On the other hand, Liza could feel that pride and admiration, and missed her mother all the more – although, since Judy had two Academy Award nominations (for *A Star Is Born* and *Judgment at Nuremberg*) but never had an Oscar of her own to put on the family mantelpiece, she might well have been more envious than proud. The nearest Judy got to handling an Oscar in public was in the scene in *A Star Is Born* in which she accepts her Award, while her husband, the drunken Norman Maine (James Mason) causes uproar in the hall.

Judy would have behaved herself, but would she have quite enjoyed seeing Liza standing on the podium at the Academy Award ceremonies, accepting her little gold statuette? Probably not. Certainly not as much as her ex-husband, Liza's father. For him, it was the loveliest night of the year – and possibly of any year. There were tears rolling down Vincente's cheeks. In his own book he recalls the first time he saw the picture. 'It's one of a kind,' he told her. 'Truly one of a kind... and so are you.'

Despite all the plaudits and all the excitement, it was a difficult time for Liza. The studio's publicity department were milking it for all its worth – and a great deal that wasn't worth much, too. Stories started appearing in the newspapers to the effect that Liza's own bank balance wasn't benefiting from the movie, as everything she earned was going to pay off Judy's debts. It was not true.

There was also studio politics. Her rivals for the Award of Best Actress were Diana Ross for *Lady Sings The Blues*, the ice-cool Scandinavian beauty Liv Ullman for *The Emigrants* and Cicely Tyson for *Sounder*. All four girls were instructed by their various bosses to behave as though they were mortal enemies. When they met at business parties, they were meant to ignore each other. Asking Liza to ignore anyone is like suggesting that she spends ten minutes without talking. She treated the instruction with the contempt she believed it thoroughly deserved.

She had failed to get the Award the last time out – so very recently, when one considers how many top stars spend lifetimes trying to win an Oscar – and had played the studio game all along; she hadn't campaigned the way other stars did, but she did all the necessary publicity appearances, said the right things at what seemed to be the right places and took advice. Now, though, she only wanted to win on her own merits. She also knew that if she couldn't get it for *Cabaret*, she ought never to get one. She left the established practices for the awards night itself.

Liza wore a stunning yellow gown for the occasion at the Los Angeles Music Center. Her father noted that it was his favourite colour. It was an eventful evening – the night Marlon Brando told the Academy what it could do with his award for *The Godfather* and got a young pretty American Indian girl to say so for the benefit of her cause and the cameras.

The only mild shock from Liza that went through the audience at the Music Center was when she insisted that the Award was hers for herself and not because of her parentage.

Nothing, however, could blunt either Liza's excitement or the complete approval of ninety-nine per cent of the audience when Gene Hackman announced the result.

The movie itself failed to win the Best Picture Award, but there were Oscars, too, for Bob Fosse and Joel Grey as well as for the musical director Ralph Burns and the cameraman Geoffrey Unsworth.

Liza was swept up in the madness of it all, not least of which was the posing for photographs. 'Then you pose by yourself. Then you pose with Joel Grey, then you pose with your dad, then you pose with your dad and Joel Grey...'

Later she asked Vincente how he felt. 'Never take me to one of those things again,' he told her. 'I will never go through that again. I feel like I've been through World War Three.'

There was one more photograph for which Liza had to pose – with Desi Arnaz Jnr. He was her new fiancé.

Chapter Fourteen

DESI NEVER really looked right for Liza, although she firmly believed that he certainly looked right *with* her. His background wasn't all that different from hers. If there were a special blood group for people from show business families, both of them would have belonged to it.

It was both a great and a tough time for her. As she once said: 'My childhood was abridged and kinda delayed. I didn't get into the swing of childhood until I was in my twenties.'

Now she was the swinging child at last. And she was behaving in a swinging, childish way. There had been trouble in New York that she couldn't have predicted. She found that her advisers had not paid her credit cards. Her electricity was cut off because the bill hadn't been paid. 'I was so distraught,' she said, 'that I went off to Cartiers and bought a watch.'

So Desi seemed to offer her the comfort she needed. He was good fun and he enabled her to forget her problems. Like Liza's, both his parents were stars. Like Liza's, his mother was the bigger star, although – again like Liza's – his father was eminent in his own field, which was closely related. And like Liza's, Desi's parents were divorced.

His mother was Lucille Ball, a one-time top film comedienne who, nevertheless, only really came into her own on television. *I Love Lucy*, in the early years of television sitcoms, was one of those programmes around which families planned their lives. It wasn't just a block to social engagements; meal times were arranged on the schedules of Lucy transmissions. Business deals were postponed because the executives wanted to see how Lucy's husband's tough boss managed to get round the zany illogical logic of the red-head who made Gracie Allen seem like a college professor.

His father was Lucy's screen husband as well as her real spouse.

Desi Arnaz was mainly a band leader, but with *I Love Lucy* he found a new career for himself – not least of which was partnering Lucille in the Desilu company, a TV and film production outfit that became so successful it was to buy the old RKO studio lot. Such was their success and such was the atmosphere in which Desi Junior was raised. Liza recognised every childhood story he told her.

She also realised that he was unhappy about his relations with his mother. Lucy thought he was going off the rails, especially in his love life. A child had been born to one of the young actresses with whom he had an affair.

When he met Liza, he was eighteen. She was twenty-four. He was doing well in films himself, but she was the bigger star, a star so big that her biggest problem was fencing with the studios who kept foisting scripts on her, 'rotten scripts' that they shoved down her throat, because they were convinced she was going to burn herself out before long and wanted to get her in their clutches before it was too late. That wasn't Desi's problem, but he wanted Liza just as badly.

In the end, their age difference would tell. So, too, would Liza's huge success which, again, was beyond the reach of her fiancé. But once more, she was saying that she loved him and once more nothing was going to stop them setting up home together – happily ever after.

Lucy was not going to stop that. She welcomed the prospect of Liza joining the family like any other mother would when faced with the prospect of a highly eligible girl entering her son's life. She not only found Liza a good catch, she enjoyed her sense of humour, admired the way she looked and dressed and could catch the resemblance to her mother, whom she had known and admired, although she was much older herself.

She also knew that she couldn't dismiss that easily a girl who had just won an Oscar, had had a nomination a year before and was earning $60,000 a week in cabaret. Not only that, but the British and French were as much in love with Liza as were the Americans. That was precisely the sort of girl every mother-in-law-to-be wanted for her son.

It was going to be a marriage of dynasties. But more important than that, it was going to be a marriage that Lucy could talk about at the clubs and society soirées she patronised. One would have imagined that a star of dimensions so huge wouldn't worry about that sort of thing. But she did. To her, it was as important as the noughts on the cheques she received. She didn't need the kudos any more than she needed the money, but the prestige was important. It reflected on her herself. It showed that she was still an important person who was courted by others.

Liza may have been sought by her son, but Lucy made it seem that this bright, successful star of a new age was paying her homage.

Liza Minnelli was a catch – if only because it was a relief for Lucy to have a young woman to whom she could talk, a funny, articulate, intelligent woman who would discuss politics. If in the middle of a sentence about Richard Nixon she suddenly started talking about Fred Astaire, well, that was part of her charm. Charm and intelligence. It was a winning combination for Lucy. So, it was, of course, to Lucy's son. This was going to be the catch of catches.

There was, however, that one great problem – of Desi and his mother not being exactly on the best of terms. Now there was a new rôle for the prospective daughter-in-law to fulfil.

Even more significant was the fact that Liza had wanted to patch things up between Desi and his mother. She said that there had been enough dramas in her life without seeking any more in a second marriage. Lucille Ball appreciated that. It showed a degree of maturity in Liza which she respected. If she couldn't put Desi on the right track no one could.

It really seemed that she achieved just that. Friends in the older Hollywood set were exceedingly impressed at how the two women got on together. When they smiled in public for the photographers, they really did seem to mean it – which was no ordinary achievement. The one way in which actors and actresses could betray the fact that they were only acting was in their smiles. Somehow you could tell when it was, in fact, just an act. These smiles, though, seemed real. The ladies liked each other.

Maybe they wouldn't have done so, if Liza hadn't been doing so well. She was enjoying her freedom – because, as she said, she had never had any before.

It was going to augur well for Liza's future and that of her fiancé. And nothing was going to spoil it in any way at all. Certainly, not drugs. Liza said that she never used them – words that would be eaten eventually when she admitted that this was a lie – and that she only drank moderately. (Dean Martin used to joke that he kept a crate of 'Moderately' in his dressing room, but Liza was not being flippant.)

On the other hand, she had done so well playing Sally Bowles, that it was proving more difficult than ever to convince people that she *wasn't* Sally Bowles.

People saw her in the street and expected to see her raise her skirt high enough to reveal those luscious thighs and the suspenders that kept up her stockings. If they saw her in bars, they knew that if she weren't drinking prairie oysters, she would be choosing something else that was equally divine and had just a touch of wickedness about it.

Someone put out the story that every day, Liza downed a bottle of Grand Marnier, a liqueur to which, according to the cognoscenti, she was known to be not a little partial.

'A bottle of Grand Marnier!' gasped Liza when the matter was put to her with the seriousness of a question about her views on the Hollywood studio system. 'Are you *crazed*?' Part of the image of Liza-Sally Bowles-Minnelli was of the girl who would invent her own vocabulary. It seemed to sit well on questions like this.

'I don't even enjoy drinking. Oh, I may have one on occasion...' And, she assured Guy Flatley in *The New York Times*, she didn't mean one whole bottle. (It was part of her status that writers from important newspapers could joke with her like that. You couldn't do so with youngsters who have either failed to make the grade or who were on the way up – it seemed superciliously patronising – and if you did it to an older, more established performer, it would be rude and would indicate that the only way that person was going was down.)

Like many another young woman, she was attracted to drinks that came in pretty colours and had 'silly' names. But she didn't really like their taste. Neither was she in the least bit attracted to the hard stuff. But she did enjoy wine – and before long, she was drinking a lot of it.

Not that she thought it had any effect on her. She was the strong one. There was no need to worry about drinking wine. It never made her drunk. It made her feel good and she liked the taste. But have any adverse effect? That was silly. Certainly, not the way she drank it. If people thought she was drinking excessively, that was silly, too.

Liza concluded that she was 'disappointing' to people who wanted to read about her. They were hoping for scandals and couldn't find anything to say about her. So the Press made it all up. Well, other stars had been subjected to that sort of treatment and did not like it any more than Liza did now.

She was staying at the Plaza Hotel in New York. That should have impressed people. They didn't like scandals at the Plaza, and didn't usually get them.

'I must be truly boring to people who are looking for the dirt. Probably, if I suddenly decided to run stark naked down the street, screaming at the top of my lungs, they'd say, "See, we told you about her."'

People were telling other people about Liza Minelli, but what they were saying more often than not was how much they admired what she was doing.

She wasn't sure now that she would make another big film for some time. But to a lot of the public and to the less reputable newspapers, she was still Sally Bowles.

One of the papers suggested that she was involved in the sexual exploits of a group of Brazilian transvestite dancers. 'That stinks,' said Liza. 'In the first place, the dancers are gay... too ridiculous. They were a great group of dancers, an adorable bunch of people and they weren't doing enough business in Paris. So I said, "Look, why don't you use me? Give a special show and invite me and we'll get a whole bunch of Press people to come and it'll generate some excitement for you." Their show was terrific. It wasn't a drag show, really. They weren't transvestites. I mean a lot of the guys dressed crazy. They were sort of saying, "We're not men, we're not women, we're people." So I helped some terrific artists and the Press turns it into Liza's having an affair with Brazilian transvestites.'

She was going to live for herself now. When she came back from Germany and when she knew that *Cabaret* was going to be a hit, she decided to celebrate – by having her New York apartment redecorated.

Decorator Richard Orbach decided he had to plan a place suitable for a woman who never sat still – one who would rather cook spaghetti than send for room service, was the way he put it – so he gave it all a temporary, easy-to-live-in look. In one room, a couch was shaped like a pair of 'hot lips' in a colour described as 'vibrant lipstick'. A piano stood under a canopy, given pride of place in the centre of the room like a dining table. That was a tribute to *Cabaret* and in case she wanted to have any cabarets at home. In another room, everything was made of basketwear. It seemed suitable for someone who had experienced the fragility of life. That had been the principal lesson from her mother. She wasn't going to forget any of it. Or at least, that was what she was saying. In fact, she was moving into drugs in a way that the experience of her mother, to say nothing of the others involved in what laughingly was called the 'culture', should have told her was not just stupid, but downright dangerous.

Like the others, she thought it didn't matter, that she could get away with it. After all, she was so strong and drinking hadn't ever affected her. As she was to say: 'After a night on the town drinking, I was always the one left standing. I could drive everybody home and still be ready for more.'

She didn't take her pills for fun. She did it to keep her going when she was feeling a little fragile or unsettled – and sometimes, particularly when things were going hard with Peter or if she worried more than usual about her act, she felt a lot like that. Tranquillisers really did . . . tranquillise. But other people had found there were difficulties in that. And like the others she found it was draining her life.

It had all started with the Valium at Judy's funeral. Before long, she was addicted, although she would claim she didn't know it. After all, she had grown up with pills around her, not just the uppers and downers that Judy had been given at MGM, but the sleeping pills she took as though it were some part of a religious ritual.

She wasn't into barbiturates and she had always hated smoking pot or the idea of taking LSD, or any of the others. As she said, she was the survivor. What she was taking now just didn't matter – and they had 'nice sounding names' like Librium and Dalmane, to say nothing of Valium itself. If she wanted to go into drug taking, she wouldn't have confined herself to pills – pills with names that were chosen to make it easier for people to use them.

Liza was to tell *People* magazine: 'You think that if you're smart and lucky you won't get dependent. But luck and brains have nothing to do with it. You're dealing with chemicals that are baffling, cunning and powerful. You can get dependent.'

When she thought she was getting too dependent on the Valium, that was when she moved over to Librium. She was in the process of kidding herself and that was as dangerous as the tablets she was pouring down her throat. But at this stage, she was taking things as they came. There was nothing but highs for her now.

Vincente was happiest of all about this. He was finally going to direct a film starring his daughter. It would be a movie version of the novel *Film of Memory* in which a chamber maid gets to know a great deal about life from her employer, an Italian countess. It was the start of a four-year battle to get the project – and the opportunity for father and daughter to work together – off the ground. Meetings were held, Vincente and Liza talked about it and statements were published in the trade Press. But for the moment it didn't happen. And for the moment, Liza wasn't disturbed. She had her other work. 'You've got to go step by step each time. And if it works, that's thrilling. Anything that comes out of a negative energy thought – "I'll show them" – that's as far as you can go... This is a business built on sheer fantasy. To open yourself up to delight is dealing with emotions that this business isn't there to give you.'

Her second TV special, *Liza With a 'Z'*, was now being nominated for an Emmy. It was one of those times when she felt she had a lot for which to be grateful. Life was still good and looked like remaining that way for quite some time. And she had her Desi.

What she had not yet asked herself was why she had Desi. There she was with what a later generation would have called her 'toyboy'. The answer is easier to understand now with the passage of time than it was then. She was still chasing her missing adolescence. With an eighteen-year-old on her arm she had a young man who wouldn't try to dominate her and would allow her to fit almost naturally into his world. There were no cares, no responsibilities when around him.

She had business managers and agents and gofers to organise her working life. Desi was fun – the kind of fun she should have had when *she* was nineteen, a time when the sweat was pouring off her brow as she pushed harder than ever with that best foot forward.

Not that that was the way she wanted people to think of him – as young and irresponsible – and she did care what people thought of him; she was old enough to know that public reaction to someone like her was very important indeed. 'Desi is older than the calendar shows,' she said. 'He understands the need for calmness the way I do.'

That in itself was news. Calmness was the thing one would have thought Liza knew very little about. As for the need for it, that only seemed evident every time she pushed some Valium down her throat.

But Desi had a 'steadiness' that she considered very important. 'I hate abrupt changes of emotion and I can't live in that kind of atmosphere.

'He's so understanding. He really has a much greater understanding of people than anyone I've ever met except, perhaps, a psychiatrist or a psychologist.'

It was a typical Hollywood arrangement. They were living together – at Lucille Ball's house. 'Lucy's a genius. I adore her. Wherever I am, she calls me up to see if I'm taking care of myself. For Desi's sake, especially, I'm glad I moved in with her. I thought it was stupid of him to be paying rent for an apartment when he's making movies all over the globe.' (He was making *Billy Two Hats* with Gregory Peck in Israel.) Liza continued to live at Lucy's house.

Would they get married? At first she had said that they would, that it was just a matter of time. Later, they contented themselves with what the romantic novellas used to call a 'marriage in the eyes of God'. They went to bed together and they wore each other's wedding rings – a symbol of their 'bond of union and understanding'.

'I believe in grabbing at happiness,' Liza said. 'If you have to pay later for a decision you've made, that's all right. That, too, is part of living. But at least you can't say you didn't get a chance. It's the immediacy of something that appeals to me.'

When they went together to Puerto Rico in 1972, there were rumours that they had, in fact, got married. The story was published in newspapers on the island and almost immediately flew across to the mainland and everywhere else that professed interest in Liza Minnelli.

In fact, Liza was now saying she wasn't sure she wanted to marry anyone at all. 'I don't want any really serious love affair in my life right now. I put so much of myself into my rôle in *Cabaret*. I believe it will not only change my career, but perhaps the direction of my life.'

That could not have pleased Desi very much. She was still living with him. But that statement was the beginning of marching orders.

But there were other 'family' problems for her. The relationship between Liza and her younger sister was always problematic, but Lorna has been willing to admit that there were moments of kindness from her. The year was 1972 and Lorna was performing at the fashionable Palmer House in Chicago. The highlight of the tour was the night that Liza came to cheer her from a table in the audience (at which I was also present – along with four men Lorna described as 'gorillas' and who looked as if they had just stepped out of a frame of *The Godfather*).

This seemed to be a new Liza Minnelli, a much tougher one than people had known before. She wasn't allowing anyone to talk about Judy now and, to her credit, few were. She was there on her own looking tough. 'But my toughness is there only when I need it.'

She seemed to need it most when love got complicated and then she adopted the old philosophy of regarding the best form of defence as being a solid attack.

Desi said they were getting married. Liza said they were not – not yet, anyway.

Chapter Fifteen

THE AFFAIR between Liza and Desi was not that different from a Hollywood publicity campaign – a huge boost for a production which, several months later, turns out not to have been made yet. Yes, it will happen, the PR boys say, but not quite yet. 'We'll keep you informed.'

For the moment that was the best anyone could hope for. Desi would have loved to have fixed it all up. Liza wasn't sure – even though they shared Lucy's home and when he was in New York, Desi lived with her in her apartment.

He was making quite a name for himself now, too. He was starring in a film being made in Japan called *Marco* as well as having second billing in the Gregory Peck movie.

Liza had wanted him to share billing with her in a TV special, but Lucy vetoed it. She thought it might harm his movie career, his star status. But there was no question of their affair coming to an end, she said.

Things weren't going so well for Liza. A planned picture, *I Never Promised You a Rose Garden*, was left on the shelf and Liza didn't fancy the same fate for herself.

So when would there be a wedding? That was the question Liza was constantly asked – and for which she had a constant answer: 'You'll know when you get your invitation.' That ranked fairly close to telling her mother she'd come to her next wedding.

Yes, she insisted, there would be a wedding before long. After all, Desi was 'the swellest', which sounded a little like a song from the 1930s. But then when you were Liza Minnelli you could make up your own vocabulary with impunity.

After all, she was winning awards as quickly as she could find new work, and there was never any shortage of that, even if it wasn't always the right film. She was the winner of the Best Actress Award from BAFTA, the British Film and Television Academy, the nearest thing to Britain's own Oscar.

Desi, for one, wasn't in any doubt. He had been linked with older women since he was fourteen, he said. His baby son was proof of his knowledge of the world. But Liza was so different. He knew from the moment he had first knocked on her Las Vegas dressing room and introduced himself that she was the one – and it would be for keeps. As late as March 25, 1973, Liza was saying much the same thing.

'Meeting Desi,' she said, 'has changed my life.' He had given her the impetus to carry on with a tough lifestyle.

'You'd like Desi if you knew him,' she would tell friends who went to her New York apartment and could see his photograph on the piano close to one that said, 'For Liza, with my love as always – Lucy'.

Somehow, Liza gave the impression of caring as much about Desi's mother as her young fiancé himself.

As she said: '[Lucy] is a genius of humour who can affect people on their own level without condescension. For a while, our generation seemed to lack humour, but it's coming back.'

More than that, there was so much in common between them all. A Los Angeles doctor was boasting about having assisted at only three births in his career – Judy Garland's, Liza Minnelli's and Desi's. It took a little believing, but it seemed important to Liza.

'We complete the circle,' said Desi. 'Liza is one half of the circle, I am the other.'

On the other hand, Liza could see the complications and the anxieties.

She also found the need to defend him both for himself and for her relationship with a youngster whose reputation about town was one which would not make him seem terribly eligible to most prospective mothers-in-law – which was precisely why Lucille Ball was so happy to have Liza in the fold.

As Liza said: 'I was expecting someone completely different when I met him. After all, I'm like everybody else. I had read the same stuff in the fan magazines, trying to make him seem like the gay blade of the town because of the lack of enough teenage idols. He's been through a lot of crap and problems. But when we met, more than a year and a half ago in Las Vegas, I thought, "Hey. Wait a minute, he's nothing like I've heard. He's so nice. He's so sensitive and so kind."'

He was intelligent, too. 'He's taught me how to deal with this business of being a movie star. He knows the meaning of attention paid to famous parents and he has helped me to handle that with some kind of perception, not to be bugged and to insist on what I want for myself.'

That was Liza Minnelli talking in her now customary articulate, intelligent way – except that one couldn't help wondering if she knew what she did want for herself.

The answers that she sometimes gave acquaintances or told reporters were not the real ones that she felt. Very often, she didn't feel like saying 'Terrific! ' But she said it just the same. She didn't want anyone to suspect that occasionally everything wasn't quite as terrific as she said.

When she really felt that she could talk to a woman who a day before had been a total stranger, she would give a warning: 'Don't let people take advantage of you.' It could have been Judy talking.

She was basically so insecure that she would go into a cold sweat when she contemplated her future, no matter how successful it seemed to outsiders or those who just read the rave reviews of her concerts. She suffered from palpitations. Her hands went cold. She didn't conceive that the real cause might be the drugs she was shoving down her throat like a stoker pushing coal into an old steam engine. She only knew the fact about her that was her secret. She worried. Sometimes, she worried that she was about to die of a heart attack, that the body was so vulnerable, that one shove and she'd be taken to the morgue. Thereafter, she had to fight it. So she would get up and dance. Corpses couldn't dance, could they?

She knew the difficulties she was facing without having the answers. 'I didn't set out to be Girl of the Year. That's not what I want to do. It's terrific. But if you think of it only that way, there is a futility. There are 365 days to a year and everything you do is different and what you build for the future is the answer.' What she didn't understand was how to put that theory into practice. And Desi quite clearly couldn't help her.

Her success in *Cabaret* had plainly made her think about herself, but the conclusions were, to say the least, confusing. Success had taken her into different circles, more mature than those she had faced on any large scale up till now. *Cabaret* had made her a film star as well as an entertainer. Did she want to be a film star *per se* or did she intend to devote her career to the live performances to which she was so perfectly suited?

For all she was saying, Desi plainly wasn't able to help her resolve those difficulties. But then nobody could. She didn't know her own mind. When she did know it, the old story was repeated. The romance was off. For good? No one could say.

In fact, all that Liza would say was 'Things are a bit rocky for Desi and me at the moment. I don't want to say any more now. I shall have to speak to some people first.' At the same time, the old stories of affairs with other men were circulating. One of those was Charles Aznavour who told me at the time: 'Maybe there is, maybe there isn't.' And then he explained: 'It is the same as I had with Piaf – not exactly love, but then not friendship either. Very much more than that.'

She wondered about the effects that marriage had had on her parents, not so much on Judy but on her father – and here again the perhaps greater influence of Vincente Minnelli came into play. Judy had, she believed, caused much of her own downfall. Vincente had been badly used by his first three wives. 'What he's been through in his three marriages! He spoiled rotten every woman he's ever been married to. And they left him. And I watched it happen, watched women taking advantage of him.'

When she asked him why he gave them everything they wanted, he replied: 'I thought that's what women were for.' Liza wasn't going to be that sort of woman and if the only way of guaranteeing it was not marrying again, so be it.

So the best thing to do was to concentrate on that blossoming career of hers – the kind that got NBC to postpone *Bonanza* to make way for her special, *Liza With a 'Z'*. (They hadn't done that with her mother.) By now, she liked television a lot more than she once had.

'In television, they're always drying you off. They're always patting you with towels and powdering you and combing your hair. You know the way I work, hair matted, sweat pouring off me, make-up running. I've always thought television was a medium that could get a person and show him real and whole. Well, that's the real me. That's what I've always wanted them to let me do on television.' And that was what that show was all about. To be allowed to do her own kind of show was stardom, too. The National Association of Theater Owners thought so, and was why they awarded her the title of 'Star of the Year' in 1972. It was also why CBS named her 'Entertainer of the Year' (on the same programme, Lorna Luft was named 'Rising Star of the Year'. Both girls wore identical halter-neck dresses.) The Golden Key Foundation of the Reiss-Davis Child Care Center in Los Angeles held a party in aid of their funds and said it was all in honour of Liza. The only problem was that they didn't give her enough notice of the date and when she was invited, she was out of Los Angeles recording. So Vincente took his daughter Tina along and apologised on Liza's behalf. Because she was a big star, everyone understood.

At Harvard, the Hasty Pudding Club – the most prestigious of all the university's organisations – decided in 1973 to name her Woman of the Year, following such illustrious names as Mamie Eisenhower, Jane Fonda and Dionne Warwick.

It was greeted as warmly as the nomination of Jack Lemmon who had been at Harvard, and head of the club himself, as Man of the Year. Showbusiness cleaned up. Whenever that happened there was a peculiar sense of satisfaction for its practitioners to be included in such a list.

She arrived, wearing a black trouser suit, with Desi on her arm. In Liza's honour, the students blew up 1,000 helium-filled balloons and released them over the campus. The Harvard Band came out to play for her and she was swamped with flowers.

It gave her an opportunity to reflect on her own education and its weaknesses. 'College is a wonderful slice of life, but somehow I just never was in the right country,' she said. 'I've hardly ever been to school.' As an old girl of some twenty schools, she was speaking qualitatively rather than quantitatively.

When she appeared on the Ten Best-Dressed-Women's list, for her Halston creations, that was because of her stardom, too. Stars collected honours and citations every time they left their front doors, but there were other honours that were bestowed simply in recognition of their talent. And that was why she went on stage at the London Palladium for that year's Royal Variety Performance. Honours in her kind of show business didn't come very much higher.

She always seemed happier in London than in most places, although the British audiences hadn't yet discovered how to handle her. Was it such a crime to always think of her in terms of Judy Garland's daughter? They were fighting words, but her loyal London fans weren't anxious to scrap, so they cheered and Liza had to hope they were cheering her for her own sake.

Not that it was difficult to adjust to life in the British capital. She still had fond memories of the city and there was much about it that appealed. She found, in any case, that every girl there looked just like she did.

Meanwhile, Andy Warhol asked her to assess her best features. She said: 'My eyes and my legs. People love my tits, but I'm always trying to hide them . . . they are coming back into style.'

She wrote a letter for his magazine *Interview*, and they printed it exactly the way she wrote it, complete with self caricatures and ink blobs. When the phone rang in the midst of writing the opus – which was not the sort of thing that would have interested *Private Eye* – she scribbled, 'That fucking phone.'

She found Bob Fosse 'sexy' – and then explained: 'Anyone who is intelligent and creative is sexy. But, of course, it all depends.' It was nevertheless an interesting assessment.

Cabaret, of course, had whetted her appetite still further for more films. Still, the good scripts and accepted movie ideas were not that easy to find. She wanted more than ever now to do the Zelda Fitzgerald story – with Vincente, but he wasn't able yet to even get *Film of Memory* underway. And she was still talking about Joan of Arc – whom she considered as kooky as Sally Bowles. In fact, she had formalised her feelings on St Joan now.

'I want to do it my way. I think she had a big chip on her shoulder, but my concept of her is that she had total belief in her belief. She was a cuckoo, but a good cuckoo.' Not enough of her devoted fans in France heard that to be offended at her assessment of the country's principal heroine.

As she said: 'I think I pick the roles I do because I believe that no matter how crummy a thing is, there are people who come through. The interesting time is when they stumble but get up.'

People occasionally stumbled and got up when they spotted her out in public. But by 1973, Liza could deal with that a lot better than she had been able to in her early days; the times when, even when she hadn't wanted to, she sounded just a little too puffed up for her Paris-made high-heel shoes.

She went shopping in the supermarkets of New York and Los Angeles or, occasionally, the towns and cities where she was playing. It was not only a convenient place in which to buy her groceries, it also taught her a certain amount of sociology. 'It's the great equaliser. You're just women on common ground in them. Oh, sometimes ladies do point and come up and say hello. Nice.'

She was also finding out which supermarkets had the cheapest goods. Surprising, but that was important to her, too. As she got to the check-out one day, there was a delay over the price of a box of paper towels. The cashier didn't know how much they cost. 'Thirty-nine cents,' said Liza. 'They went up.' She could afford to be honest.

Dinner party guests at this time would see the result of her shopping even if they didn't get to use the paper towels. 'I cook a mean roast,' she said. No staff to do it for her – or to open the door to the people who would be sharing that roast. When she was hostess, she believed in showing she did it all herself.

After the roast had been digested. and the after-dinner mints consumed along with the coffee, Liza would then be the entertainer all the guests had known her to be. The piano would come into its own and Liza Minnelli was in her private cabaret again. She gave out and she sweated every bit as hard as she did at the Empire Room in Las Vegas.

She enjoyed her holidays, too. With no romantic attachments, her affair with Desi having finally petered out, she went to Paris – and then realised she didn't know anybody. In fact, when she arrived at Orly Airport, she could only think of one hotel, the Plaza-Athenée, so it was there that she asked a taxi driver to take her. When they arrived, she demanded to see the manager.

She was given the best in the house – Liza Minnelli was the kind of guest the hotel wanted to foster. Ensconced in the suite and with the porters tipped, she sat on the sofa – and wondered what the hell she was going to do. As she had first thought, she didn't know anyone in Paris.

So she phoned Kay Thompson in New York. Kay gave her some advice:

'Go instantly out into the street – and shout, "Paris, you are beautiful – and so am I".'

That was precisely what she did. The doorman wondered a little about the crazy American woman who he had just seen enter and register, but it cleared Liza's lungs for her. She was happy – and felt free. Paris was thereafter there to be enjoyed.

And how she did enjoy it! Marisa Berenson was in Paris, too. She was of French extraction and as a granddaughter of Schiaperelli knew everyone.

Marisa, who had played the supporting rôle of the Jewish girl in *Cabaret*, suggested taking Liza along to a party at the Rothschilds' – on the Riviera. So she went. It was just like anyone else's beach house, she said – which might or might not have pleased Baron Guy. The Baron invited her to have a drink.

'Well,' she said, 'I wouldn't mind trying the home brew.' She was referring to the produce of his vineyards and the château that went with them, but Baron Guy de Rothschild didn't appear to take offence. In fact, he introduced her to all the right people. Which gave Liza second thoughts. Everyone was dressed in the most elegant styles she had ever seen. And there was she, she would say, looking like Punk City. That really didn't worry her until she was given another introduction to the Baron Alexis de Rede. He asked her out. Liza said yes, but she had to attend to one or two things first.

What she had to attend to principally was her wardrobe. Well, that was not all that difficult. After all, everyone who was anyone went to Paris to have their clothes made. Liza, though, flew straight back to the United States.

In New York, she demanded an urgent meeting with Halston, told him her problem, that she needed a few little things for the races, for visits to the casino, for parties and receptions . . . just little occasions like that.

Halston supplied the items as though he were responding to a demand from MGM for the following day's shooting – and Liza flew straight back to France, her excess baggage bill bulging as much as the suitcases.

The Baron was at the airport at Deauville to meet her. It was one of the times of her life. 'Just good friends,' Liza protested and then showed everyone she knew the little diamond ring he had given her. 'Regardez, darling,' she said.

If she left with the ring, she left with the clothes, too – and no ties. The Baron wasn't anxious to make Liza a baroness and she wasn't totally convinced she wanted to be one either. The air of freedom was still fairly heady for her and she wasn't totally anxious to give it all up. Even for her own château.

They were all, for goodness sake, just people. As she said, when she was a child she didn't believe that the Queen peed. Now she knew that she did. And so did baronesses.

If there were things that really upset her, it was still the Judy Garland legacy. She hated her mother's last husband Mickey Deans and everything he said made her run for the Valium bottle. Deans claimed he had eliminated forty years of pain for Garland. 'That's just bull,' said Liza and she was hurt to have to say anything. But it couldn't rule her life.

It had to be more important for her to go on stage to the sound of 'Cabaret' as her signature tune and then give out with 'Liza With a "Z"' before settling down to 'Maybe This Time'.

Maybe this *was* the time – that she would find her real love. In May 1973, she was back in London. Officially, she was there for a concert at the Royal Festival Hall. Unofficially, she had a date with another man called Peter.

Chapter Sixteen

IT WAS ONE of those infatuations that seemed to indicate more than anything else that at twenty-seven Liza Minnelli was emotionally immature. A much older man had fallen in love with her and suddenly the world, if not a cabaret, was certainly a carousel in which she wanted to spin round and round without having to get off.

There also had to be the suspicion that after the end of her longish affair with Desi and the realisation that there was no permanent future with the Baron, she was desperately seeking a new love; someone who was important enough to tell the world that he loved her, too, and have the world interested. There was one.

The man in her life now was Peter Sellers, who had graduated from stand-up comedian at London's 'We Never Closed' Windmill Theatre, through a radio impressionist's act, to the *Goon Show*, to Ealing comedy films and eventually to what was not lightly called superstardom. He would later become internationally famous for the *Pink Panther* films in which he played the inept Inspector Clouseau and his penultimate picture, *Being There* – the film with Shirley MacLaine for which he received an Oscar nomination, although no Award – finally confirmed him as an outstanding actor.

Sellers' friends and business associates first became aware of his infatuation with Liza when they sat with him at her Festival Hall concert. He was taking pictures of the performance, quite illegally, of course, but when you are Peter Sellers you can do anything.

The way he reacted to her act – telling everyone who would listen that she was a wonderful artist – revealed all.

As for Liza, Peter Sellers was at this moment a combination of lover and father figure. He was everything that the French Baron had been. He was also very funny, very intelligent – those Clouseau

accents and the thousand other voices he had recorded didn't come
out of thin air – and in the business. As we have seen, to Liza that
was all very sexy. He was also twenty years older than she was. After
years of being with younger men, it felt good for her to be able to
metaphorically snuggle up to an older, protective person. It didn't
matter that he was now in the midst of his third marriage – it had
only begun three years earlier and was destined to end a year
afterwards – or that he had a record of severe heart problems which
would eventually kill him.

She told herself that she needed someone like Sellers. The fact
that she also found him sexy was a bonus.

He was making a picture called *Soft Beds and Hard Battles* at
Shepperton Studios. The morning after the Festival Hall concert,
she was with him in his dressing room – at 6.30 in the morning.

John Boulting, the movie's producer, told Alexander Walker for
his masterly biography of Sellers that he was worried about the
effects of the affair on the actor. He was up half the night at Tramp,
the nightclub, managed perhaps one or two hours' sleep, and then
had to be in make-up at six. It was telling on his performance and a
not very good film was being made much worse.

Liza was saying to people that she considered Sellers to be a
genius; while Sellers, according to Boulting, was saying: 'At last I've
found the sort of woman who will come and take care of me.'

Marriage, both said, was only a matter of time – and he took her
to see his first wife Anne Levy, which was roughly equivalent of a
prospective bride being escorted to his doting mother. On the other
hand, his current wife Miranda Quarry said: 'I know nothing about
Peter and Liza Minnelli. It's really none of my business.' She and
Sellers were planning an amicable divorce.

(Britt Ekland, the second Mrs Sellers, was suitably bitchy. 'He
must have used one of his disguises on her,' she said.)

Together, they went to the memorial service for Sir Noel Coward
who had died shortly before. They were mobbed by both fans and
the world's Press at the Savoy Hotel, where Liza was staying. They
were seen all over London together that May of 1973, walking hand
in hand, Liza in a trouser suit, Peter wearing a cardigan over a sports
shirt and slacks. They were found sitting on the grass in the park.

'I fell in love with this man and I am pleased to say he is in love
with me,' said Liza. 'I am really terrifically happy.' They went to cosy
West End restaurants. At one, they got up and gave an impromptu

duet. Peter was saying they had known each other for a long time. Liza didn't see any need to lie. 'But I've been an admirer of his for years.'

Now, once she had completed a professional engagement in Chicago, she was going to also complete their marriage plans. They would live in London.

He had a pet name for her: 'Flash' – which he had inscribed on a mini tape recorder he gave her.

'I associate with everything Miss Minnelli says,' replied Peter less than enigmatically. 'We both believe in humour and having good times. We haven't found anything we disagree on yet.'

Together, they were seen cooing like teenagers in love. Always, they seemed to be laughing. Then one day, it was obvious that everything wasn't so perfect. Liza moved out of Peter's Belgravia house and set up at the Savoy, where her father also had a suite. He was in London on a private visit, but now found himself acting as his daughter's spokesman.

'The house was just too small,' he said, trying to explain the reason for Liza's change of address.

The Press wouldn't let her alone. A knock on the door from 'Room Service' usually meant a reporter was there. They dogged her wherever she went. 'Look,' she said as though talking through her 'Flash' recorder, 'I fell in love with a lovely man. Now will you please go away.' So perhaps this was not a woman scorned. If it were, hell's fury was a lot worse than hers.

Peter, meanwhile, was in the midst of a ten-day break. Boulting had allowed him to try to catch up with his biological clock and with his own intentions. Peter left Liza's suite looking distinctly uncomfortable. Somehow, Liza managed to escape. She was next seen leaving Sellers' home. A little later, she was spotted in tears. It was the end of the affair.

She rushed back, still weeping, to the Savoy and Vincente's suite. She stayed with him until he caught his plane to Los Angeles. Originally, she had said she would go with him, but when the time came for them to leave, Liza decided she couldn't face up to all the airport formalities which would have to be conducted under the gaze of reporters. The thought of walking through the long corridor leading from the departure lounge – even from the one set aside for VIPs – to the plane with photographers racing after her and blocking her way was more than she could face.

She decided to take a house in London. She thought she could do so quietly and secretly. But that said little for her knowledge of Fleet Street. The Press found and hounded her. Liza, however, was trying not to admit it. When a reporter asked her what was going to happen, she snapped, 'That's bloody private.'

It really wasn't. Both she and Peter had seemed to enjoy being seen in each other's arms. Besides anything else, it was good publicity – two attractive figures in the business of letting people know they were still attractive and virile. It had lasted a month.

Later, she admitted: 'Yes, it's over. I have no regrets.' Someone asked her if she remembered what their last words to each other had been. She said, 'I guess it was "Goodbye".'

She was much less happy than that flippant reposte indicated. No doubt about it: she was looking for love and couldn't find it. Sellers was in a line of glamorous showbiz lovers. As we have seen, Desi Arnaz was in that line up. Before long, Martin Scorsese would join it. But none of them lasted or offered any kind of real satisfaction.

The one person who seemed happy about the break-up was Desi, who was not accepting that his engagement – which was the way he looked upon it – had already ended.

'Something seems to have gone sour,' was all he had been prepared to say about his relationship with Liza when she was in London. But then he added: 'There's no way I want to take her back.' Now, though, it looked as if he would be doing just that.

The 'souring' got sweeter when Liza was back in the States. Desi had dinner with her at Vincente's home and then followed her to Lake Tahoe, Nevada, where she was appearing at a night club. But the reconcilliation was short.

What Liza still needed, it seemed, was a confidante, someone on whom she could depend. Once more, she turned to Kay Thompson, who became Liza's personal manager. It was a job she had held once before – to Judy. 'Mama knew what she was doing when she made you my godmother,' said Liza giving Kay a suitably warm and large hug.

And there was still a lot of career to manage. In the autumn of 1973, she flew out to entertain the troops in Israel in the midst of the Yom Kippur War. Entertaining troops had been one gap in the Liza Minnelli career – but it was an important audience and those who had gone out to play to soldiers in previous conflicts regarded it as an experience not to be forgotten. She wasn't Jewish, but this, she decided, was her war.

There were more peaceful battles for her, too. A few months earlier, Liza saw her TV show *Liza With a 'Z'* get the Emmy most watchers of the scene had predicted. She herself, though, did not get an award. After the *Cabaret* Oscar and everything else, it didn't matter that much to her.

The response she got at the Winter Garden on Broadway in January 1974, however, did matter – a great deal. She got $300,000 for her three weeks at the theatre and the management considered it was worth it. She made more money there than any other entertainer ever brought in. Liza said she felt sick every time she saw an empty seat in one of her theatres. She certainly didn't see any at the Winter Garden, one of the loveliest theatres on Broadway, which Al Jolson used to regard as his own 'house'. Now it was going to be Liza's – in a show in which she really didn't need to do any of her routines. Like Jolson – and like the younger Judy Garland – she could have recited 'Little Miss Muffet' and still had the audience eating out of her palm.

The theatre marquee had just one huge word scrawled in rough script on a vast white background – 'Liza'. Next to it was an outline of a silhouette that was instantly recognisable.

Her show had a limited run of twenty-four performances and they were all sold out within thirty-six hours of the box-office opening. It had never happened before. The *New York Times* said that it was generating 'the kind of electricity in this energy-starved theatre season [this was the legacy of the Yom Kippur War, an energy crisis worse than anything the world had experienced since 1945] that can't be provided by all the oil of Araby.'

Mayor Abe Beame of New York came to the opening night and so did the Secretary of State, Henry Kissinger.

She even got down on one knee and sang 'Mammy'. That hadn't been done there since Jolson did it. He would have regarded it as *chutzpah*. The audiences thought it was delightful. The similarities between the great old star of the past and the great young one of the present were not lost on the audience, a sprinkling of whom had seen the original artist performing that same number and could attest to the fact that the amount of applause in 1974 was not too different from that heard there forty-five years earlier.

She sang the title song from *Cabaret*, naturally enough, and 'I Can See Clearly Now', and there was a French medley with lyrics in English supplied by Fred Ebb. But a great deal of the repertoire was from the 'Mammy' era, with songs like 'Shine On, Harvest Moon' and 'Bye Bye Blackbird'.

This wasn't just a variety performance. That's why it had a title – *Liza* – and was directed by Bob Fosse. It was written, of course, by Ebb and John Kander, and Marvin Hamlisch was musical director. Those were formidable ingredients and Liza shook them up in the anticipated manner. Columbia recorded a cast album and that sold about as many as anyone would have expected, which meant in the hundreds of thousands.

Clive Barnes in the *New York Times* loved it. 'Stay longer next time and then even the management will spell your name right on the tickets.' The Shubert Organisation had spelled Liza's surname with only one 'n' on the tickets, which worried Mr Barnes more than it did Liza.

The show was not totally successful, however. In the song and dance numbers, Liza mimed her own pre-recorded voice, a technique fairly common at the time. But some members of the audience felt more than a little cheated as a result.

The New York *Daily News* concluded that it wasn't as great as it might have been, although Douglas Watt's assessment was based on Liza's reputation and was the kind of review that would have satisfied many another artist.

'Winning though she is,' he wrote, 'Miss Minnelli's turn palls long before it is over as the carefully manufactured aura of triumph becomes cloying. She is brimming with health, energy and enthusiasm and she is undeniably talented. Now all she needs is a little fresh air.'

Flowers also need fresh air, but the stage of the Winter Garden was swamped with them at the end of the show. It was an appropriate reception for a woman who was feminine if nothing else – despite the number of homosexuals in her audience.

There were flowers a few months later, too. Liza won her second Tony for the show.

It was the time when women were burning bras and when Jane Fonda was still pleading the cause of women's lib, if in a more restrained way than at the height of the Vietnam War. Liza didn't see any need for a campaign for the cause.

'It's fabulous to be a woman. If women realised that they were women, they'd be liberated already. Ladies were made to have men bring flowers to them and all that kind of stuff. Like having your hand kissed. It's terrific.' That was something that might have struck home to the *Los Angeles Times* who reported about the Winter Garden to its readers 2,500 miles away that Liza was so good that her theme song ought now to be 'Liza With a "T"' – for Terrific.

Liza felt happy enough with it all to celebrate her opening night with a party in the Rainbow Room in the Rockefeller Center, at which she turned up wearing a man's white suit and black shirt, white tie and wide fedora hat. In September 1974, the *Daily News* was a lot kinder than last time. In fact, it found a lot to be pleased about when her show transferred to Carnegie Hall. 'These nights, she's putting on her own act with a show that manages to combine humour, good spirits and intelligence, excellent musical values and a tasteful selection of songs, a good book and a well-constructed programme that showed off her considerable talents to great advantage.'

So she had found her fresh air. And she was planning to get that fresh air with a new film. *Film of Memory* was now going to be called *Carmela* and was being written by Frederic Raphael. Vincente was directing, as before.

'It's very exciting to me,' she said. 'It's like a little girl's dream. I've watched him direct since the age of four.' But this film would be put off, too.

In the meantime, Liza was having other problems of her own. She was having trouble with her weight. Those who called her '*La petite Piaf Americaine*' because of her resemblance to the French singing 'sparrow' would now have to reconsider it because the sparrow was getting fatter.

Liza's solution to the problem was the worst she could have chosen. She started taking diet pills. They then began swilling around her system along with the Valium and the other downers and sleeping pills and the variations on the theme that was taking over more and more of her life.

That being so, her body was becoming increasingly tolerant of the drugs. She no longer needed to worry about how much she could take – or so she thought. She was taking more and more pills and the more she took, the more she thought that she could take.

She was convinced she was strong enough to resist everything everyone said about drug taking.

Later she would say: 'All the time I was telling myself, "See Liza, you're not dependent on Valium. You just quit."' Now she was kidding herself she could quit taking the diet pills and the various cocktails that came with them. 'You fool yourself for years. I sure did.'

Was her problem simply one of insecurity? Her stepfather Sid Luft always believed it was. 'There was now a real lack of real men in her life.'

One of the things that Liza would have to accept was that things were changing for her. She and Desi had had another row and this time, things really were over between them. She might have wondered about her career in similar terms.

In show business you were as good as your last show and Liza's last show had been stupendous, despite what the *Daily News* said.

But for all the success of *Cabaret* people were beginning to ask, 'So what have you done recently?' They were not lining up to give her new *Cabarets*. The only cabarets were the sort she was making an art form all of her own at the Winter Garden and on tour. She really wanted to be able to expand. Once having starred in four media at the same time, it was natural to want to do it again – and keep on doing it. Yet films were not growing o any sort of trees, especially since *Carmela* was hardly blossoming yet.

She had, however, had an opportunity of getting across once more to the much wider movie audiences. MGM was making a splendid tribute to the days when musicals were a way of life, full of luscious extracts from the studio's catalogue called – what else? – *That's Entertainment.*

It was a glorious movie monument to Judy as well as a tribute to people like Fred Astaire, Gene Kelly and all the others who made singing and dancing seem no more difficult than lining up for a bus. Liza introduced one of the film's sections.

She also introduced herself to the film's producer. Although they had known each other for years, this was an opportunity to be closer than ever before. His name was Jack Haley Jnr.

This was a distinct connection with her past. In *Wizard of Oz*, the Tin Man had been played by Jack Haley. Now Liza was being escorted everywhere by his son. She and Jack Haley Jnr really were that celebrated 'item'.

Chapter Seventeen

WHAT NO ONE seemed to realise was that, for all the love affairs, the engagements, the romances, Liza was still married. After she and Desi had split up, she was being squired around town by Edward Albert Jnr and there was considerable talk that they would be married before long.

That worried Liza's friends – she was flitting around too much. That and the exhausting work schedule she had established for herself were having an effect on her that wasn't exactly healthy. Couple that state of affairs with her drug taking and Liza was on the way to being sick. Add to that all the mental strain revolving around the fact that neither she nor Peter Allen had got round to the tiresome formality of organising an official divorce, and the complications looked distinctly unhealthy. It didn't seem to matter to either of them. However, by early 1974, it became more important. Liza had moved into the West Los Angeles hill-top home of Jack Haley Jnr. Haley and she had known each other since early childhood, but they first met professionally when he directed the 1973 Academy Awards show. He wanted Liza to do a spectacular number that she wasn't at all sure about.

Most of her friends had advised her that she was getting 'overexposed' – in the strictly professional sense – and shouldn't do it. So Haley flew to Las Vegas, where Liza was appearing, inveigled himself into her dressing room and after forty minutes of persuasion in the locked room, she agreed to do the spectacular.

Their own personal relationship became equally spectacular after that. Before long, she was living with him.

'I found out what a hell of a bachelor he was,' she said. 'I had some very jealous ladies to deal with. They came out of the woodwork and they were all mad at me. Jack tried to warn me, but he wasn't always around to deal with it.'

He was equally unsure of her. He had heard about her various romances and wasn't clear how he fitted in.

To Josephine Bell in *Good Housekeeping* magazine, Liza told how they both discovered they fitted in. They were having dinner when Jack looked at her and said, 'This is it, isn't it?'

In July 1974, they told everyone else what 'it' meant – when Liza announced that she was marrying Jack Haley Jnr, twelve years her senior and as active in the movie business as anyone in Hollywood.

Peter seems to have been the one to have spurred things along. 'I only know what I read in the paper,' he said. But once having read it, he put matters right. As he said: 'When you've been separated longer than you were married, it's time to get a divorce.'

If Peter did not know, he was far from alone. Both Liza and Haley had kept their romance very quiet indeed. The experience of being in the public eye everywhere she went with both Desi and Peter Sellers had taught her an essential lesson. If she really believed it was none of anyone else's business, she had her part to perform – to keep things to themselves.

They had worked together on *That's Entertainment* and had found out that they had more in common than merely wanting to pay homage to Judy Garland and the image of MGM and the great musicals those letters represented.

Mickey Rudin, Liza's lawyer, was instructed to organise the divorce as soon as he possibly could. That was in June 1974.

Liza had an engagement ring made up of a five-carat diamond surrounded by a cluster of emeralds that caused almost as much excitement as that which had been given by Richard Burton to Elizabeth Taylor. Hollywood wiseacres suggested that it symbolised the love Judy had had for Jack senior.

Liza meanwhile took off for a six-week trip to Europe, taking in Paris, Venice and then Leningrad and Moscow. Her 'escort' was Kay Thompson who said she was going mainly to buy caviar and a pair of boots.

Perhaps it was more of a testing trip than anything else – to see whether Liza still felt the same way about Jack. They spoke on the phone every day and the prospective bride returned saying that she had no doubts that this was for real.

Even so, she was constantly reading about other romances of hers that never were – with Bob Fosse, with Marvin Hamlisch, and with a score of men whom she only had to meet once to have their names linked in the newspapers.

By September it had all been settled. Liza and Jack decided they *did* still care. On September 15, the two were married – a stage, as more than one paper was pressured to remark, on the Yellow Brick Road to Romance.

The wedding ceremony was up to everybody's romantic standards at a little Presbyterian church by the sea at Montecto, not far from Beverly Hills society's favourite weekend watering hole, Santa Barbara.

Appropriately, Liza arrived late – an hour late. But Haley, who had never been married before, still cradled her head next to his shoulder after the ceremony, which was attended only by nine guests, their closest family and friends.

Jack gave her a diamond-studded bracelet on which was inscribed the legend: 'I offer you all my worldly goods, my name and my heart.'

The ceremony lasted twelve minutes.

Liza's Halston creation was a cardigan trouser suit. It was in yellow – which was not just Vincente's favourite colour, but the one which Liza had now decided was what she wore on all important occasions. It brought her luck at the Oscar ceremony – more luck than at her previous outing to an Academy Awards evening – and so she hoped for the same magic for her marriage. The guests then went on to a party at Haley's father's house.

For a small private party at Vincente's garden the night of the wedding, she wore silk, a jersey caftan – in yellow, too.

Later, there was a party jointly hosted by Vincente and Sammy Davis Jnr and his wife. It was at Ciro's, just about the most fashionable Hollywood nightspot in the 1940s and 1950s and the proprietors were grateful for the refurbishing of their image. Lorna helped with her strapless black velvet dress and the train that went with it. Some 1,400 people who were not invited, including every photographer and reporter for miles around, turned up to see the proceedings.

Those who did have invitations included Fred Astaire, Gene Kelly, Jack Benny – on about his last outing; he died three months later – Rita Hayworth, Shirley MacLaine and Elizabeth Taylor who came on from a David Bowie concert.

Liza looked happy if slightly bewildered. Jack Haley was smiling so widely you almost couldn't see his beard. Partly, one suspects, because he and Liza had kept the whole thing so quiet. People who considered themselves to be among their most intimate friends professed to have heard nothing of it before they met at the Santa Monica courthouse to collect their licence.

Was this Oz? People wondered if Liza was still looking for something unattainable, without any corny references to that rainbow. They had spotted a new Liza trait – every conversation with her tended to end these days with, 'Do you love me? Do you really love me?' Had she now left all that behind?

Indeed, Liza – suitably gowned by Halston – wore a pair of slippers that were specially modelled on the ones her mother had worn in *The Wizard of Oz*. Sammy Davis asked her what she was giving Haley for his wedding present. 'A tin suit,' she said.

If Liza protested, as naturally she did, that this was no ordinary romance then, in her terms at least, she was right. Haley was too solid and steady a person for it to be an infatuation in the Peter Sellers' class. He was more mature and intelligent than Desi Arnaz. And, truth be told, he was very much more successful than Peter Allen had ever been.

This added up to the sort of man for whom Liza had been looking, a husband on whom she could depend, not one who was given an inferiority complex every time they spoke, let alone when they made love. She needed a man to be in charge of her life. She had done her women's lib thing too long ago.

She was to say about him: 'I'm married to the most wonderful man, totally male and always has been. Jack is very big – he's like a corner I can hide in.' That statement to *McCalls* magazine's Barbara Grizzuti Harrison was off the cuff, but it said more than most prepared quotes ever could.

On the other hand, she did sometimes wonder about the rôle of women in this world and she confessed that in a girls-together aside to the same writer. 'Women get old, they lose their beauty and then they're nothing, they're thrown out on to the streets for garbage. Poets and statesmen are revered when they get old, but a woman?'

So this was a woman who worried about the future – and the what might have been. 'I'd have been dead a long time ago if I hadn't been a self-preserver. You have to say when it's enough. *Basta!* It's hard getting through life, but you've gotta, you just can't cave in. You've gotta keep going – you can't give way to despair.'

Both she and Jack were busy telling everyone this was for keeps.

Vincente was planning to get married himself. His fiancée Lee Anderson was almost as ecstatic about her prospective step-daughter's marriage as about her own. She decided that Jack was a stabilising influence on Liza and that just about said it.

Others, however, enjoyed a filling diet of sour grapes; for instance, Lucille Ball. Nothing was heard of Desi, but his mother said: 'Liza does have a knack for altering her affections. I could probably make a pretty accurate guess as to the month, the day, and the hour she grows tired of this marriage to Jack. The only thing I wonder is how she will work her way out of this involvement. I'm sure that should be no problem for her, however. She does have a knack of working her way out of involvements, you know.'

Lucy's picture was summarily removed from Liza's piano.

Desi was rung up by his former fiancée and asked to attend the ceremony. He declined. Sammy Davis rang Lucy and then called at her house to ask her to come. 'I told him thanks. But I thought I'd just as soon pass.' It was hardly surprising. Lucie Arnaz, Desi's sister, did come – and told everyone how much Liza and her brother still loved each other. 'They're better friends than they've ever been.' Not many others came to that conclusion.

Meanwhile, Jack and Liza each had their work to get on with – Jack to produce another movie, Liza to do a TV special – *Liza In Love From A to Z* in which she co-starred with her old 'friend', Charles Aznavour.

Then there was a new film for her called *Lucky Lady*. She seemed to be that all right. More lucky certainly than she would be with the film, which was based on the premise that she and a couple of shady characters were busy smuggling illegal hooch into the USA from Mexico during prohibition. Liza would have to wear a wig for the film in which, the world was told, she was expected to co-star with Paul Newman. It was to be another one of those Watch-This-Space situations – after all no one had been saying anything recently about the picture which was going to be called *Carmela*.

She went to Europe for a series of one-night concerts and came back into Jack's arms, telling him how much she had missed him. She really had.

There were those who doubted that and Liza doubted their feelings for her. 'People don't want me to be good or happy,' she decided. 'They want me to be interesting.'

Well, interesting she was. Liza tried to find more time to think

about other things. She was changing, people noted. She now lived
not in Beverly Hills, but in a large house in West Los Angeles –
close to Jack's work – and the girl who had said such unkind things
about the artificiality of California was now spouting about her
dislike for the 'plastic people of New York'. That did, however, fit
into the Liza pattern of being off with the old, on with the new and
very happy to be so.

And yet there was also a chip on Liza's shoulder. Sometimes,
journalists had to ask questions that emanated from people's illusions;
the kind of things said about her before. They gave her opportunities to
deny them. She would have been more upset had they not done so.
However, sometimes when the going got tough, so did Liza.

One interviewer was very soundly rounded upon. 'Look, I'm
sorry I'm not a nut, but I'm not – so do you want to drop the story?'
The writer decided that she did not.

But was Liza being a nut in accepting the screen roles that she did
accept – not those that were being pushed down her throat like a
force-feeding tube, but the ones she accepted? While *Carmela* wasn't
getting off the ground, *Lucky Lady* was. She probably would have
been more sensible to have passed that by, too, and concentrated on
her night club and concert appearances.

At the end of 1974, the theatrical group the Masquers gave Liza
their 'George Spelvin Award' in the presence of people like George
Burns, Jack Haley Snr and Vincente.

It sounded grander than it was. George Spelvin is the name given
in American theatre programmes to actors playing more than one
role. The first they act under their own name, the second under that
of the mythical Mr Spelvin.

Much of the proceedings were enlivened by all sorts of terrible
things being said about people considered big enough to take it. The
fact that Liza was selected proved that at last she was not just a star
but indeed a superstar.

Tony Franciosa said: 'When I watch Liza on the stage I get an
incredible feeling for the human being she's able to portray through
her performance.'

Liza herself said: 'I should like to thank everybody on the dais for
saying nice things about me, funny things about me . . . anything. I
don't know what superstar means. But it's terrific to be called one.
I'm thrilled. I'm honoured and I can't say anything else. Thank you
for having us.'

Then a strange thing happened – strange, that is, for a girl who was now generally accepted to be a top, top star, although had she been just another hopeful, it would surely have been regarded as a great opportunity.

She took over another star's part, knowing it was for a limited run. The *42nd Street* story was being reversed. The star was becoming the understudy.

In August 1975, she opened at New York's 46th Street Theater in *Chicago*, not another one-woman show, but a book show and she was only a replacement in the rôle of Roxie Hart.

Gwen Verdon, her old friend, had to have a throat operation, and she was taking her place for five weeks. In a way, it was typecasting – the whore with the heart of gold yet again. Only this time, there were Chicago gangsters, trials – and great opportunities to do her thing. The part could have been written for her because she could have played it from the beginning and made it all her own.

As it was, for five weeks, New Yorkers were able to see Liza Minnelli in her first 'book show' since *Flora, The Red Menace*. And this time, the only real menace was the urgent hope among some of the people in the audience that if she didn't start singing 'Money, Money, Money', she might at least do an encore of 'Liza With a "Z"'.

In the old days, Jolson would have totally thrown away the book, gone to the front of the stage and said, 'Do you want me or do you want them?' He would have given everybody else the night off and sung his own songs until daylight.

There were indeed those who would have enjoyed seeing Liza do just that. She had the strength and the command of the people who paid to sit in the 46th Street Theater's stalls and balconies to do so.

But that would have made it a personality cult production and it wouldn't have been fair. Since she saw the show as still Miss Verdon's and because she was simply doing her a big favour by appearing, she played by most of the rules. Not a single one of her own songs was allowed to intrude even after the curtain dropped.

Because she wasn't the first in the show and because she was only there for five weeks, she asked that her name not be put on the marquee. Her wishes were respected – and, instead, a five-foot high billboard was installed in the lobby saying that the part of Roxie would be taken by Liza 'for this performance'. Replacement or not, the show was hers. She was in control and although she sweated as much as ever and bit her finger nails, she never looked anything else.

There were those who wondered whether Liza would want to take over permanently. It wasn't something discussed in late-night meetings between hard-bitten, cigar-chewing producers and equally inflexible agents. This was one star helping out another on a personal basis, showing the highly acceptable face of show business by those who could afford to be magnanimous – a situation which should not be minimised; many stars who can afford generosity frequently don't show it.

It was, generally speaking, an appreciated thing to do. Most of the people who walked the streets of Broadway realised that she was doing the theatre industry more of a favour than they were doing her. She wasn't altogether perfect in the part despite the fact that it could have been made for her, like a new pair of kid gloves. She couldn't have been expected to learn the part in six days – although she would say that that gave her no problems – and then play it only for five weeks as though she had been handed a new and highly original *Cabaret*. But she acquitted herself well and the people who counted realised that fact.

Earl Wilson noted that Liza had done 'the classy thing again', but Liza thought nothing of it. As she later said: 'People sing on other people's records and in night clubs, people step in for others. Someone gets sick or hurt, there's always someone willing to fill in for them. Gwen Verdon has always been a good friend of mine and when she got sick, it seemed like the right thing to do. And I'm glad that I did. So were the audience who again piled the stage high with flowers.'

She only had five days of rehearsal and two numbers were changed so that Liza's singing would take precedence over her dancing – she considered that Gwen Verdon was a better dancer than she was. 'My Own Best Friend' was a duet with co-star Chita Rivera in the Verdon show. Because Liza's voice was considered the stronger, she had it all to herself. 'Me and My Baby' was changed to give the singer the song.

Naturally all tickets were sold.

Officially, the critics weren't invited to Liza's opening, but they came just the same. Martin Gottfried wrote in the *New York Post*:

'Certainly on the Chicago stage, she is outperformed by her co-stars Jerry Orbach and Chita Rivera, a couple of out-and-out theatre professionals. The irony is that Minnelli has the magnetism of the true star and no audience will mistake it . . . Minnelli's star presence distracts one from the dazzle, letting one's attention fall on some peculiar goings on in the show's head . . . On the other hand, I don't imagine that anyone will much care if they've come particularly to see Minnelli.'

Liza may have hoped there would be a similar reception for a new film. But there wasn't one in sight. In fact, there was never any guarantee that she would find another movie like *Cabaret* but she was so good in her one-woman show wherever it was performed that it could be assumed that any of those performances was worth the price of the entrance ticket and of the usually indifferent meal that went with it. Liza's great success was that she could battle with the smoking, the raucous laughter of customers who had had too much to drink, and the sound of knives and forks rattling and plates crashing. There was never any such certainty when going to see a Liza Minnelli film. There weren't many of them – which was precisely why it might have been better if she were even more choosy.

Lucky Lady wasn't lucky for her at all, even though it was directed by Stanley Donen, one of the few men Hollywood legend said could never do any wrong.

Paul Newman was sensible enough to turn down the lead after all, and the male stars instead were Gene Hackman and Burt Reynolds. It turned into one of the biggest bombs of all time.

Liza's red wig didn't help. Stanley Donen was doing all he could to emphasise that this was not another *Cabaret* and needed to demonstrate it from the beginning, before people realised there would be no music. He should have been so lucky, for if it wasn't a Lucky Lady he had as his co-star, certainly he wasn't a Lucky Director.

It was as if the hairstyle change symbolised the wrong approach. Liza was as wrong for the film as the film was wrong for her. The final scene of the picture was shot twice at huge expense – when it was realised that people wouldn't accept an unhappy ending. Originally, the stars were blown up along with their boat and its contraband cargo.

It was a pity for Liza, who at last felt secure and was now in a situation in her life when people no longer wondered whether what she did was the kind of thing her mother would have done herself.

The interesting thing was that while working on the set of *Lucky*

Lady, Liza was not in the least bit unwilling to talk about her mother, sometimes initiating the conversation so that she could bring the talk round to Judy Garland, even when her fellow performers had no intention of raising what they thought would be a ticklish question.

She was as sociable a person while working in a studio or on location as she was at one of her own parties or any of the other soirées in Hollywood which she attended because she enjoyed them – unlike most people who were there simply to be seen.

There was still the little-girl simplicity about her some of the time and a great deal of the charm that was appreciated above all by the lesser players working with her.

One of those who enjoyed the experience was the actress Jacqueline Hyde.

'I found her really warm and appealing and radiating niceness.'

The charm was obvious, and it was appreciated. It couldn't have been otherwise when the big star said to an actress who wasn't yet in her class: 'I know who you are. I know your credits. Thank you for being here with us.' That made one feel good.

'I liked her instantly,' said Jacqueline.

But nevertheless, she told me she detected a 'tremulous quality' about Liza. Her drug taking was not something spoken about on the lot although she joined seemingly everyone else in sniffing coke when the work of the day was finished and they gathered either at her home or someone else's to unwind. Said Jacqueline Hyde: 'She was up, hyper, always.'

The film was shot at Guaymas in Mexico and Liza had a bungalow where she would give parties at the slightest hint that someone felt like having a good time – and since nothing ever did happen in this dead spot in the Gulf of California most people were looking for the slightest opportunity for just that. Jack would come down most weekends with a can of film, which he would show on a hastily-erected bedsheet, because there was no TV in the place.

Liza was good on these occasions. She never hesitated to ask Jacqueline Hyde to come, too, and that was appreciated as well.

The parties would usually last all night, particularly if there were a late start to filming. She believed in dressing casually, like wearing a T-shirt on the back of which she had scrawled: 'Liza's back.'

When Jack came to Mexico, Liza could be seen snuggling up to him when she wasn't dancing. Lorna was the date of Burt Reynolds.

Actually, Jacqueline Hyde noticed a difference in Liza when her new husband was around. 'She was much more pulled together. When Jack left, she reverted to being wild.

'I was convinced that she needed someone around her to keep her in check. A sort of father figure.' Jack was undoubtedly that for her. And Liza didn't need to talk about her mother when he was around. When he wasn't, she talked about Judy incessantly. Perhaps that was because she was now on the hard stuff.

When she sniffed more coke, she talked ever more openly about her past. A 'line' of cocaine would be set up on a tray on the floor and the people there would gather round it, taking what they wanted.

Some of the people there wondered about that. It *was* difficult to understand how the lessons of Judy and drugs had not struck home with her. As Jacqueline Hyde said:

'She never appeared to be totally stoned, it just made her that much more hyper and ready to talk. More Liza than anything else!'

It was, inevitably, the stories of Judy that the other members of the *Lucky Lady* crew most wanted to hear. She told them that Judy was a great mother – in the support she gave her children; and a lousy mother – who succumbed to her various neuroses.

She stayed up all night telling those stories, talking about the times they sneaked out of hotels with five layers of clothing on because they couldn't pay the bills and then she talked about her promise to be at Judy's 'next' wedding.

Liza talked about other people in her family. The one person to whom she did not refer was Sid Luft. 'I was surprised at that because I knew how long he was part of her life,' said Miss Hyde. 'It was as though he didn't exist.'

Keeping other people up all night seemed to demonstrate Liza's need to be surrounded by people. She couldn't manage her life alone, even for short periods. Spending an evening without company was her idea of hell. There was an emptiness about it that she couldn't tolerate. There was still a lack of security in this top star; probably the insecurity of wondering how long she would be that top star.

There was also the need to be loved, not just by her public but by the people she worked with, the make-up artists, the man who did her hair.

And always hyped up, except when Jack was there. 'He was a calming influence that plainly made her more dignified,' was how

Jacqueline Hyde put it. 'And I remember sensing that this was a marriage that was not going to last. He was a clever businessman, not without humour – after having a virtually inedible airline meal, he could tell the stewardess, "My compliments to the chef" – but he wasn't an artist in the sense that he had a personality that soared.'

Jack Haley was a calming influence, but one that induced a situation that was unnatural for Liza.

Probably the whole state of marriage was unnatural for Liza. She needed that father figure, that steadying influence but at the same time she needed the independence, the freedom to be able to go off the rails and snort coke when the mood got her. For the moment, however, they seemed crazily in love.

Sufficiently in love to weather the storm of *Lucky Lady* – she was so seasick during its production that tongues began wagging with the obvious surmise that Liza was pregnant. It was seasickness not morning sickness, she told her friends – and gave the impression that she really didn't care that much. The critics, however, did.

Pauline Kael, whose *New Yorker* pieces were always among the most perceptive, said about the picture: 'They're all rum-runners in the early '30s and they're meant to be adorable. This is a big expensive movie for people who don't mind being treated like hicks; the audience is expected to shudder with delight every time it hears an obscenity or sees a big movie star grin.'

They might have felt slightly better with the original ending.

The following year, *Carmela* finally got under way – except that the picture which had started out as *The Film of Memory* was going to be titled *Nina*. When filming finally started it was *A Matter of Time*.

The picture was so bad that Vincente Minnelli later disowned it. Producers Jack H. Skirball and J. Edmund Grainger cut it without his approval and what was intended to be a gesture of love from father to daughter turned out to be a huge disappointment.

Liza, for her part, did her best to make sure that everything went as it should for such a momentous moment in the Minnellis' lives. Filming was done in Italy and Liza decorated her dressing room with pictures of herself and her father together on film sets since the time she would be carried on and allowed to 'ooh' and 'aah' at the pretty dresses worn by Cyd Charisse and the others.

It was an obvious moment in which Liza could say how closely she and her father felt. 'He always listened to me,' she would tell people gathering around in that room, wanting to know more about their relationship. 'He had an absolutely iron, iron belief that I knew what I was doing. When that happens to come from a parent, it is very, very special.' What they had for each other, she said, was a 'puddle of love'. If so, the puddle didn't splash out into a great success for their movie.

Certainly, nothing like as great as the picture she discovered was showing in Rome and which she made a number of trips to see. That really was a puddle of love, *Singin' In The Rain*.

Lorna came to Rome to see what she was told would be the fun and helped make it a family occasion. When their escorts round the local nightspots – a couple of local actors trusted by Vincente and Jack Haley – got into a fight, the girls took a taxi to their hotel suite.

Not even Ingrid Bergman, as the countess, and Charles Boyer as her former husband, in one of his very last roles, could help get it going. That was partly due to the script, but the direction, it has to be said, didn't greatly help.

In the end, it was not written by Frederic Raphael, but by John Gay. Just about the only critic who liked it was that of the *Hollywood Reporter*, who said in October 1976 that the picture was 'a charming, nostalgic return to the days of elegant, stylistic film-making.'

There were a number of flashbacks in the film, but they didn't encourage people to enjoy it very much. Frank Rich wrote in the *New York Post* that it was a film that was 'so spectacularly crazy that if Minnelli could only persuade Mel Brooks to put his name on it, *A Matter of Time* might yet be the comedy sleeper of the year.'

Mel Brooks wasn't so persuaded. But he did get Liza to perform a cameo rôle, playing herself in his picture of the same year, *Silent Movie*. It made a great deal more sense than *A Matter of Time*.

It was obvious that it would be just a matter of time when it would all be forgotten. But not Liza's feelings for her father. When she thought that Vincente needed a new swimming pool, she paid to have one put in, as her birthday present.

Meanwhile, she and Jack – now head of Twentieth Century-Fox's television division – both said they were determined to put down roots. They had their house. Soon they would want a family.

As Haley said: 'Liza's never been a loner. She needs to feel some kind of familial relationship all the time. I suppose it's because she's been on her own so much of her life. She's always seeking the home environment she never had, and having people around to whom she feels close helps fill that need.' Both undoubtedly knew, however, that that was, perhaps, asking too much. A woman determined to go on being a star could not then any more than now expect to do that and be a mother at the same time – and without making any sacrifices.

Once a year, they decided they would give a big party, to give all their friends who were so busy through most of the year a chance to meet each other. They chose Ciro's. The memory of their wedding party was too good not to want to renew. But she believed she played her part as the consort of the head of a big TV empire. It was, as she put it, a new hat for her. She turned that, too, into a Paris creation. 'I wear it pretty good,' she said. 'I get out the Baccarat crystal and all that stuff and I enjoy it because I like to make my husband proud of me.' She was undoubtedly a tremendous asset when it came to having business dinners at home. There were not many people in the business who would turn down the chance of being hostessed by Liza Minnelli, even if they thought they didn't want to do business with Twentieth Century-Fox.

A lot of people were already talking about the marriage not lasting. That was not the way either of them thought about it. 'Marriage is hard work,' Liza said. 'But it's not *just* hard work. Jack and I are having a divine time.'

Even so, Liza still felt there was more to do. She didn't want domesticity to hinder that.

It certainly did not affect her getting the prestige rôle of one of the hosts in the TV spectacular, *Life Goes to the Movies* based on the book published by Life magazine in which the world of cinema recorded by the publication during its first magnificent incarnation was recalled as glossily as only a magazine could. Gable, Monroe, Astaire, all were there. Liza – as well as Henry Fonda and Shirley MacLaine – introduced the various extracts, a job not unlike her performance in *That's Entertainment* and almost as successful.

She hoped that would be the case with the show she was going into. It would be called *In Person* and although that sounded rather like a one-woman performance, it wasn't exactly like that. There would be a book, specially written for her and with music by... Kander and Ebb, of course.

It was scheduled to open at the Los Angeles Music Center's Dorothy Chandler Pavilion in August 1977, as part of the Los Angeles Civic Light Opera's fortieth anniversary season. One of the other highlights would be Debbie Reynolds in *Annie Get Your Gun*, the biggest of all Irving Berlin hits, and the one that had given Judy so much anxiety. Liza's show would be about a young performer with a compulsive drive to get on in show business. That, at least, sounded familiar.

Actually, she was much in demand for anniversaries. When it came to celebrating the hundredth birthday of the telephone, the Bell Telephone Company asked Liza to join Bing Crosby in hosting a TV special called *Jubilee*. It seemed to have everything: Maurice Chevalier – on film – singing 'Louise', Errol Garner, Benny Goodman, André Previn, Steve Lawrence, Eydie Gorme and Joel Grey recreating his Broadway rôle as George M. Cohan.

Liza's next big-screen movie however, looked more exciting than her last two. It was called *New York, New York*.

Chapter Eighteen

LIZA LIKED TO say that both she and Jack were in love with New York. New York was fast. So was she. Life was a cabaret, old chum, and nothing should ever be made to change it. No one seemed to doubt that she meant it. She was the number one guest in the party set when she went to Manhattan and everyone knew that she was buying a great deal of the stuff negotiated in the dark corners of the clubs she frequented. She drank a great deal, but that wasn't anything to worry about. Ask her how she felt and she would reply, 'Terrific' – and then would ask, 'Do you love me?' She wanted the obvious answer. If she got it she felt better. It convinced her she really did feel terrific.

Of course, she worried about her career. It couldn't be enough just to be a cabaret artist, even the best there was. *New York, New York* would have to be the answer. It wasn't.

It was to be a story straight out of the age of the big bands, a tale about a saxophone player and his love for a girl singer who goes across the country and turns into a Hollywood star.

Liza, of course, was the girl. The saxophone player was a young, thin Robert De Niro at the stage when he had first taken his personality and the mole on the side of his face to considerable stardom. *Mean Streets*, *Taxi Driver* and *The Last Tycoon* had already made him a formidable actor. Before long, audiences would see him as the young Marlon Brando in *The Godfather, Part Two*, but it was *New York, New York* that made him. He and Liza did a lot of shouting – in fact, it was almost as prevalent as the music. The director, Martin Scorsese, said he loved the reaction he got. De Niro would throw a line at Liza and she wouldn't hesitate to return it. Indeed, watching them was like seeing a fine rally at Wimbledon.

It was a gruelling twenty-two weeks of filming. 'I can't remember ever sitting down once during that entire time,' Liza was to say.

She played a band singer, and looked even sexier in her dresses with the wide shoulder pads which emphasised her curving bust and hips than she had when wearing half the clothes in *Cabaret*. It was an opportunity for a new kind of Liza Minnelli, band singer as well as talented actress. Somehow, it required a different technique from the sort of singing she was used to doing. She was quite clearly not singing à la Liza. In fact, she sounded much more like Doris Day in the opening moments of the movie. By the time the picture was over she described her style as being more like Helen O'Connell. By that time, however, she had used her voice telling De Niro to get off. After all, that was the way to treat a man she thought was a 'Class A Bastard'. She was referring to the character and not the actor.

The film did something else, too: it gave Liza a new signature tune that, before a week of the film's release, would eclipse 'Cabaret' and even 'Liza With a . . .' you-know-what.

The film was being produced by Gene Kirkwood for United Artists. But the influence felt most was that of Martin Scorsese.

There was a lot of talk of romance between Scorsese and Liza and romance meant an affair. Both tried to scotch the rumours. 'A lot of my problems,' said the director, 'are because I like women who are very intelligent, very bright, their own person. The others just don't interest me.' He had to admit that Liza fitted comfortably into that first category.

She herself complained about the 'treachery' of Hollywood. How else could anyone suggest that she and Jack weren't in the middle of a marvellous marriage?

Part of Liza's trouble was that she was always living the life of the 'kook'; even when she wanted to be taken seriously, she still seemed to behave outrageously. In her less outrageous moments, she behaved as though it were necessary at all times to be an original. Her favourite tipple of white rum and soda, to which she introduced fellow guests at an Andy Warhol party, was considered terribly exotic – and was immediately taken up and used in advertising by the Puerto Rican Rums company.

If people had thought that Liza Minnelli had been 'over-exposed' before, they certainly could not say that about Liza, the movie star. The film was certainly no *Cabaret*, even if it were better than her last couple of efforts.

In fact, she was maturing now and looked good in practically anything. No one could be surprised that when *Vogue* magazine held an exhibition called 'Women Observed', featuring more than 100 pictures from the magazine over fifty years, Liza's face should be among those staring out from frames in Saks' Fifth Avenue store. It was another reason for her to like singing 'New York, New York', which in addition to being Liza's own was also borrowed by Frank Sinatra – who made a take-over bid for the number himself and shared the song as his own signature tune with her. Not only that, it had now taken over as the unofficial anthem of the city in the title, supplanting the song with the same title written by Leonard Bernstein for *On The Town*.

She said that not only did she herself love New York, so did Jack. 'He's a New York man. Never stops. He's filled with energy and he's got that New York humour.'

Both Jack and Liza had ambitions to set up home in the city that was already known as The Big Apple. But that was for the future – the film was being shot in Hollywood.

There were those who were now saying that Liza was a little confused. She said all those nice things about New York, yet Hollywood had made her a superstar. One had the feeling that perhaps she was not really sure that she wanted to be a film star and was happiest in cabaret. Yet this wasn't true either. She wanted everything – and needed everyone to know it. That was another reason why she still sometimes ended her sentences asking, 'Do you love me?' On stage, she could be sure that they did. On the film set, she really couldn't be certain.

Jack, for the moment, gave everyone the impression that he admired Liza as much as he loved her.

Stupidly, people asked him how he liked being called Mr Minnelli. That was always an upsetting question to Peter Allen. To Jack, who was very much his own man at the top of a very public organisation, it was just stupid. He answered intelligently, but without sneering. 'I'd sign Vincente and be proud,' he'd usually reply, which was a cunning way of turning the question around and answering it in a way that was not offensive. He wasn't recognising that anyone would think he was a mere appendage of his wife. If people were mistaken in asking it, he reasoned, they could only be confusing him with his father-in-law.

There were those who wondered about the company Liza kept, why she was, even with her marriage to the he-man Jack Haley, friendly with a bisexual set led by artist Andy Warhol. She usually answered by saying that she was entitled to the friends she chose.

But that was only part of it. The truth of the matter was that her marriage was turning into a replay of everything else in her life at that time – expectations dashed into failure.

Everybody had had romantic high hopes of the relationship. After all, it was a vicarious reunion of the *Wizard of Oz* gang by osmosis – a generation removed. The daughter of Dorothy married the son of the Tin Man.

But the romance didn't last. Liza, who was not beyond taking a drink herself, was married to a man who went on the booze seriously. Every morning he had a new bottle of whisky in his desk drawers.

Sid Luft recalled in an interview for this book: 'I was over at Fox at about 9.30 in the morning and he was already hitting the bottle. It was tragic. A clever guy, but whisky killed him.'

Jack Haley was to die in 2001.

Liza was so busy that some people wondered how she could do half the things she did without some sort of help from tablets. She continued to deny it, though, and continued to work – her one-woman show, now labelled simply *In Concert*, and benefits for hospitals, like the show in memory of Rosalind Russell at the end of 1976, called 'For Roz with Love'.

And there were comforts, particularly the support of those close to her, like Lorna Luft. 'I've more than once been very jealous of her,' Lorna admitted to me. 'But Liza has been wonderful for me. When she saw things were hard, she gave me an introduction to her agents and made them work for me. How could I not be grateful for that?'

Liza was in Japan when Lorna opened at Houston, Texas. Liza flew in in time to make sure that she was there during the show's run.

People were anxious, she said, to see them pulling each other's hair out. 'So you know what I tell them? "She's just my best friend." And if anyone wants to hear nasty things about a girl's best friend, they're not hearing them from me.'

Both girls had been invited to consider playing their mother in films. Both turned down the offer flat. It would be in excruciatingly bad taste, they decided.

Some people thought that about a few of the possessions that Liza so obviously enjoyed. Her chauffeur dropped her in a Rolls Royce – with the initials 'LM' delicately inscribed on the door. It stands for 'Lotsa Money', she said.

There was no guile about Liza now, which was perhaps her most endearing feature. As she said: 'I knew I was going to make it when I started feeling free to turn down lots of shows. Now I never do anything for the sake of doing it.'

That sort of honesty did not stop the rumours, particularly those about Liza's romantic attachments. She was said to be having an affair with dancer Ben Vereen – she said that they were good friends, since both were trained by Bob Fosse. Another name with whom she was linked was that of Assaf Dayan, son of the Israeli general.

Not that people were no longer tying her to Martin Scorsese. He was not only directing her in *New York, New York*, but also her forthcoming show, called *In Person*. Before long, the title had been changed to *Shine It On* before settling down as *The Act*. By then, Mr Scorsese had been replaced.

The new show was the talk of the town, mainly because of the hot language used on stage when it opened in Chicago and San Francisco. Certainly it wasn't all honey and roses.

There were stories in the papers of how, when faced with less than flattering reviews outside New York, the cast fortified themselves with tales of how disastrous both *My Fair Lady* and *Hello Dolly* had been in their own out-of-town try-outs. One of the people involved said that there had been so much interest in the show's progress – or perhaps lack of it – that it was covered in the New York papers every day. So much so, that wits began to christen the *Daily News*, the 'Daily Minnelli'.

Liza hoped that they would talk mainly about her performance and how good she looked in Halston's dresses. Scorsese hadn't directed a stage musical before the show opened at the Dorothy Chandler Pavilion at the Los Angeles Music Center, later going on to the Majestic Theater, New York, on October 29, 1977.

The show's fault was mainly that it concentrated on providing a vehicle for Liza, playing a once-famous Hollywood star who is aiming for a come-back at Las Vegas. The musical numbers – by Kander and Ebb – were mainly those she sang in cabaret. The non-musical scenes were the ones that illustrated her life between careers.

Liza had her work cut out trying to prove that the woman she played, Michelle Craig, was not really meant to be Judy Garland.

Her co-star was Barry Nelson, a man with a certain reputation on Broadway, but not generally considered to be in the Liza Minnelli class. Nor, to be fair, was the show itself.

'*The Act*,' wrote Dan Sullivan in the *Los Angeles Times* when it opened at the Pavilion, 'looked more like the rehearsal... Liza Minnelli just missed getting conked by some falling baubles from Tony Walton's scenery, lines went awry, spotlights couldn't hold their aim, there were these weird thumping noises.'

That apart, how did Mr Sullivan enjoy the show? In truth, he didn't. What was there about it? 'At best, a shiny dance floor, a big band and Miss Minnelli as in Las Vegas or one of her TV specials. At worst, the dumbest backstage musical ever, to the point where you figure they've got to be kidding.'

It was reminiscent of *A Chorus Line* in that it tried to show how the star got into her present predicament. But, the critic added. '*A Chorus Line* knew how to play the past against the present without stopping, while *The Act* goes dead every time it pauses to look back. Meaning that when we return to the floor, Miss Minnelli has to crank the show up all over again.'

Not much of this affected the box office. By the time it opened on Broadway, all tickets were sold for months ahead – mostly because of Liza – and there were substantial changes.

There were the predictable headlines: 'Minnelli Gets Her Act Together' and 'Miss Minnelli Caught In The Act'. All audiences apparently wanted to see was Miss Minnelli, live on stage. What it was she did, really didn't matter. The management was very clever to get her to star in their show.

The show had the highest ticket prices in box office history with prices of $25 a seat on Saturday nights, and $35 for the première and for New Year's Eve, traditionally a good night for business on Broadway. The *Hollywood Reporter* noted: 'Princess Margaret's visit to NY paled into insignificance compared to the arrival of Liza Minnelli, sole heiress to the crown of Queen of the Musical Comedy Theater now that Ethel Merman, Barbra Streisand, Gwen Verdon and Lauren Bacall have rejected Broadway for other fields.' That was nothin' but the truth.

So, all in all, the show was going to do better than the out-of-town reception appeared to indicate – despite the stories that permeated to Broadway from the Mid-West and West Coast.

By now, it had a new director, Gower Champion – who was later to do incredible things to make *42nd Street* the huge hit it became, and would die just before opening night – had taken over from Scorsese. The original director was still given full billing credits, but was being advised to stick to hit movies like *New York, New York* and *Taxi Driver.*

Fewer people were now saying the names Liza Minnelli and Judy Garland in the same breath, but when audiences greeted her with the call, 'We love you Liza', the memories were strong.

Variety said of the show: 'After several months of reports of drastic try-out doctoring, *The Act* finally arrived last Saturday night at the Majestic Theater as pretty much what everyone had said – a personal triumph for Liza Minnelli in an overblown formula musical. It seems likely to prosper on Broadway... Minnelli gives an almost unbelievably dynamic performance as the magnetic center of all thirteen musical numbers and incidental story scenes of a production that runs approximately two hours and fifteen minutes, excluding a single intermission. Except for a few quick costume changes, she is never offstage, which is clearly just as well.'

The respected 'Broadway butcher' Walter Kerr put it succinctly: 'Liza deserves more than a floor show.'

As he said: 'If she must perform so uninterruptedly that she hasn't time for a sip of water, a nibble on a sandwich or an unflustered costume change (some are made on stage by ripping her apart or basting her together in more or less full view) she can still get something out of that.'

There were problems with the songs, too. Not that Liza didn't sing them so strenuously that at times her voice broke, but she had to cope with dancing just as toughly. So those songs were taped and Liza lip-synched them as she would in a film. Several people claiming to be purists wrote protesting their shock to the management.

New York magazine was even more disturbed. In fact, for practically the first time since *Best Foot Forward*, Liza got a stinker of a personal review. John Simon's piece was headed: 'Liza With a Zzzz' and went on to criticise her face which, he said, reminded him of a 'beagle'. He even said that her appearance was unredeemed by talent. 'Miss Minnelli has only brashness, pathos and energy... The brashness is of the manic variety, a mask for insecurity, self-doubt, hollowness; as such, it appeals to all fellow sufferers of inferiority feelings, deserved or not.'

Worse was to come: 'What did the crowds roaring inside and thronging outside the Majestic Theater care about *The Act* or Michelle Craig or anything except the blooming, bleeding, barnstorming ego of their darling Liza? Liza, Liza, a loud and barely talented near-nonentity born to Judy Garland and Vincente Minnelli and borne aloft by waves of bad taste that never ebbed.' Which, naturally enough, left room for a pun or two about Fred Ebb.

Time, of course, was kinder. It couldn't have been much else. But she had cause for concern with what its reviewer T. E. Kalem said: 'She had been labelled a "superstar", which seems to be part of the mandatory hyperbole of the age. Let's just call her a star, a title she deserves since she has that special X factor of personality that sets stars apart from other top-ranking talents. But as a star whose gifts include singing, dancing and acting, ought she not to be extraordinary or unique in one of those categories? Liza is not.'

The magazine's rival, *Newsweek*, saw *The Act* more as 'The Game'. As it said: '*The Act* has at last completed its broken-field run across the country, bouncing off bad reviews, to fling itself gasping across the goal line onto Broadway. Touchdown? No. Someone forgot to give Liza Minnelli the ball – a show, that is. But Liza's run to daylight is unquestionably the trajectory of a star. At $25 top ticket, it had better be.'

The player, however, was injured. Liza was ill with a viral infection which turned into a serious bout of flu, and had to miss two weeks of performances. Because she had no understudy – that, itself, was a huge demonstration of her own power – the Shubert Organisation lost almost $400,000. She went off to a Texas health farm to recuperate. Later she returned against her doctor's advice. Then she missed a matinée. No one was told until fifteen minutes after curtain-up, which, as the audience complained, was too late to find another show. She made the evening performance, however – which distressed the unfortunate matinée-goers even more.

No matter how strong the box office, there were still those who had doubts. It wasn't until the following April, six months after opening, that the original-cast album was recorded. Nobody had shown interest in doing it until the DRG label decided to sew up the various legal difficulties and satisfy the people in the lobby asking for records.

The problems with the show were not the only ones for Liza. In January 1978, it was announced that she and Jack had 'agreed to live separately and apart'.

The announcement came in the midst of a busy time for Liza – taking part in the Golden Globe Awards one moment, appearing on

CBS's *Who's Who* the next, and following that with a TV special called *Tribute to Bette Davis*.

The trouble was that Liza had fallen in love with the show's stage manager Mark Gero, who was also a sculptor. Liza said she found him 'caring' at a time when she was suffering from all the pressures, felt tired and was more lonely than she normally wanted to let on. When she had needed Jack with her, he had been tied up in Hollywood. That was when they decided to make their separation official.

Newspapers and magazines had a field day – actually, they had several field days – with stories about their affair. But Jack Haley didn't. He felt humiliated and filed for divorce, saying he 'wasn't going to be made a fool of by Liza'.

People saw Liza and Gero together. What they did not know were the details of what had led up to it – the Valium and the sleep it helped induce. She would stay in bed until late in the morning – a textbook symptom of depression when its sufferers can't get up to face the traumas of the day. When she did rise, she would take a cup of coffee – and then decide to have another sleep. Then she would turn on the television. Liza Minnelli could have won any quiz on American soap operas – until, that is, she decided to stay in bed all day till it was time to get up and go to the theatre and pretend that the world was perfect and she was its queen. By then, there was an end in sight to *The Act*.

Gero seemed to help her. They were never seen apart. That seemed a very familiar story. Except that there was also someone else on the horizon. She was spending more and more time now with Mikhail Baryshnikov – to an extraordinary degree. While she was playing in New York, he was dancing in Washington. So every night, after her show, she flew to the capital to be with him. And she'd stay in Washington until it was time to fly back to Manhattan for the next show.

When, after 239 performances, the stage show closed, their own seemed only to thrive.

Chapter Nineteen

SOMEHOW, THIS was an Act that wouldn't come together. The fiery feminine Minnelli and the beefy, masculine Baryshnikov – not at all the usual image of a ballet star – appeared to be ending the affair before it really had a chance to catch on. With no big show in which to perform, Liza could have afforded to sit back and let things happen in her private life. But she liked challenges. Now, when it looked easy, they both lost interest.

So Mark Gero came back into the picture. It was not taken for granted that Liza and Mark were going to set up a joint life together, even though they had been seen around for so long. But he did seem to inhabit her world. The trouble with Haley had been, so their so-called friends said, that he wanted to go to bed at night while she wanted to play, and just as he was starting to yawn, Liza was waking up and feeling ready to go dancing. So the scraps between owl and lark made it intolerable to carry on any longer.

The papers were still tipping her ending up (or at least settling down for a time) with Scorsese. But he seems to have been the opposite of the people who had previously been in her life – neither a potential Mr Minnelli, nor a soft, protective teddy bear into whose arms she could cuddle, but a man of extraordinary strength, stronger than she was herself.

People wondered about that. Others saw her in the company of Al Pacino and decided that the idea of Liza with Al was a good one.

In May 1978, the marriage with Haley was officially at an end. There were always new men alleged to be in her life. For a time it seemed again as though she would end up with Baryshnikov. Together they went to a party and he accompanied her to the Tony awards. That was a good evening for her. Liza won her third Tony for *The Act*.

There were worries about her, though. No one could doubt that she was a big, big star, for all the rude things written about her during the early days of the show. But one always had the feeling that she was running a race that might end up at a brick wall. She felt vulnerable and she looked it. She was fed up with being regarded as a sort of person-made-royalty; hated the thought, as she said, of the same audiences who had said 'We love you, Liza' telling her to 'get outa it, you bum.' And if she did 'get outa it', did she know where she would go?

That question had to be taken seriously when one looked at the various things she was doing professionally. Why did she have to do *everything*, even when it was said that she didn't do any one of her various activities better than anyone else? The reason is that she was simply trying to prove that she *could* be better.

That could be the only reason she agreed to a weekly salary cheque of $187.50 – the Equity minimum – to star in a play at the Promenade Theater in New York called *Are You Now or Have You Ever Been?*. She didn't dance a step, she didn't lift her arm up high, grab a microphone or tell everyone she was 'Li...'.

This was a play about the McCarthy hearings. The rest of the question in the title was, of course, '... a Communist?' The part she played was of writer Lillian Hellman, a woman who always intrigued actresses – Jane Fonda played her in the film *Julia*. There was another reason for her taking the part. The play was produced by Frank Gero, the father of Mark.

It wasn't an onerous rôle, but she did it effectively – the high point of her performance was to read out a letter Miss Hellman wrote to the House UnAmerican Activities Committee, explaining her refusal to testify before it.

She had a little legal trouble of her own in May 1979. The Riviera Hotel in Las Vegas sued her, alleging that she failed to fulfil her contract – by only appearing there for a total of twelve weeks between August 1973 and the same month four years later, instead of the specified twenty-four weeks. The hotel was asking for damages in excess of $10,000. The matter was later settled to their mutual satisfaction.

Her career, though, wasn't to her satisfaction at all. *Cabaret* was the pinnacle and she wasn't yet able to climb up there again.

She was doing a fair amount of charity work – for which she broke a rule never to sing her mother's songs. At a benefit for a child centre in Los Angeles she sang, in quick succession, 'The Trolley Song', 'Meet Me In St Louis' and 'The Boy Next Door'. It marked a sense of maturity for her. 'I guess I've finally arrived,' she said.

In December 1978, Liza was back in London, starring at the Palladium once more. 'Liza Minnelli loves us,' said Victoria Radin in the *Observer*. 'Or rather, an artful lover, she makes a deal with us: if we love her enough, she'll love us back. But mere loving is not what she's after: it's ecstasy... There were two encores, but the long fight was over and she had won.'

She ran round that Palladium stage, however, looking as if she were chasing something. Was it security? Happiness? Both – and a lot more.

Liza was in Europe in the summer of 1979 – going to Berlin, for instance, to co-star in a TV special satellited all over the world on behalf of UNICEF, the United Nations Children's Fund, of which Danny Kaye was permanent roving ambassador.

In August, she was in London and appeared at Covent Garden, a place that normally did not experience her sort of singing or dancing. She was doing neither. The Martha Graham Dance Company was performing the full-length ballet, *The Owl and the Pussycat*, and Liza was there to read the Edward Lear poem on which it was based, about the two lovable creatures who set sail in their beautiful pea-green boat. While in London, she gave a dinner at the Café Royal – favourite haunt of Oscar Wilde – in aid of setting up a National Music Hall in the East End, an effort that has still not borne fruit. It was easy to see why Liza thought that a worthwhile cause. She would have looked great in one of those big feathery hats, singing the songs of Marie Lloyd and Florrie Forde. They also had trouble with their 'old man'.

Liza, though, was continuing what she was able to do best, her concert series. At Carnegie Hall in September 1979, she drew rave notices – all of them saying how much better she was in this act than in *The Act* the year before. It was the sort of tonic she needed, particularly because it was an opportunity to have her friends around her. Halston gave her a party at Studio 54. Mark came and so did Andy Warhol, who now regarded himself as Liza's principal Manhattan guru.

Then she went off to Los Angeles to do a TV special with Goldie Hawn. It had rave reviews all over the country.

The critics in Florida, in particular, liked her. They made her 1979's 'Entertainer of the Year'. Her one-woman show was 'Production of the Year'.

Meanwhile, Vincente was awarded the *Ordre des Artes et Lettres* by the French Government and Liza gave him a party at the Bistro

Garden, the Beverly Hills establishment where the beautiful people gathered to see how less beautiful everyone else was.

Liza was by now very much part of the diplomatic set, as much as anything, one suspects, because she was now so decorative. She was always the perfect dresser, wherever she went – thanks to Halston. He made her his own design sandals, which exposed her toes. On the way out of the home of the Los Angeles-based French Consul General, she stubbed one of them – and broke it (the toe, that is, the shoe stayed in perfect condition).

Mark Gero escorted her that night. He was now officially described as her road manager. Their relationship was more than that, however.

Vincente saw it. 'You're gonna marry him, aren't you?' he asked rhetorically. He said he knew that she was. And he knew one of the reasons.

For the second time, and after two marriages and a series of whirlwind affairs, Liza was pregnant again and Gero was the father. On December 4, 1979, they were married at a candle-lit ceremony at New York's St Bartholomew's Episcopal Church, which – unlike other branches of the Anglican community – seemed to have no objections to marrying a divorcée.

Liza, wearing a full-length mink, slipped in by a back entrance. She thought she would be unnoticed. But news of that sort of thing is inclined to slip out and by the time it was all over, a huge crowd of fans had formed itself outside the church – all of them shouting the now familiar, 'We love you Liza'. They knew that this time she might not have asked them if they really did. The ceremony was performed by the Reverend Peter Delaney, 'a friend of the family', and three other ministers pronounced blessings.

Only about twenty close friends and members of the two families sat in a ring round the altar for the thirty-minute ceremony. Bride and bridegroom gave each other rings simultaneously. As everyone now expected, Halston provided her diaphanous pink chiffon gown. (Plainly, she no longer thought yellow was particularly lucky.) Elizabeth Taylor, now a good friend – how close they were would become apparent later – was there and so was Fred Ebb. Lorna acted as matron of honour.

Halston gave them a black-tie reception at his home on East 63rd Street before the couple were due to leave for a honeymoon in Jamaica. It was all very smart and very fashionable and both parties said it was for keeps. (One wonders if Judy would have returned Liza's backhanded compliment had she been alive to see her daughter's third trip to a wedding ceremony.)

When the honeymoon was over, she and Mark would try to show that they were together for keeps. Except that there was no honeymoon. Just as they were leaving for Jamaica, Liza suffered severe stomach pains and was taken to New York Hospital's Cornell Medical Center. She was sent home – and a week later, there was a miscarriage.

Liza was more depressed than she had ever been before, but she was trying not to show it.

The Geros set up home in New York, which Liza said was like a diving board. From her penthouse apartment on Central Park South – decorated for her by Tim Macdonald, with help from Halston – she could see the city before her. The people on the streets looked like those filling a swimming pool.

It was a plush apartment. In addition to the usual rooms, there were music and projection rooms, with seats covered in parachute cotton. The decorators said they were recreating La Belle Epoque. When she got into a bad mood, she just walked around. When she needed to get her voice in trim, she let out a call not unlike Tarzan's to Jane.

She was still good company, still usually said intelligent things, but admitted that there was a lot she needed to learn. She couldn't always remember names and that worried her. She couldn't recall who it was who had starred in *The Man Who Came to Supper*. It was Monty Woolley and the play (and film) was *The Man Who Came to Dinner*, but nobody quarrelled with her over that or over anything else. There was an insouciance about her that went with the kookiness and most people seemed to find it endearing.

But it was a front. The depression was worse than ever, although Liza, knowing so well the effect of such unhappiness on people in the public eye and on their fans, kept her misery to herself. Her Halston dresses were not to be worn with hearts on the sleeves and she knew it. It is one of her strongest characteristics – and because people didn't know of her troubles in the first place, they were not aware how strong that quality really was.

She said that the loss of the baby was merely 'a postponement', even though doctors had told her before that she had gynaecological problems that would prevent her ever carrying a child to full term.

Halston told reporters: 'It's the one thing she wants and needs above everything.'

But she went back to work just the same, doing a TV special with her old flame, Baryshnikov, totally unconcerned about their previous arrangement and her new situation. It was the first time for years in which reviewers – in this case John J. O'Connor in the *New York Times* – would talk about Liza 'assisting' another artist. But the show was called *Baryshnikov on Broadway* and there was no getting away from that fact. Or that they looked very good together.

Then the questions started being asked about her – never a good sign for a star who is usually constantly in the news.

'What happened to Liza's movie career?' asked *Hollywood Studio Magazine*. It was a question worth posing by the otherwise small and inconsequential journal. No one could really say what had happened to that career. Except that it was in the doldrums.

Her 1980 picture with Dudley Moore, *Arthur*, did absolutely nothing for her – except to ask whether it was worth making in the first place. As far as she was concerned, it most certainly was not.

The trouble with having a triumph like *Cabaret* was that it was going to be so very difficult to equal, let alone beat. *Arthur*, in strict box office terms, did just that. But it didn't do it for Liza. Plainly, it was Dudley Moore's movie with the dour Sir John Gielgud running a close second (and to some people's idea even first). Liza looked like an appendage to both of them.

There might have been one way of reversing the situation, getting people to think Liza when they thought *Arthur*. The trouble was that Liza was too intoxicated to give the press conference the studio wanted her to take.

It was very much another 'assisting' rôle, which was surprising for someone of her status and because Dudley Moore was not someone for whom she felt the kind of affection she had for Baryshnikov. Much of it, in fact, was reminiscent of her very first film – except that *Charlie Bubbles* had a great deal of charm. In *Arthur* she played a poor girl who gets mixed up with a multi-millionaire. They meet in the posh store where he is getting himself completely kitted out for only the second time that week and she is shoplifting for her stony-broke father.

Pauline Kael wrote in the *New Yorker* that it was an 'idea that doesn't work'. Dudley Moore and Sir John Gielgud – as his butler – were a good combination. 'But when Minnelli turns up she doesn't bounce off anybody and there's no common ground under the three of them...I haven't a clue what Linda [Liza's character] is supposed to be and I doubt if Minnelli had much of a clue.' Miss Kael was kind enough to suggest that one of the reasons was that Liza didn't have any of the good lines. The picture itself was generally accepted to be much better than was Liza's performance.

Gielgud got an Oscar for his troubles. Moore got an Oscar nomination. Liza had the feeling she was glad to have got the hell out of it. The one pleasant thing about *Arthur* for her was that the title song was co-written by Peter Allen (with Burt Bacharach), a nice renewal of their relationship. There would be no more Minnelli films for seven years. It was the beginning of a hiatus in her career as an all-round entertainer. Had she burnt out? There were those who detected a smouldering that they didn't like – accompanied by a great sense of disappointment. She still hoped that there would be another Minnelli, or at least a Minnelli-Gero.

Six months later Liza was about to begin a nationwide tour with Joel Grey, when she collapsed with stomach pains. She was taken to Boston's Massachusetts General Hospital, where she discovered for the first time that she was two months pregnant. Liza was told to go home to rest and everything would probably be all right. She went home, but just a month later she had another miscarriage.

That summer, she and Joel Grey did their postponed tour. 'She was wonderful and funny all over again,' he told me. They did *Cabaret* routines all over again and laughed together all over again. That was the best part of the show. But the audience at Los Angeles' open-air Greek Theater had other things to go on. Liza again felt able enough to take on a Judy number. She sang 'The Man That Got Away' and if there had been a roof on the Greek, Liza would have brought it down.

The Los Angeles *Herald Examiner* said: 'Liza Minnelli in concert with Joel Grey is one of the essential entertainment experiences of the spring and summer.' Everybody who was anybody in town came. Frank Sinatra sent her a note saying: 'You were wonderful, absolutely sensational and I realise I'm getting too old to sing "New York, New York". I loved you but you moved around too much on the stage. Love, Uncle Frank.'

She would admit that she wasn't always perfect, although she was most comfortable moving around. 'I'm not saying that my life is easy. It's damned hard being an entertainer, an actress and a wife and I've made mistakes in the past. But you've gotta keep plugging, keep going.'

It was a good idea, that tour. Not much else in her career was doing very much for her now. Had the Minnelli touch been lost? It began to look very much like it. She was cosseted on her tours – one writer said being with her was like being stuffed into a cotton-wadded cocoon inserted inside the funnel of a cyclone. The cyclone called Minnelli was in full thrust when she had a concert audience wanting her. The cry, 'We love you Liza' was enough.

But people worried about her. They could see that her hands shook due, she insisted, to an old childhood complaint, that curvature of her spine – and saw her popping pills into her mouth. She always insisted it was just Valium, which helped her perform. She had smoked pot and she had got drunk in her life, but neither did very much for her.

She carried on with the cabaret and concert performances in 1982 and as the year turned into 1983 she was doing much the same thing all over again. Kirk Douglas suggested that she did a show to honour Vincente on his seventy-third birthday in February of that year, and nothing would prevent her from doing so. She did her research and came up with forty songs from shows with which he had been associated in the 1930s. It was an old-style Minnelli smash.

She was going to play the part of Rose's mother in *Gypsy*, which would have demonstrated that Liza was no kid any more, but the show never happened. A new one, however, did come along. Kander and Ebb had written the score for a show to be called *The Rink* and, as a result, Liza seemed happier than she had for a long time.

She played Chita Rivera's daughter in this show about a mother-daughter feud. Most of the rows were over Liza – playing a hippy who really should have forgotten dressing in the style of the flower people long before – trying to persuade her mother not to sell the family business, a roller-skating rink.

The most remarkable thing about the show was that Liza was once again 'assisting' or rather, co-starring. Chita Rivera was the real star of the show.

The two women got on well. They spent their off-stage moments chewing the fat about Broadway, Hollywood and their respective real mothers. Half-way through the show's first night, they embraced each other. The critics liked that more than they did the show itself.

Perhaps that was why Liza used to try to go into the theatre incognito, dressed differently each day, sometimes wearing a baseball cap. 'I see myself mainly as an actress,' she said now – explaining, perhaps her willingness to play second-fiddle to the veteran of *West Side Story*.

She had other things to do, though, like co-starring in a TV children's show for a cable network, opposite Tom Conti in *The Princess and the Pea*.

Nevertheless working on *The Rink* recharged batteries that were, to any insider, plainly wearing out. No one yet knew why. Liza tried to explain her search for energy and the results that she achieved, even so: 'It comes from within. It's like you're a conductor of energy. You take what you're getting from the audience and then the energy comes out in a very thin line, like a laser beam. It's specific purposeful energy, not frenetic energy.' The articulate Liza had not lost her form. But things weren't right for her.

Despite her professed happy marriage, she had never felt so lonely. And the drugs were getting to her more than ever before. When she told a doctor about her insecurity, her loneliness, her inability to sleep, he doled out pills, as she said, 'like candy'.

At weekends, she had cares she wanted to forget. So that was when she had her 'party drugs'. There were stories of a dishevelled Liza being poured by Michael Jackson into a limousine, laughing hysterically. People who had been in London in the late 1960s and witnessed a woman not that much older in the same state would have had a sense of *déjà-vu*. Her hands were *constantly* shaking now – more than they ever had.

'I was addicted to relief,' she would say. 'I couldn't understand why everybody else felt so good. I wanted to know what they were taking', she told writer Bob Colacello. 'Little things. Like getting up and going to the market. I thought it would be miraculous to have the energy to do that during the day and perform at night.'

Early in July 1984, she had to temporarily leave the show, which she said she loved doing more than anything else in which she had performed in recent years. A lump was discovered on the back of her neck. It was removed and found to be benign. Her mother had had a similar problem, but she had worried that it might have been serious. When it was found to be all right, she decided she needed a rest. Soon, she was off to Monte Carlo to do a show with Charles Aznavour, which would lead to a European tour. (Charles liked to talk about the way they felt for each other; Liza had one of his shirts, he said – and she still wore it.)

After six months in *The Rink*, she had had enough. She left the cast later that month. But her lifestyle stayed crazy. After one night's performance, she took a bunch of the cast down to the Sounds of Brazil club at Greenwich Village and stayed there with them until four in the morning. Then, she brought the entire staff back to her apartment. No one left till after daylight came.

A few days later, Liza checked in to the Betty Ford Center in Rancho Mirage, California.

Chapter Twenty

BETTY FORD was arguably the one First Lady to become better known and better remembered than her husband, the President.

Gerald Ford was Richard Nixon's Vice-President and succeeded him after Watergate in 1974. He remained President until beaten by Jimmy Carter just over two years later. His wife, Betty, however, went into history simply because of her intense bravery. She was the first First Lady to admit that she had breast cancer and therefore needed a mastectomy. She was also the first to admit that she had a drink problem. Not only that, she was the first to do something about it – and at the same time try to help others like her.

She set up the Betty Ford Center for Alcoholism and Drug Addiction on the premises of the Eisenhower Medical Center. Soon after its establishment, Elizabeth Taylor went there for treatment for her own problems. So did Robert Mitchum.

Liza was very much more worried than she let on. The girl who used to have an answer for everything, who would claim that life was terrific, now didn't even kid herself that she really believed that any more. She still said that the real difficulty was Valium. It wasn't. She had got used to the 'hard stuff'. She tried equally hard to wean herself off them. It wouldn't work and she knew there had to be something more seriously done.

That combined with everything else she was facing made life virtually unliveable. Her closest friends were just waiting for what they assumed would be the complete return of the Judy Garland story – only this time, perhaps the overdosing wouldn't be quite so accidental.

She and Mark were having the by-now customary marital difficulties. They never usually talked much about their relationship when it looked like going off the rails. They just sat silently and waited for the final derailment. Now they had decided to separate.

But her health was even more crucial a problem and both she and Mark knew it.

She was so worried about her drug problem that she thought at one stage she was dying. It wasn't just a moment's fright that comes to people who have no medical reasons for thinking that. She really believed it. She read a lot. She had a lot of medical friends who threw around hints without doing anything. Liza put it all together and came to the conclusion she was suffering from either mononucleosis or hypoglycemia.

None of the doctors she consulted on a professional basis could find anything wrong with her. But then, she hadn't told them about her drugs.

It had been Lorna's idea to go to the Betty Ford Center. Years later, Lorna would reveal that she had had a drug problem of her own, but now she was happily married and had a baby boy. Liza seemed to be enjoying the rôle of favourite aunt, except she wasn't really well enough to enjoy anything.

Lorna was worried about Liza. She spoke to Elizabeth Taylor about her and wanted details about the Betty Ford Center. Elizabeth said that she wouldn't do any persuading. Liza had to make up her mind for herself. Lorna decided to take on the responsibility of the persuasion herself. It took a lot of heart searching.

Liza and Mark had been separated for four days now. But it was he whom she now felt she needed most. A phone call and he was by her side, encouraging and sympathising. There was no hesitation now. She would go the Center. But she didn't go with Mark – who said he had a problem of his own. He was 'CD', chemically dependent. But the Center thought that adding marital problems to her drug difficulty was too much. So Liza turned once more to her sister.

At least, that was the story at the time.

It's not difficult to see that the relationship between Liza and Lorna has been delicate. She could not have liked the fact that her younger sister had talked about her health so much. Especially about the time when she was starring in *The Rink*. That was when she convinced herself that she had cancer. Her doctors said that she didn't have the dreaded disease. But Lorna knew how dreadful Liza's psychosomatic condition was and begged the New York Hospital to take her in. She was told that the only way she could be admitted was through the psychiatric ward, the last thing she wanted for Liza.

The truth was that all the drinking she had been doing had taken its toll. She had put on weight. She was plainly depressed. When she saw herself in the mirror, it wasn't the girl who in black stockings and suspenders had driven millions of men to swoon. Now, though, it was worse. She thought she was dying. After considerable pleading, the hospital agreed to give her a private room on a general floor.

Lorna took her to the hospital, trying to cover her sister's face as she thrashed around in the car. But people recognised her. 'Yeh,' Lorna shouted after them in true Garland family style, 'half the drag queens in the city look like Liza.'

Finally, she was convinced that, no, she didn't have cancer. But everyone around knew that drink and drugs were taking away every quality of life that she had known. That was when Lorna and Liza's secretary together talked about getting her admitted to the Betty Ford Center. But it wouldn't have happened without the help of an old family friend.

Frank Sinatra was a man of extremes – intolerant, greedy, wicked (there is overwhelming evidence that he had rubbed out people who didn't do things His Way), womanising and yet kind, considerate, generous, friendly, fatherly. To Liza, he was all those things in the second category. So now, in 1984, he came to her aid at just the time when things were going from bad to worse.

Sinatra heard about the Betty Ford Center option and, using the fatherly Frank technique – the kind which you should not try to ignore – made her an offer she could not refuse. He made the arrangements and made his private Lear jet available for the journey to Palm Springs.

Not surprisingly, Liza didn't want to go. Lorna was forced to kidnap her to take her to the airport. According to the younger sister, Liza was virtually asleep in the car. When she did awake to a semblance of consciousness, she cried out: 'I want a hot dog. I want a fucking hot dog.'

As she said, riding with Liza was not an experience to savour.

Lorna was less than pleased with her responsibilities when they arrived at the centre. She expected simply to leave Liza behind. But she had a task to perform before she could go. She was told to write down a list of the problems, as she saw them, that were affecting her sister.

Lorna never said so, but she had been there herself and was easily able to distinguish them. It was not a happy chore.

In her extraordinarily incisive memoirs, Lorna talks about bringing Elizabeth Taylor into the picture and asking her advice. She says that Taylor told her Liza would hate her for making her go to the centre, but it was the right thing to do. 'She'll be going through a lot of changes,' said the older star. 'She may resent the fact that you're clean and sober and that you have a child, that she can't be like you.'

But not everyone, Lorna says, was so considerate. She castigates, for instance, the behaviour of Liza's lawyer, Mickey Rudin, which was, she claims, a lot less understanding. Lorna says that she left his office, feeling 'disgusted'.

Mark Gero, however, responded to it all by entering a 'family programme' in which those close to a patient are asked to help deal with their loved one's problems, rather like husbands in an antenatal class.

Lorna says she was clear that Liza was very angry with her.

She and Lorna checked in without hiding anything. 'I've a problem,' Liza said. 'And I've decided to deal with it and seek help.' It was perhaps the hardest of all the things Liza had done in public. But going to the Center at the highly fashionable township of Rancho Mirage in the hot, dry desert near Palm Springs fulfilled two vital functions: it weaned her off Valium and other drugs that had been cascading through her system at a rate of knots – and it helped draw attention to the severity of a problem that, with pain and effort, was curable.

Liza's own problem had been getting worse than ever. She liked to say that it was all to do with the show and the work it involved. Sometimes, she would not disagree with those who thought that the pace and manner in which she played had as much to do with it. She wasn't even joking now – except that she sometimes allowed the typical Minnelli humorous articulation to surface. 'My eyeballs are twirling,' she said. If you looked at her closely, they almost were.

Both girls were also facing up to another fact – whatever happened now, they would be compared with Judy. That was the hardest part of all: not only would the world outside their own circle be saying that they were going along the Garland path, they themselves had to worry that perhaps they were, that more than just a love of singing had been inherited. Liza didn't follow the usual pattern of being sent to the Eisenhower Medical Center first to be 'detoxified'. She had been working on her own 'cold turkey' treatment long enough for most of the toxins to be removed. Once at the Center, she was suffering all the usual withdrawal symptoms of depression and tears.

In addition – and this came as a shock to those who had envied the coterie of hangers-on who were always with her – she was more lonely than she had ever been before.

Certainly, there was no luxury there. She slept in a ward with a group of other women, from all sections of society. As she told *People* magazine. 'All of us had the same problem. This is not a picky disease.'

The staff kept her on the go all day; a day that began at what was for her just about twilight, the beginning of the night – 6.30 in the morning. It stopped only at seven o'clock in the evening.

She was told she had to do her own 'chores' – make her bed, clean around it, the kind of thing she hadn't done since she was at school and last slept in a dormitory. She kept a diary, so that she could catch up with herself. There were lectures. She went into group therapy. Learning just how much this was not a 'picky disease', how many other people suffered from the same symptoms, had the same problems, even if they had nothing like the material success of Liza Minnelli, was a cure in itself. As she was to say, she was used to living with survivors. Now she was in the company of women who hadn't all done well, who weren't sure that they had survived.

There was good reason for this approach. One of the great problems of addiction is that the sufferer thinks he or she is totally alone. No one else knows the way it feels. Now she knew that there were others out there who knew very well.

Elizabeth Taylor visited her, to show the effects of the treatment. She was, she said, totally better. Liza seemed impressed.

She told her she didn't really know what her trouble had been till she went to the Center.

Years later, Liza recalled: 'I faced my personal demons and nearly ran away.'

She was at the Center for less than two weeks. When she came out, she had a new outlook on life. She would go to 'chemical-dependency support group meetings' for a year after treatment.

'You don't just get fixed,' said Liza. 'You work on your programme all the time and you develop a good set of values. It's a

clarifying experience. You're allowed to think about yourself and
work on yourself – it's a luxury, but it's also scary. Who wants to stop
and look at themselves? But I'm very grateful now that I've done it.
I'm dealing with my feelings. I'm no longer burying things that are
going to come up and mug me later.'

She was told to rest for a year. That was taking the cure too far.
She couldn't live without planning the next tour. But she was going
to think more about herself – and then go to work.

She couldn't pretend that everything else was 'terrific'. Work was
fantasy and an escape from reality. The Betty Ford Center may have
persuaded her to give up drugs, but not her dependence on the
crutch of the fantastic. Facing life without applause was asking for
much more of a cold turkey cure than she was prepared to even
consider. But she had been told to take each day at a time and that
she was now doing. And, as she pointed out, she had taken stock.

As if to demonstrate the change in her life, she went to church –
Christ Church, New York – where she became a Dame of the Sacred
Order of St John, Knights of Malta. It was a gesture of recognition
for what she had done from an organisation that did not normally
go hand in hand with the sort of thing for which she had become
famous.

Nor would it have been particularly happy with the marital state
of its new Dame. In August, it was announced that Liza and Mark
were to file for divorce. The papers were submitted – and then
withdrawn. They decided to try again. Somehow, marriage itself
didn't mean very much to Liza any more. It had never been her
strong point – and the only man she had really ever loved to
distraction was her father.

Vincente was now seriously ill. He had had an operation for
kidney cancer and when the Rome Friends of Filmcritica awarded
him their 'City of Rome' award in November 1984, Liza went to the
Italian capital to collect it on his behalf.

'I always thought my father was the best,' said Liza telling nothing
but the truth. 'And it's wonderful to have the most beautiful city in
the world agree with me.'

Before long, she was back on the road. She really couldn't have
done anything else. This time, she said, she was going to appreciate
all that she had. 'I'm going to celebrate people's human-ness.' she
said. They knew what she meant. The old self-deprecating Liza
Minnelli humour was there, along with the talent. If she had burnt

herself up before, this was a phoenix in concert. In Chicago, she began her act with Jerome Kern's 'Pick Yourself Up'. The audience burst into applause. They saw she was dusting herself off and starting all over again.

Chapter Twenty-one

LIZA WOULD have liked people to think that she was now settled. She wasn't. But she had a new attitude to it all. Instead of worrying what people thought, she knew that she was helping other sufferers in talking about her problems.

She began to recognise the reason for them. Acquaintances would brave the question: with a mother like Judy, why didn't you *learn*? Her answer was sound: who are the child molesters? Those who were molested themselves. It put the matter into the mid-1980s perspective and she was, unfortunately, quite right.

The Betty Ford Center didn't say, in the way that Alcoholics Anonymous groups do, that once a drug addict always an addict, but that was the general idea. She had thousands of letters to answer and she did. When she travelled abroad, she would visit other support groups, sometimes in strange places – and always with members who were surprised out of their seats to see Liza Minnelli join them.

She went to Alcoholics Anonymous sessions too, revealing finally that it was a double problem.

She would go into the Betty Ford Center itself and talk to patients usually introducing herself (as if any introduction were in the least necessary), 'Hi, I'm Liza.' This was an audience who didn't say, 'We love you Liza', but were scared, and she appreciated the fact.

There was another factor, too: her drug and drink problems, at around about the same age as her mother had experienced hers, gave her, as she put it, her first opportunity to 'really bury' Judy, fifteen years after her death. If she had never been her own person before, she was determined to be so now. She had seen the glory of the coming of the Lord and she wanted to wait a little longer. She tried to show that she had a new sense of values. The marriage to Mark was doomed from the beginning. Lorna would say that she believed that he was taking advantage of her sister, partying at her expense, and she blamed him for her increasing dependency on drugs. There were constant rows between them. Eventually, he left.

'I was a drinking, drugging misogynist macho dago jerk,' he said of himself.

Liza would spend a lot of time with Lorna, living a normal existence in a normal house with a normal husband and a normal baby called Jesse. Lorna had told me that she envied Liza. Now the Paris-made shoe was on the other foot.

There were the traumas. In 1985 Vincente died and with him died a part of Liza, too. It isn't a trite thing to say: it was true. In a way, over the years since, she has built a shrine to his memory that she never created for Judy. Her mother was the visible parent and although Vincente was himself a great director, few talked of Liza as Vincente Minnelli's daughter. Now there are photographs of Vincente all over her home; there are none of Judy.

His influence had been tremendous from the time he first took her to those film sets. Now she was recognising the fact.

It was a time for reconciliation, too. She had had a big row a few years before with Sid Luft – when he organised a sale of Judy's effects, which Liza (and friends like Debbie Reynolds told me they felt the same way) thought ought to have been kept. The night before Vincente's funeral, however, 'Poppa Sid' had dinner with his stepdaughter and with Vincente's widow, Lee.

'We made it up,' he told me. 'I'm very, very proud of Liza.'

She was still anxious about her career and where it was taking her. In October, 1985, she branched out, and in her first dramatic rôle for television, *A Time To Live*, she played the mother of a boy dying from the effects of muscular dystrophy. It was a hard rôle to play, based on the life of a real woman. With her she went to a muscular-dystrophy ward. The effect was numbing, but it showed in her performance.

'I'm ready for a change,' she said. 'I want to grow in a new direction. In the future, I'd like to be more in the area of drama and comedy. They're not making too many musicals these days.' She said she drew on her father a great deal for the way she played the part of Mary Lou Weisman. 'You can't blame any of this on Mama. Not this time.'

But she did do the old things, too. She continued the concerts and people said she had never been better. She got a standing ovation at the Kennedy Center in Washington in October 1985.

In March 1986, she took the show to the London Palladium. The concert was taped and was shown in America on the Home Box Office network two months later. The title of the show said it all: 'Standing Room Only – Liza in London.'

It was her fortieth birthday, and she was celebrating it there in London. Lorna would report that she was in fine fettle and stone cold sober. But shortly afterwards, in the midst of a stage show with Elizabeth Taylor, she was once more under the influence. This time, she checked herself into a Minnesota rehabilitation centre. Lorna said she rang her to tell about it – in tears.

Basically, it was the same sort of Liza performance, but she paid a certain tribute to more contemporary artists. She greatly admired Madonna and said they were good friends.

In the early summer of 1987, she was back at Carnegie Hall and every seat was booked for the three-day run. This was a totally new Liza. As sure of herself as before, but more mature. She did the old routines, but there were new ones, too. Half way through the performance, she came on stage wearing a demure red dress and a hairstyle that was close to being sedate Edwardian. She sang old ballads, including an operatic version of 'Buckle Down, Winsocki.' Her audience were standing in their places, screaming for more.

It was a more mature audience, too – people who gave the impression of being regulars at 'the Hall', who were as at home there at a Leonard Bernstein concert as at a Liza Minnelli performance. There were the usual sprinkling of homosexuals in the audience – not a few who had come to Carnegie Hall in the final stages of AIDS – but everyone there seemed to have in common an admiration for an entertainer who was perhaps a throw-back to a previous generation and they were grateful to have been able to catch her in the process.

She sang 'Love For Sale', a number she said her father had taught her when she was four. Once more, it was Vincente she talked about. She said that he had read Colette to her when other fathers were telling their daughters the stories of Heidi.

When she sang 'Ringa Dem Bells', she put on her spectacles. Liza was now forty-one. In six years, she would be as old as her mother ever got.

She sang 'I Can See Clearly Now' and not a few understood when she added . . . 'If I can make it, now that the pain has gone . . .'

By the time it came to the finale, the audience was willing her to sing the now inevitable 'New York, New York'. It was her town, she seemed to be saying. She had lost the little town blues. There was no reason, though, why she wouldn't sing it wherever she went – like again in London the following November.

There was a lot of the old Liza in her. In her 1987 film *Rent A Cop*, she played . . . a hooker; once more a supporting rôle, as a side-kick to Burt Reynolds. She said that she believed the time had come to go back to Hollywood – which was perhaps why she drove a car with the number plate, EXCITEMENT. There was also excitement in her next product – a sequel to *Arthur*.

One thing was sure. Nobody now was asking her to think about what was going on over the rainbow. She had been there.

But the rainbow was losing its brighter colours. These were clearly the hardest and cruellest years in Liza's life, a decade or more of trying to recapture the great moments. In her 40s, she was looking too much like a backnumber, a woman with a following; a following, sure enough, that guaranteed standing-room-only audiences wherever she played. But there was too often the question to ask: So what have you done lately? If the words roller coaster could be applied to a human being, Liza was riding one and all too often looking as though she was about to fall off.

It wasn't easy for Liza being a Garland daughter. It was even harder for Lorna. She had to get used to being introduced not only for the Judy connection, but as 'Liza's little sister'. The trouble was, as she wrote in her revealing book *Me And My Shadows* that Liza's name (as in 'Liza Minnelli's sister') was bigger than hers on all the posters and other billings. That was an old showbiz problem, recognised by siblings of more successful performers in the same business. Harry Jolson, Al's elder brother, was always being billed that way, with the more famous Jolson getting the bigger lettering.

Lorna always said that she was proud of her sister and that there was no sense of competition between them.

In her book, Lorna said that she could never be sure whether Liza was her 'normal' self or just giving another performance. She said there was a blurring line 'between truth and performance'. Her stay at the Betty Ford Center hadn't changed her, even though she was no longer stoned. That was one difference between her and Judy – who had lived in a different world – or at least, so her younger daughter believed, simply because of her 'condition'. An interesting thought, that.

In 1988, Liza embarked on a gruelling tour that put her very much in the public eye, but it was not a huge success for her and she retired exhausted.

Of course, anyone would have been exhausted once they had taken on the mantle of being an honorary Rat Packer – which was, in effect, what she had become.

The original pack members, Frank Sinatra, Dean Martin and Sammy Davis Jr, had had a reunion but 'Dino' couldn't take the pace and Sinatra asked Liza to step into his shoes.

She would have been better off saying no – but then Sinatra and Davis would have been happier if they'd never asked.

Liza's domestic life, for a change, wasn't any happier. Her marriage to Mark Gero was officially over in 1992 and was no better than any of the others in her life.

'I never liked him,' says Sid Luft. 'He called himself a sculptor. I never knew who he was. He was just a user.'

It was Gero himself who divorced her after they'd been together for ten years. 'She paid him off and he went back to Italy on her money,' was how Luft put it.

Money was never important to Liza, at least not the way it was for other people. Yes, she had demanded and got the top dollar that was hers almost from the moment the curtain went down on *Flora, The Red Menace*. But she was of the I-Gotta-Sing, I-Gotta-Act, I-Gotta-Be-Seen school and the fact that she had an opportunity to sing, to act and be seen was enough. Her agents fixed the details of how many zeros there would be on her cheques. But the toll it all took on her was tremendous.

Her most regular appearances were at meetings of Alcoholics Anonymous. She impressed people. Going to the sessions at which she had to declare her alcoholism to an audience of people who couldn't have been more different from herself required a great deal of bravery and she showed it every time she went. It took a long time to work, but eventually it did, even if only in stops and spurts – a tribute to the philosophy of the organisation but, above all, to Liza herself.

She tried to show that life was still a cabaret old chum. She lived life to the excess of a star who had everything and wanted everyone to know – if she didn't have the big stuff, how could she still be a big star? To prove the point, there were four portraits of her by Andy Warhol hanging in the foyer of her luxury apartment on New York's fashionable Upper East Side.

She continued to make movies, always hoping that there would be another *Cabaret* around the corner. But you can't find a good cabaret these days anywhere and maybe that's why she couldn't make it.

Her list of films in the late 1980s and early 1990s reads like a shopping list and will be no more remembered than details on a list taken to the supermarket. *Rent A Cop, Arthur 2, Stepping Out* (a British-made musical co-starring Julie Walters, which led to a series of stage shows at the Radio City Music Hall, using that title) and *Parallel Lives* contributed nothing to her happiness and less to the history of Hollywood.

There were always attempts to show that she was still as good as she ever had been. At the 1993 Tony Awards ceremony, she was the hostess – and sang a medley of hit songs with Lorna. It was a brief moment of rapprochement with her younger sister. Although both would deny it, there was a continuing sense of rivalry between them, much like the one between Judy and Liza.

A few months later, she was in Moscow – part of the hands-across-the-Volga (to say nothing of the Black Sea and the Atlantic Ocean) relationship with the new post-Soviet Russian federation. Liza was featured in the D-Day 50th anniversary celebrations there.

But that was Russia. What about at home? Liza plainly needed a boost to her career. The best way of doing that was to make another film, better than all the others. When she heard that Andrew Lloyd Webber was looking for a new Evita for the screen version of the hit musical, she was tested. It was not a good idea and she didn't get the role that years later went to Madonna.

It was clearly a bad time for her – and one that was getting worse.

In 1995, things improved slightly when she co-starred with Shirley MacLaine in the TV movie, *The West Side Waltz*.

She was at her nadir in 1996. In London, she appeared on the *Big Breakfast* TV show and was supposed to jump on to a double bed in the company of a rather large lady called Vanessa Feltz, which was, of course, a matter of taste. Getting on to the bed, recalled Ms Feltz, wasn't the problem, it was getting up the stairs to the studio. She reported that Liza fell up the stairs on the way to the studio – which, to be fair, could happen to anyone missing a step. But, claimed the newspaper columnist, 'though charming, she seemed distracted, dazed and confused'.

It seemed only a matter of time before her career declined into oblivion.

In February 1997, she was welcomed back to Broadway in her own right. Julie Andrews had had another of her triumphs on stage, in a live version of her movie role of the female impersonator (a woman who pretends to be a man who pretends to be a woman – easy, once you think about it) in *Victor, Victoria*. When she decided she needed a holiday, Liza was invited to take over from her.

She not only accepted happily, she was thrilled. And so was the theatre-going public. The producers of *Victor, Victoria* couldn't have been happier. It was only for four weeks, but those four weeks brought the biggest audiences to the Great White Way. She was so sensational, so fully getting into the spirit of the occasion, that Ed Vulliamy wrote in the London newspaper, *The Guardian*, it was 'like watching motorcycle racing'.

There was a greatness about her on the stage sometimes. There was also a sense of gaucheness. She made mistakes singing songs or reciting speeches, but even they always seemed to be part of a script.

The four weeks made her seriously ill – and didn't make the other members of the cast feel too well either. She and her co-star Tony Roberts, a Broadway and Hollywood veteran, hated each other and it was said he pretended he was ill so as not to have to face her on stage. He claimed that she got into tantrums, and complained about her 'flamboyant interpretation' of her role.

But, much to Mr Roberts's relief, Liza couldn't have continued. Polyps were found on her vocal chords and they were removed by a surgery that no one could guarantee would ever allow her to sing again. Yet sing again she did – with no apparent repercussions from the operation. Before long, Ms Andrews herself was to have the same operation, but with disastrous results. Liza was so much more lucky that, after resting on her own doctors' orders for a month, she said that she would always be happy to go into the role again – but Roberts would have to be well out of the way. That opportunity did not present itself to her again.

There was a great series of comebacks scheduled for her in Britain in 1998. She was going to set the nation alight. Alas, it didn't happen. Serious concerns were expressed for her health and the tour was cancelled.

The following year, she was feeling better and was saying that all her previous problems were behind her. There were no more drugs, no more booze in her life.

She was no longer married and saw no reason to go to the altar or the Justice of the Peace's offices again. Marriage had brought her no happiness. She had even been denied what she wanted most – the chance to have children. But now at the age of 52 she still wanted to have them. No, she wasn't going to seek fertility treatment via an anonymous donor. She simply wanted to adopt. Undoubtedly, the question of adoption was deep in her heart. She put it nicely. 'When one's been through and learned on the way, the least you can do is pass it on to an unloved child who has lost its parents.'

The question in more than one mind was simply this: just how much had she learned 'on the way'?

Her closest friends were brought into the picture. Mia Farrow and Rosie O'Donnell had both adopted babies – in Mia's case in the glare of publicity. 'The only thing missing in my life,' Liza declared, 'is being a mother. I've had it all. Now I want a child to share it with.'

A 'friend' was quoted at this time as saying, 'Liza is the godmother to two of Mia Farrow's children by André Previn and Mia has been whispering in her ear for years that adopting a baby would change her life. When it comes time for a big holiday like Thanksgiving or Christmas, and the family is supposed to get together, Liza never gets invited.'

Why? Because she had no children to bring with her? No, the less than friendly friend explained. 'This is because she has been at war with everyone.'

There were plenty of people willing to give evidence to that effect, one of whom was Liza's half-sister, Lorna – who was not always known as the easiest person in the world either, especially to her father, Sid Luft, who even now shrugs off the relationship by saying things like, 'Well, you know Lorna.'

There were stories of the two women not talking to each other for four or more years – a break that also affected Liza's relationship with Lorna's children, to whom she had been close, saying that she always loved them as much as had they been her own.

The truth was that Liza was mainly at war with herself. The pills and the drink were not good for her. But much of her problem had nothing to do with her own mistreatment of herself or neglect. Indeed, she could have said they were caused by the end of that apparent self-destruction.

It was the spring of 1999 that she gave yet another comeback performance in New York. In *Minnelli on Minnelli*, she paid tribute to her father, a one-woman show based on numbers connected with his movies. People liked the show, but that, too, was to have its share of disasters. On stage, she fell and severely injured a spinal disc as well as her left hip. She was rushed to hospital and the hip was replaced, just another example of the medical jinx in her life.

Was it all just another of all those similarities between Liza and her mother? It is all too easy to see the similarities. 'I don't buy that,' said her stepfather, Sid Luft, early in 2003. 'Not really. Liza is her own person and Judy was hers. Her problem was that she [Judy] was a pill taker, like Marilyn Monroe. Actually, Judy and Marilyn were telephone pals. They'd make midnight calls to each other.

'These people sign up, go to AA meetings and so on, still there's always that fear that they had of getting off the wagon, so to speak. Liza's problem was not pills. Liza's problem was alcohol.' But, actually, there were pills, too.

She put on weight – more weight than people could imagine the formerly sexy Liza ever getting. The weight had disastrous effects on her. She was unable to sustain her posture and, as a result, damaged her back. At the same time, she severely hurt her other hip. Before long, both hips were replaced. The problem was complicated by more operations on her knees.

Liza was still, though, full of the show-must-go-on spirit. 'I feel fabulous,' she said before going down to the operating theatre to have both a hip and her back opened up. 'I've been in and out of a wheelchair. But I feel healthy. I feel like a bloody ox, darling. I feel very good. I'm so happy.'

At that stage no one knew why. Things, however, would only get worse. The sight that Liza presented in 2000 was not one that gave any pleasure to the people who had worshipped at the Minnelli shrine. She was rushed to hospital on a stretcher, suffering from what, nobody was willing to say. The truth of the matter is that nobody actually knew what was wrong with her. When, while staying in her luxurious villa in Fort Lauderdale, Florida, she collapsed in a series of convulsions, the doctors assumed she had had a stroke. They knew she still had trouble with her hip, but this time it was not merely orthopaedic. She looked sick – no colour in a face that was severely bloated.

It wasn't the girl from *Cabaret* that they remembered. Not the star in the scarlet dress that barely covered the essentials whom they recalled cheering as she threw out an arm and belted some of the great numbers of her career. Now, she couldn't belt out anything. If she spoke at all, it was in a mumble, but she wasn't doing much in the way of mumbling.

She was so desperately ill that doctors recommended that her family and friends should be called.

A few days later, it was revealed that she was suffering from an illness that could be fatal and, yes, doctors said, she was now close to death. She was suffering from viral encephalitis, a sickness that can have desperate effects even if a recovery happens. In layman's terms, it is an inflammation of the brain and is as horrific as it sounds. Exactly what the effects are depend on which part of the brain is affected.

The encephalitis was much worse than the public were led to believe. But the doctors kept little back. They told Liza, not that she would never dance again, but that she would never even walk. It depressed her. When it seemed all behind her, she said that she laughed it all off. 'I'm just a cockeyed optimist,' she said, quoting the line from the *South Pacific* song. But just how true that was at the time – or at any time – she wouldn't say.

Liza was very seriously ill, but she was left with none of the effects that can strike – a loss of memory, a loss of speech, of hearing, of sight or of balance. People catch it as a result of measles or chicken pox (it can be a severe form of shingles). In Liza's case, it was said to be caused by a mosquito bite.

The bites of the Press at times seemed almost as severe, but Liza and those close to her kept the details to themselves.

Something rather strange and surprising did come out of it all, however. The illness saw a reunion of Liza and Lorna – for the first time since the Betty Ford Center catastrophe. Lorna was sitting by her bedside when she awoke from a near coma.

It seemed that there was no way forward for her. As in most cases of encephalitis, there were complications, the worst of which was a difficulty in breathing. Her lungs were in a terrible state, although nobody could be sure that that was a direct result of the illness or of the attack of double pneumonia that went with it. This was a gal who suffered.

The results of all this caused as much inward suffering as the sicknesses themselves. She was warned by the doctors that she had to rest for a year, live like an invalid or else suffer the probable consequences, like losing her singing voice altogether.

Incredibly, she agreed to comply and shut herself up in a Florida villa. The only time she went out at all was to make an occasional visit to Disney World or to go to local restaurants with the closest of close friends.

Few people recognised her, which was probably the way she wanted it, now that food was her principal indulgence, to say nothing of addiction, and had by then put on so much weight that she now tipped the scales at 14 stone.

Yet a year later, she was up and about – almost. She was in a wheelchair and again people were shocked to see her. The once sexy figure, if you could see it, was bloated beyond almost all recognition. She smiled when spotted, but it was a false smile, a smile that kidded no one that this was really a happy lady, a lady with two or more chins.

You didn't have to be too clever to realise that the effects of her medication had taken their toll, although less tactful people said she simply was eating too much and couldn't stop her addiction – no longer to drink and drugs, but to banana pies.

Yet in May 2001 she was seen in public again. Still in a wheelchair, she went to the first night of the new Broadway production of *42nd Street*.

But she was seemingly making a remarkable recovery.

After the planes flew into the World Trade Center on September 11, 2001, she joined in the I-Love-New York tributes. She sang – well, of course, she did – 'New York, New York' at the city's Shea Stadium

In December that year she was having more anti-addiction treatment, this time to break the spiral of painkillers. She could not give up smoking, however, although she promised she would do so.

But things were looking as though they were getting better. She had a new man in her life, the TV and spectacle producer David Gest.

It had all the marks of a transformation – and all the ingredients of one of those show business occasions which were all show and little serious business.

People had been there before and they knew that Liza had, too. She was full of excitement, full of exuberance, full of telling the world that past troubles were over. She had found her man and she was sticking to him, just as he was staying with her. Cynics, as cynics would, worried about her. People who had been there before worried, too. Her closest friends and members of her family were the most concerned.

But when she announced her engagement to David Gest she said she had never been happier and there seemed, at last, reason to believe her. At least for the moment.

She and Gest had known each other for 15 years – ever since they were introduced by Frank Sinatra at his Palm Springs home. But it was when Gest produced the Michael Jackson TV special in which she was making a guest appearance – it was to mark his 30th anniversary in show business and turned out to be the most successful show of its kind for 10 years – that they started becoming, to use the Hollywood expression much abused in today's media, 'an item'.

He had gone to Liza's house to discuss the idea of her being on the show. And, here was the surprise both for him and for everyone else concerned, he was there to tell her he didn't want her to appear at all. He had heard all the stories that she was overweight and too addicted to the booze and drugs. 'I didn't think [she] was in the right physical condition to compete with Whitney [Houston] and Luther [Vandross] and a lot of the people.'

Then, he said, he heard her sing 'and I looked at this little girl with the sweetest heart in the world. I knew right then I was in love.'

By all accounts, David gave her a reason to start living again – and to get rid of all those pounds. 'You have everything to live for, so shed the weight,' he told her.

He knew that she was never happy off the stage, but she had to slim down to avoid getting nothing more than a sympathy vote – if she were ever able to go back on the boards. They say that nobody since Vincente had given her as much encouragement or a bigger push. Gest became her manager and, before long, her lover.

He told her to study the contemporary pop singers and note the present show business scene. She couldn't afford simply to rest on her laurels. They were no longer comfortable enough to rest upon. She had to be bigger and better than ever before.

'Liza has won every award,' he said, 'done everything it is possible to do in show business, but there is still so much more she can do.'

He had known all her troubles – which was a considerable achievement in itself. He also knew something that nobody outside of an AA chapter did. She was still hitting the bottle, although she did try to climb on to that wagon. 'I kept saying,' Liza would report, 'I think I am going to drink' and then added: 'I'm going to get help'.

The biggest help came, as promised, from David Gest.

Sid Luft, in an exclusive interview for this book, told about the time Liza came to introduce David to the man she always regarded as a second father.

They spent about 15 minutes together, but it was enough to convince the older man that he liked his step son-in-law. 'I thought he was very pleasant, but rather shy,' which is perhaps surprising for a man who was used to putting on Broadway and TV spectacles, to say nothing of shows in Las Vegas. Anyone who could manage Michael Jackson, as he had in his shows, had to be used to handling problems.

On this occasion, it didn't look as if there were going to be serious difficulties – particularly with 'Pop'.

'We were up at the Ritz Carlton Hotel on the Marina [the Marina Del Ray, just outside the suburban Los Angeles sprawl]. All the boats were tied up as she looked out.'

She had, she told him, an important announcement to make about her present state of health.

'Pop,' she said, 'I'm off alcohol and I'll never drink again.' Sid hoped that she meant it. It was, after all, the oft heard statement of all alcoholics who had managed to mount the wagon and looked firmly enough settled on it to not seem as if they were about to fall off. And her health seemed robust. Nobody – unless she was actually hiding something – would guess that she had been so close to death. Sid, who had seen at close quarters the effects that booze and drugs had had on Judy, thought what everyone else had allowed to enter their minds: that Liza was inevitably going to go the same way. Yet there were no obvious signs of anything. No facial paralysis, frequently a symptom of encephalitis, no difficulty walking – amazing for someone who had left hospital a cripple. No problems speaking, the curse which had dogged her early days of slow recovery.

She had lost an incredible 100 lb in weight, despite the addition of an artificial hip or two. As Sid Luft said, she not only looked good, but she had, to use his words 'got all her marbles together', a suggestion perhaps of just how upset she was by the way things were going for her.

But the real point of the meeting was to introduce him to David.

He wasn't about to ask for her hand in marriage, although for a sneaking moment 'Pop' hoped that he might. But he was happy to concede that David seemed good for the girl he still regarded as his own daughter.

'Well,' he said, 'this guy is a miracle. You have been so sick with your back, your bad hip and how he does it, I don't know. I think he is wonderful for you.'

The wedding was just a month away.

At 56, Liza was marrying for the fourth time, which in Hollywood terms was nothing very special. The occasion, however, was more spectacular than any of the previous occasions.

When it happened, the world gasped. Literally. Television, newspapers and celebrity magazines treated it as the event of the year. In London, *The Times* had it about right when it reported that 'New York celebrates what in American show business circles is undoubtedly a royal wedding'.

It had all began a couple of days earlier with the bridal shower – a little intimate gathering with Donna Summer singing for the ever-growing Liza female set.

Actually, it all began with the invitations – and the accompanying wedding list. Anyone who doesn't care for being told what to give and how much to spend for a bride or bridegroom would have had a marvellous case to build on. They were told that the bridal list was held at Tiffany's – well, of course, where else? Actually, also at those downmarket emporia called Bergdorf Goodman and the Lalique store. If anyone wanted to know what to give the couple who had everything, the safe answer was 'don't ask'.

As an idea of what they were expecting – 'hoping for' would be inadequate – the listings ranged from silver tureens at $4,000 each (a mere snip, except you had to guarantee to give a set of four of them, and, in any case, there was a 'sold' sign above those if you decided that was your choice) to a soap dish at only $495 – that would probably have guaranteed a place at a table next to the kitchen. On the other hand, you could have given one of the $39.95 'emergency lanterns' that they wanted (even better, they were in the sale at $14.99). The downside to that was that they required 100 of them, and wouldn't accept anything less. Mind you there were napkin rings at $250, but they required 16 of those. Or butter knives at $65 each. They didn't specify how many they needed, but you couldn't have got away with just one. If you were feeling pinched financially, they would have been happy with a pair of silver candlesticks for only $2,300.

The wedding itself wasn't just a glittering occasion for the showbiz fraternity. Liza arrived in a black dress, but changed into white (designed by Bob Mackie) and the guests had to produce specially-designed black invitations to get in.

It had all the spectacle of a Broadway opening or of Oscar night in Hollywood – an Oscar night that cost $2 million.

And one that proved, despite calls for restraint after the terrorist outbreaks of the previous year, that September 11 made no difference to things if you were rich and celebrated. As one of the onlookers noted: 'Someone should have explained that those twin beams of light shining into the night sky are not footlights'.

The Marble Collegiate Church, which follows the Dutch Reformed rite, was the ideal setting for the ceremony on March 16, 2002 – not because either of the couple were used to worshipping there or at any other church on Fifth Avenue for that matter, but because it looked like something out of a Hollywood screen wedding spectacle.

There were 16 exquisitely dressed bridesmaids. And since this was going to be that Royal Wedding, they weren't just any old friends of the bride wearing dresses she had chosen for them from a catalogue.

You could be kind and say the assemblage of bridal assistants was a gathering of some of the greatest names in show business. You could also say they were the oldest bridesmaids ever seen – ranging in age from a totally acceptable 26 to an unconventional 78. Certainly, it was a wonderful assortment of the Misses Yesterday, who were told to 'wear basic black'.

One was the former elfin Mia Farrow, ex-Mrs Frank Sinatra and ex-lover of Woody Allen, with whom Liza went to school. Janet Leigh, who had starred in *Psycho* more than forty years earlier, was another. Petula Clark, Gina Lollobrigida and Claudia Cardinale were among the others. Just to show, however, that Liza knew what was happening in the world of today, the list also included the *My Fair Lady* star and *EastEnders* player Martine McCutcheon, and Chaka Khan, winner of seven Grammies. Cindy Adams, the *New York Post* columnist, who described the whole junket as a 'zoo' was another. She said: 'There's no celebrity left unturned. If they could get a bigger name, they'd bounce me from the wedding party.'

To complete the picture of having only the most important stars as bridesmaids, Esther Williams, who had once done impossible things in the MGM swimming pool (alongside a lighted candelabra that was seen to come up, with all candles blazing, from under the water) was invited to complete the team but, without anyone knowing why, decided not to come.

But almost everyone else did. As Jack Warner, the Hollywood mogul, once put it 'Who's Who and Who's Through' was there – including Michael Douglas and Catherine Zeta Jones, Michael's father Kirk Douglas, Sir Andrew Lloyd Webber, Sir Anthony Hopkins, Donny Osmond, Andy Williams, Elton John and, in his last expedition before his death, Dudley Moore, unable to speak, walk or eat.

Mickey Rooney described it as 'one of the most thrilling weddings I've ever been to'. He should know – he's had eight of them himself.

The newspapers had a field day, exploding in delicious sarcasm (irony would have been too kind a word). Cindy Adams gave an insider's view: 'I haven't seen so much hype since Donald Trump's last catered divorce'. And there was this from the *Boston Globe*: It's the wedding of the century after three weddings last century'. The *New York Post* summed it up beautifully: 'Liza's Nutty Nuptials.'

There was a rehearsal, which, if everyone had come – which they didn't – would have been an occasion in itself. *Brides* magazine editor Millie 'Martini' Bratten said it was all 'over the top', but was probably salivating as she said it.

Guests had to pass through metal detectors to enter the church and the following reception – not because any of them could be suspected of carrying bombs or guns, but – even more worryingly – of sneaking in cameras.

OK magazine paid $400,000 for the photographic rights, which helped to defray the cost of the shindig (the presents would have gone a good way to do so, too). To make sure that they got the exclusive rights, no other guests were allowed to produce either still cameras or camcorders. There was obviously a serious attempt to make sure there was no recurrence of what had happened at the Douglas-Zeta Jones nuptials – the pair ended up suing *Hello* magazine for publishing unauthorised snaps.

The centre point – appropriately enough – was a stage-like structure on which stood the minister, surrounded by people Liza regarded as her close friends. Matrons of honour were Marisa

Berenson, who had appeared with her in *Cabaret* and – here, the announcements seemed to gasp – Elizabeth Taylor, to whom she had been close for years. She was given a private plane to fly her from Los Angeles. Quite appropriately, Michael Jackson, who seems to have taken on the role as comfort and confidante of ladies who have recovered from the depths (Ms Taylor's last wedding was held at his Neverland home) was given a place of honour, too, as best man.

He was there as much for David as for Liza. As he said, 'People don't really understand Michael Jackson. He's not the soft type of person people think. He talks very kind of loud and a little bit more harsh and he knows what he is doing. I think people have been very cruel to him when he has given so much.' They had lived near each other in the California town of Encino and had been friends since they were 12 years old. They played baseball and basketball with each other.

Liza saw in Michael a soul brother who had been abused by the media – even if she didn't exactly put it like that. 'He's been hurt too much. Rotten things have been said about him.'

Jackson's brother Tito, who was described as 'second best man' – which didn't mean he was only second best – was one of David's closest friends. The three other former members of the Jackson Five – Marlon, Randy and Jacky – acted as ushers. Others were the actors Tony Franciosa and Robert Wagner, neither apparently too worried about being low down in the billing.

Jackson was the one everybody was looking at, Sid Luft maintained. 'He looked very excited, as a good friend would. They are always very lovely to each other.'

Sid Luft sat in the front row with his wife, Camille, and Liza's brother Joey. Lorna was not listed among the people who were there – which seemed to confirm the impression that they were still not all that close, although Sid maintains that they are now friends.

Perhaps in a gesture to show that she was very much her own woman, neither Sid nor anyone else gave her away. She didn't walk down the aisle in the traditional way either.

The ceremony began with Whitney Houston singing 'The Greatest Love of All'.

The ceremony was followed by a reception at the swanky Regent Hotel in Wall Street, just a piece of rubble's throw from Ground Zero, site of the Twin Towers destroyed in the terrorist action of September 11, 2001. The hotel was one of those buildings that likes to think it has ancient and olde worlde values, at least as close to being as ancient and olde worlde as it is usually possible for Americans to be. 'She was happy as a lark,' recalls Luft. 'Very affectionate.' She also needed to be very tall, which she was not, to even contemplate cutting the 7-ft high cake.

She was affectionate to any or all the 300 guests who were there. That was the official figure. Other reports claimed there were 900 people there and Sid Luft said he was one among 2,000.

Whatever the actual number of people present, there was no doubt that the 'show' was spectacular. David Gest brought 54 entertainers (including Dionne Warwick, the Pointer Sisters and Gloria Gaynor, who sang what was regarded by some as Liza's own personal anthem, 'I Will Survive') and an 80-piece orchestra, but the real show was Liza herself, whose contribution to the entertainment was to dance on the tables.

'I'm the happiest I've ever been,' she was reported as saying. 'Everything I've been through was worth it to find David.'

Inevitably, people started keeping diaries to record just how long the marriage would last, picking on the fact, no doubt, that they had signed a prenuptial agreement, just in case they turned out to be not quite so happy as they appeared to be.

But at that moment, happy was precisely what they were.

They were happy, no one doubted that. When people made comments about David or his potential as a satisfying husband she responded angrily and took his part. They wanted the world to see how happy they were.

The couple went to London for their honeymoon – a deliciously happy couple of weeks marred only by a thief trying to snatch her diamond necklace as she leaned out of their limousine in the West London district of Holland Park. (It was a huge cross, given to her as a wedding present and said to be worth £10,000.)

She was on the way back from the BBC TV Centre where she had been recording an interview with David on the popular Jonathan Ross show. The car stopped at a red light close by Holland Park tube station. The attempt was foiled by the alert chauffeur who closed the electric window, giving the prospective thieves the choice between getting away or having their arms chopped off – or being dragged along the road. The man at the wheel knew more about life than Liza. She thought the gang merely wanted her autograph.

It took a time to get over the scare of the attempted mugging, which shocked them because they said they 'weren't aware that these sorts of things happen' in London. But Liza, who did everything extravagantly, did so in a somewhat unconventional way. They sat down and drank – cappuccino in a Starbucks coffee shop. When they got back to their hotel, the plush Lanesborough, they hung a notice on the door, saying 'Do not disturb until teatime'.

As she said, 'I'm a New Yorker after all'. She was still having a 'great time' in London which was 'my second home'. The would-be thieves were 'just a few kids fooling around'. No one can even be sure that those 'kids' knew who she was. They just saw a sparkling jewel that looked good for the taking.

That didn't stop the Gests announcing that they now intended to make London not just their second home, but their first home. She had always loved England and its capital. Besides, it seemed to be the fashionable thing to do. Madonna had led the parade, setting up home in London, and so had Robert De Niro and Tom Cruise.

How true were those stories? Not very, because they also said they were going to spend half the year in France – and the other half in New York. As Liza said: 'I learned about France early'. The main thing that got her going, she said, was when her father got the Légion d'Honneur for *Gigi* and *An American In Paris*.

Meanwhile, Liza was bolstered by the reaction of audiences to the show she gave at the Royal Albert Hall, as well known as a home for the world's top entertainers as it was for classical music and opera performances. It was the beginning of a European tour. Seemingly, she believed in working holidays and a working honeymoon had to be no different. It would help further defray the cost of the wedding junket and was calculated to make sure that Liza, the woman who was only happy when performing, really enjoyed herself.

Not that it was that easy to organise. She had rehearsed back in New York and found it very uncomfortable. She said she once more had nodules on her vocal chords, the familiar singer's curse. But she still took the Concorde to London and had no reason to regret going ahead with the Albert Hall booking.

David knew that she had made the right decision – and so had he. 'The reason why life is great is that a) we are in love, b) Liza wanted to get better, and c) she's got much more to give.' Yet nobody pretended that her voice was as good as it had once been. She quivered and quaked a bit more than usual and getting to the high notes was a bit like a woman of uncertain years climbing a steep staircase.

But, conversely, nobody seemed to worry all that much about it. Audiences had never seemed happier. The stars turned out, too – led by Tony Bennett, who clapped, shouted and joined in the six standing ovations that greeted her appearances. David was in the front row as a kind of cheerleader for it all.

There were so many people wanting to get in, the story was that all London's gay bars closed until after the concert finished. They dominated the audience that night and, appropriately, comedian and TV chat show host Graham Norton was the warm-up act. 'It's like a rent-boy convention,' he noted. And if the audience were embarrassed about that, he had the right words soon afterwards. 'We are in the presence of a legend,' he declared, and you had to admit that there was no gainsaying that.

Certainly, it was an amazing event. So amazing that the press, both in Britain and across the Pond, couldn't contain themselves. It wasn't every day that a legend comes out on stage in April wearing a floor-length white mink coat. The spangles were revealed a little later.

Glyn Brown in the *Sunday Telegraph* was a little too honest about it all. 'At the end, she tells us again and again how much she loves us. No one – apart from her mother – was ever so needy.'

But the audience gave every impression of being just as needy of her talents.

In London's *Observer* newspaper, David Benedict reported: 'Liza is a cabaret, old chum'. He compared her with that shouter and screamer from a previous generation, Ethel Merman, for whom audiences 'sat up and listened' when she sang 'Some People'. He could have added 'There's No Business Like Show Business'. But this was a show business event *par excellence*, and even La Merman couldn't match this kind of audience reaction. The only difference between the kind of response she had achieved and that which greeted every Liza number was that this time the audience stood up. 'Correction,' he wrote, 'they leaped up and yelled.'

They didn't even mind that she fluffed the occasional line. They loved her all the more for it. It wasn't a concert, said the writer, it was a revivalist meeting. They liked everything she did – even, remarkably, when she mimed a recording of 'Losing My Mind' along with the Pet Shop Boys.

What they liked most apparently was her moment of autobiography. It wasn't the kind that her mother had told – you know, about being born in a trunk in the Princes Theater at Pokatella, Idaho, which wasn't really true at all. Liza had all the facts to lay before her audience in a specially written song: 'I took all the pills and flushed them away/I emptied the booze and I went to AA.'

Everyone knew that she had done just that, but the admission before 6,000 people was in itself riveting.

And there was a great sense of occasion about it all – not just the occasion of Liza's performance, but of what was happening in Britain at that moment. The Queen Mother had just died and Liza managed to mention the fact. She said she remembered when she sang for the old queen. 'I'm so sorry for your loss,' she said as though she had come visiting a house of mourning, even if this one was perhaps the residence of quite different kinds of queens. But nobody was mourning that night, apart from hazarding a wish that she had concentrated on what she could do best. 'New York, New York' was indeed that. But 'I'll Be Seeing You', supposedly one of the Queen Mum's favourites, jarred. Not that you would have noticed.

She ended in fine form with an adaptation of her *Cabaret* refrain. 'When I go, I'm NOT going like Elsie.' The audience went crazy.

Surprisingly to some, she and David went on the TV talkshow circuit – if only to counter all the rumours about the new Mr Minnelli (she couldn't resist that one) being a homosexual. It was *Vanity Fair* that first proclaimed David was gay. Neither he nor Liza – especially after her earlier experiences – was happy about that.

The effort was made to emphasise that she wasn't going to go down that lane again. Gest had one distinct advantage in his favour – Peter Allen was always surrounded by gays. David was happy to allow them to form the core of his wife's audiences and that was all. But people persisted. After all, wasn't he unmarried and had never been married when he and Liza first met? Didn't he collect Lalique glass – now there was a sign of something or other – and, worst of all, didn't he pluck his eyebrows and have a permanent tan? That all also added up to something, although what no one could be really sure.

Sir Elton John had a lot to answer to in that regard. He was on TV in the run up to the wedding and was asked what he would be giving as a present. 'A heterosexual husband,' he replied.

She sang on the David Letterman show – a difficult song which Sid Luft recalls as having 'flowed like her old talented self. It flowed . . . as easy as I had ever seen or heard her before.'

On the Larry King show, Gest pledged his everlasting devotion.

'We are going to beat the odds,' he said. 'We're going to die in each other's arms, I promise you.'

What was there about David Gest that made him seem so different from the other men in her life, Larry King asked her. 'He's the most brilliant producer,' she said. 'Also, he's so funny. He's very special. We knew we really liked each other. As a musician would say, "We dug each other".'

People heard that and waited to see how long that would remain the case.

'We're going to beat the odds,' she repeated. 'We'll die in each other's arms.'

As was only to be expected, the press were sceptical.

There was always that running battle with the press. In kinder moments, she recognised it and said she was reconciled to the problem. As she once noted: 'It sells papers. I'm very glad I sell papers.'

There was now an opportunity to give advice. People phoned in to the show and wanted to know more about how she had conquered her problems and what they themselves could do. She told one woman: 'You're not going to enjoy this news very much. If I was you – and I have been you and you know it or else you wouldn't be asking me this – I would bite the bullet and go some place, to go off all the medications, so I knew what I was really feeling. Then there's help everywhere. But it comes from within – it takes some real work. But you won't believe how you'll feel. You know, I can move anywhere I want to, bend any which way I want to. But it took a while…'

Then they announced what Liza had wanted for so long – they were going to adopt a three-year-old girl whom they knew was called Serena.

Why a three-year-old? 'Because,' she told Larry King, 'that's quite a luxury, to get a child at birth. I think that a child that hasn't had the chance yet to be loved and supported and somebody to laugh with, that's OK when somebody who is already here and doesn't have anything. That's why I thought an older child was more understandable for my age.'

David said he thought she was going to be 'the greatest mother in the world'.

But would it happen? Only time would tell – about them and about the marriage. For the moment, it looked like everything was perfect for them – and for Liza in particular.

Sid Luft is still ecstatic about the way his step-daughter has conquered her previous problems. 'She is good natured and very generous.' She was always particularly generous to her half-brother Joey and frequently helped him out of his various financial problems.

Certainly, she was a sight for sore eyes. She looked wonderful and it would be churlish to say that that was simply the work of a studio make-up department. As Sid Luft said: 'I was so proud of her. Her legs had slimmed. She looked stunning in a short dress.' To prove the point, he sent her two dozen red roses – to join the dozens of others that had found their way to her New York apartment.

Luft picked up on what others had noticed: David Gest had taken charge. 'Kind of domineering as if he were running the show.' But his step father-in-law would insist that he was not perturbed about that. 'It didn't bother me because I could see that she was now a brand-new woman. That is incredible. I thought, 'Liza, keep it going and you'll own the world one more time.'

The most bizarre chatshow was one in which Liza 'interviewed' David – or was it the other way round? – on the *Entertainment Tonight* show. They were described as 'New York's most outrageous couple' – and judging from the way they carried it all out, that seemed only reasonable.

'OK, David,' she began, 'if you could change one thing about me what would it be?' Gest replied that what he had in mind was the 58th hair on her head, which was 'a little slanted'. That was about the level of it all. He also told her that he thought her best physical feature was her nose and her left breast – not that he wasn't just as enthusiastic about her right breast, which we were all much relieved to know. He was laying it on the line that he was not a man to have favourites.

He was annoyed that she would interrupt an important phone call by asking for his opinion on a new dress or her hairstyle. Oh yes, she told him she loved him because he was so 'loyal'. It was time to break up and get a hamburger. No, said David exercising his influence, he preferred a turkey burger.

We were so glad to know all that, too.

Certainly, on the chatshows both in America and Britain, she had all the confidence of someone who really did own the world. But her love affair with television was short-lived. In November, she and David were in the midst of a huge row with the VH1 TV company, who had set up a series of weekly one-hour 'reality television' programmes, featuring the pair.

It set out to be a remarkably frank fly-on-the-wall series of one-hour programmes that included almost everything but the couple in bed or in the bathroom. There was talk of them even allowing the cameras in on Liza's AA meetings. This notion was rejected because Liza said it would invade the privacy of other members.

But it didn't work out according to plan and was called off after the newspapers carried the first advertisements for the series.

They said they gave more time than that to which they were contracted and complained that the crews had wrecked their furniture and damaged the walls and ceiling during 60 hours of abortive filming, in which they built a virtual studio inside the house.

The whole thing came unstuck over a dinner party, which one might have thought was the simplest of the things that could have been screened. But the TV company weren't happy with the guest list – although Ray Charles and Luther Vandross were among those who accepted invitations to be featured on screen, eating Liza's food and ready to enjoy her singing.

The Gests said that 60 technicians invaded their house. But they denied that they had insisted that the TV people wore 'surgical bootees' while working there.

It was while she was indeed singing 'Maybe This Time' at the dinner table that the trouble broke out. It got worse when she went into an aria, 'And The World Goes Round' from her film, *New York, New York*. Gest later said that the show's producer wanted to know why Michelle Branch and Kelly Rowland, singers then top of the pops in America, hadn't turned up – and if he couldn't guarantee they would come, he was cancelling the whole series.

David said that one of the TV people was 'screaming in my ear' and was 'jabbing and poking me' during the row. He was, he said, 'very, very rude'.

They complained that if it were really a 'reality' show they should be allowed to invite who they wanted to their dinner parties, not those nominated by the production company. But they vociferously denied that the whole thing was organised simply to get more presents. As Gest said, they had 1,000 gifts at their wedding, why would they want more?

On the *Larry King Live* show on CNN, David said he was hit in the arm as the producer made his demands. The next day the man rang to say that the show was cancelled.

Meanwhile, the company said they weren't given sufficient co-operation, with the couple stationing bodyguards outside their house gates to keep camera crews out.

Later, they filed a legal case that said the boot was firmly on Gest's own foot. He had at one time insisted that a VH1 assistant put her head in a gas oven – we were not told if she did so, or why he would have wanted her to. The real problem seems to have been that Gest insisted on flying in his own hair stylist from Los Angeles – not Liza's, but his own – at a cost to the company of $60,000. He explained that he was not going to appear on the small screen when he was not looking his 'personal best'.

People inevitably accused the Gests of simply being greedy in seeing an opportunity to make another fortune, even willing to go to the extent of having a copycat Osbournes show made around them. That was not the highest of compliments.

Liza said she saw it as an opportunity to show how someone could recover from drug or drink addiction. As she said: 'Let's say there's a kid in a hospital bed, or a drunk or a woman, a woman in her 40's, lying on her couch, drunk. She doesn't have the energy to do anything. She thinks she'll wait until she has another drink to do it. I know. I have been there.'

And even now, in the midst of what she insisted was their happiness, there was what could only be described as a cold streak in them both. It was so cold, in fact, that you didn't have to be a marriage counsellor or a psychiatrist to perceive that all was not so very well in the Gest household. Was the idyllic marriage quite as idyllic as both had made out? Why did they hug and kiss so much in public? Was it some kind of evidence that both did protest just that little bit too much about how much they loved each other? There were those around who could swear they heard them shouting at each other. There were others who knew about certain bookings being made in Liza's name – for a rehabilitation centre or two. Liza may have denied it, but she was clearly on the sauce again. Not too good, that, for the man who said he had got her to quit.

But if they were in the mood for quarrelling, seemingly they had plenty to fight about.

David was forced to deny that, while they were away in Europe, he had arranged to put down Liza's 18-year-old Scottish terrier, an old loyal Minnelli friend during her bleak years.

She said she had agreed to it happening. But what happened next was a lot less understandable. Soon after her marriage, a lawyer called at the Beverly Hills home of a 94-year-old woman. Lee Anderson Minnelli was Liza's step-mother, a woman whom she called 'Mummy'. That did not mean that they had any kind of relationship. When Liza indicated that she wanted her father's old house for herself, the aged woman decided to sue her. She said she had been guaranteed a home in which to spend her last days by her late husband and, while Liza was away, had been forced to live alone in the dark. Then came the announcement that she wouldn't sue after all. Liza, relieved, phoned her. 'I'm so glad you're not suing me, Mummy,' she said. But before Lee could say anything more, Liza added, 'Be out of there in two weeks – and we'll go and have dinner.'

The story behind the row was as complicated and as bitter as such things can be. It turned out that Liza had tried to sell the house while her step-mother was still living in it. But the real fight was with Mehrdad Saghian and Stephanie Jarin, a couple who said that she had backed out of a deal to sell them the four-bedroom house for $2.7million and were suing.

Lee said that while the sale appeared to be going on, she was determined to stay where she was. So she herself sued Liza too – for 'Elder abuse and breach of contract'. Whatever the rights and wrongs of the case might have been, it left a sour taste in the mouths of fans who had been so glad to see Liza happy again.

And there were other developments that made them wonder. In December 2002, the stories that the ever-happy Liza was anything but began to surface more frequently. Even worse, a so-called eyewitness claimed to have seen her burst into tears at an Upper East Side restaurant in the course of downing three glasses of scotch. If that were true, it was evidence enough that she was tumbling down from that wagon again.

Alas, true it was. All the old symptoms of Liza's existence were there. The roller coaster lifestyle was once more hurtling on the downwards slope – with just the occasional climb upwards.

In July 2003, both she and David appeared on British TV, on Ruby Wax's show – billed as 'Liza Minnelli and Husband'. Protesting too much about their love for each other? This was not just a protest, it was a revolt. Considering how much they swooned over each other, the whole thing was pretty revolting indeed.

Neither appeared to be the most articulate individual who had ever been seen on television. They said practically nothing and what they did say was about as exciting as a note to their milkman. They walked in Hyde Park, they served fish and chips – would you believe? – to punters at a famous London eatery. Then they went shopping for themselves – well, where else? – at Harrods. Liza fell in love with a trinket, a diamond encrusted cross. 'Do you like that?' he asked, trying not to be blinded by the sparkle under his sunglasses. 'Yes,' she said. 'OK,' he said. 'We'll take it,' adding that they were very Christian in their household. 'I love you,' she said.

She gave him a big kiss in front of the sales staff, in front of Ruby Wax and in front of the cameras – which then switched to a woman making a phone call. Mr Gest wanted a discount. He looked as if he were going to get it. After all, when you are willing to shell out £80,000 for a single piece of jewellery, you are entitled to get the best deal possible.

But did either of them get the best deal possible? Nothing on that totally vacuous show seemed to indicate that they did. In fact, there was something rather pathetic about it all – a word which seemed to sum up their marriage. Liza wanted to throw a party for David at the Dorchester Hotel. The showbiz set turned up in their hundreds – but there wasn't one who knew either of them well. One guest, the artist Tracey Emin, arrived and said she had been asked by a party organiser to come. She had never met either one of the couple. That apart, the only interesting thing was when one guest asked David to take off his sunglasses. He did so briefly – and it is possible neither he nor his newly found friend enjoyed the experience very much. Liza has very big eyes, David doesn't.

But they were in love, Liza and David. Both told us so – interminably.

What we didn't know was that things were getting violent – if David was later to be believed.

According to legal statements he would make four months after the London visit, he was in the midst of a wife beating incident. Beating *by* the wife, that is.

He claimed that she hit him constantly while staying at London's highly dignified Connaught Hotel. It was during a drunken onslaught that she threw an expensive lamp at him – so hard that it shattered. His claim seemed to indicate that his head was almost as badly damaged as the lamp.

Court papers alleged that this followed an outing she took while he remained at the hotel. She had said that she was going out for a Chinese takeaway – not quite the cuisine to which she had become accustomed. According to Gest that, actually, was not what she went for.

Instead, she had gone in a car driven by a woman named Catherine Adams, to an off-license and there bought two bottles of vodka. She had, he said, consumed one of them in the car. When she got back to the hotel she was, he further alleged, totally under the drink's influence. She began, he said, 'running erratically from room to room'.

The papers submitted to the court she said she 'began beating the plaintiff about the face and head with her fists without relenting'.

None of that was then made public. But a week after the British TV show, we had the first confirmation of the big love affair being anything but that.

They announced their separation. It really was the old Liza pattern. The daughter of Judy Garland was following in her mother's footsteps all the way to the rehabilitation centre into which she had been booked a short time before. If one were really playing at detectives, the fact that they had cancelled a tiny, intimate bash for 1,200 of only their closest friends in New York's Times Square – to mark their first anniversary – might have given some indication that there were problems ahead.

He went off to stay in Hawaii. She drowned in her tears at their Manhattan apartment.

Actually, people in the business had had their radars more finely tuned on them from the moment they had heard that the couple had cancelled yet another appearance on the Larry King show – in which they were expected to look into each other's eyes (well, David would have looked into Liza's eyes and Liza would have seen her reflection in those sunglasses).

It was a mere 16 months since the nuptials and the amazing wedding list. People didn't speculate about getting their presents back. Neither did they spend too much time worrying about the causes.

Sure, there was the occasional sly dig at all the talk there had been about David being gay. Liza had always done her best to put that to rights. 'He's a real tiger in the sack,' she said. As for David, he contented himself by assuming that people would take his comments about Liza's breasts (made yet again on Ruby Wax's show) as being sufficient proof of where his interests lay. Was it really, though, because David was putting his commercial interests first? After all, there had been talk that they were going on tour – and that had to be cancelled.

Or was it her drinking that had done it yet again? After all, the rehabilitation centre in rural Pennsylvania was offering an 'eight-week self-help programme'. Maybe David thought he was helping her by ending it all.

It was in late October 2003 that it became obvious that, now, it wasn't primarily his wife's welfare that he was thinking about. It was then that he officially charged her with the beatings and demanded $10 million in damages for the trouble she had caused him. He sued in the New York Superior Court, as a 'victim of domestic violence' – violence that had left him, said the papers, with 'virtually unrelenting pain in his head' and 'vertigo, nausea, hypertension, scalp tenderness, insomnia, mood dysphora, photosensitivity, and phonophobia' – which was defined as a fear of voices and telephones.

He had to have CT and MRI scans, as a result of which he had to take 'steroidal antiinflammatory medications, anti-epileptic medications, antidepressants and intravenous analgesic infusions'.

He was plainly deeply upset about it all.

She is supposed to have told a security guard: 'I have no friends. My husband is using me to be a star. I am the star.'

Perhaps the bitterest charge of all was that, contrary to all that was said at the time of the so recent wedding hoopla, he had married a woman whose career had 'eclipsed'. As for her being as beautiful as he had professed in 2002, she was 'alcoholic, overweight, unable to be effectively merchandised' and, toughest of all, she 'could not get insurance to perform concert dates on stage or any other artistic' media.

And then other events were rolled out – such as, he alleged, she had bitten Gest's security director Willie Green on the chest. She had also, he alleged, attempted to strangle Steven Benanav, Gest's production manager.

'She's stronger than any woman I've ever seen,' Benanav was quoted as saying.

It was also charged that she caused more trouble at New York's Hotel Plaza Athenee when room service operatives refused to deliver three glasses of vodka, after she had been drinking at the bar.

She fell asleep, it was said, in a drunken stupor. When she woke up in the middle of the night, she fell over in the hotel bathroom and gave herself a black eye. The press were told that she had had to have a cancerous growth removed from under her eye. Gest said he had made up that story.

Liza, meanwhile, charged that he was making up the stories on which he based his charges. His lawsuit, she said, was 'stupid'. She then sued for divorce.

She said in a statement: 'I hoped very much that the end of my marriage would be handled with mutual respect and dignity. The allegations in this lawsuit are hurtful and without merit...I will continue to focus on my work, my sobriety and my friends and fans who have been so wonderful to me.'

In truth, that was always her most reliable crutch. The friends would despair of Liza, but the fans would never fail to be 'wonderful' to her.

Epilogue

How should we think of Liza now? Her step-father, Sid Luft, inevitably draws the comparison with his former wife, Judy Garland. He disputes those who think – or who would like to think – that the daughter is a copy of the mother.

'I think she is wonderful. But no similarity at all. Not at all. When you talk about singing, Liza has a lovely style, a great deal of energy. She's kind of smokey. Judy, to my way of thinking, was the greatest singer who ever lived. When you go back to when she made her first movie, the years before she made *The Wizard of Oz*, you would have to agree with me. There was only one Judy.

'I think that Judy knew that Liza had really control of one thing and that was herself as a dancer – and, later on, she learned her craft as a singer and then she mixed the two and became a singer-dancer professional.

'Now she has reached a station in life, over 50, she is back where she belongs and it is a miracle.'

The comedian Jerry Lewis, in an interview for this book, looked at the new Liza and said: 'Being with Liza is like going to a place that advertises "if you are without energy, we will inject you with all that you need". That's Liza. She has the most incredibly wonderful spirit.'

As he said: 'I'm not going to talk about Liza's appearance because she's gorgeous. I'm not going to talk about Liza's ability as a singer because she's the best. I don't even have to discuss the fact that she's Judy's daughter. What I do have to talk about is the one individual that I know in our business who has a consummate professional approach to her energy and her output. She never allows the public to see that she's down. And I've seen her at times when she's down. But she musters whatever is necessary to bring you an energetic picture of a performer and I respect her for that. And I love her for it. Because it's wonderful selflessness on her part and she's always been that way. Ever since she was a little girl. And whenever I'm with her, I feel uplifted.'

She was resilient but 'she's also vulnerable. Terribly vulnerable. And I want to go and make sure that nobody offends her or hurts her. I feel as protective of her as I would be for my daughter.'

After David's lawsuit she needed all the protection she could get. And, if his court papers were to be believed, so did he.

Lewis saw differences between Liza and her mother. 'Judy wasn't as pure as Liza. Judy was manufactured by Metro. And Liza has created her own persona in spite of all of that. And I think she's been wonderful in spite of her mother. And that has to be said because her mother was so prevalent, so in the foreground, so meaningful and now the daughter comes along and her life can be good without making it a contest. Liza made sure that nobody makes it a contest. She's so strong that you forget who her mother was, which is the best compliment I can pay her.'

The best compliment anyone can pay her is to treat her as a great entertainer, almost a throwback to a generation when an artist was expected to be able to stand on stage, throw out those arms and announce she was back for good – and allow her the chance to have an off evening without our being told repeatedly that not only has she fallen off the wagon, she was off the stage for ever, too.

The truth of the matter is that the jury is still out on Liza Minnelli. In one year she can be depressed, delighted, happy, horrendously miserable, sober, considerate and helpful – and apparently selfish and generous.

In one year, she was happier than she had ever been seen to be in her life – followed by four months of trying to hide the fact that everybody around them had long before noticed: happiness was not a couple called Gest.

She once more appeared on stage and told the world, 'I'm back. Just listen to me.' Unfortunately, she neither looked nor sounded the way she once had. Despite the loss of weight, her figure wasn't the one of old – and at 57 how could it have been? No matter how much you would have liked it to have been so, her voice wasn't the crystal-like element it had once been. But she was working and still had millions of fans who hoped that she would come back for good. Alas, they discovered that this happiness of hers, like all the others, was merely transitory.

What one has to remember is that she was named after the song

'Liza'. A line from that song proclaims: 'When you belong to me, all the clouds will roll away'.

She has for years said that her audiences did belong to her. But the clouds keep coming back. Will they ever roll away for good? If they do, this will be a different Liza Minnelli from the one we have known and many have loved.